CROSSING BORDERS IN THE ASIA-PACIFIC: ESSAYS ON THE DOMESTIC-FOREIGN POLICY DIVIDE

CROSSING BORDERS IN THE ASIA-PACIFIC:
ESSAYS ON THE DOMESTIC-FOREIGN POLICY DIVIDE

JAMES COTTON

Nova Science Publishers, Inc.
New York

Senior Editors: Susan Boriotti and Donna Dennis
Coordinating Editor: Tatiana Shohov
Office Manager: Annette Hellinger
Graphics: Wanda Serrano
Editorial Production: Jennifer Vogt, Vladimir Klestov, Matthew Kozlowski, and Maya Columbus
Circulation: Ave Maria Gonzalez, Vera Popovic, Luis Aviles, Raymond Davis, Melissa Diaz and Jeannie Pappas
Communications and Acquisitions: Serge P. Shohov
Marketing: Cathy DeGregory

Library of Congress Cataloging-in-Publication Data

Cotton, James, 1949-
Crossing borders in the Asia-Pacific: essays on the domestic-foreign policy divide / James Cotton.
p. cm.
Includes bibliographical references and index.
ISBN: 1-59033-450-7.
1. Asia—Politics and government—1945- 2. Pacific Area—Politics and government. 3. Asia economic conditions—1945- 4. Pacific Area—Economic conditions. Title.

DS35.2 .C698 2002
320.95'09'049—dc21

2002033717

400 Oser Ave, Suite 1600
Hauppauge, New York 11788-3619
Tele. 631-231-7269 Fax 631-231-8175
e-mail: Novascience@earthlink.net
Web Site: http://www.novapublishers.com

Printed in the United States of America

CONTENTS

AUTHOR'S NOTE

Earlier versions of some of the essays in this volume have appeared in journals and books as listed below. Permission to use this material is gratefully acknowledged.

'ASEAN and the Southeast Asian "haze": challenging the prevailing modes of regional engagement', *Pacific Affairs*, Vol 72(1999), no 2, pp.331–51

'The Asian crisis and the perils of enterprise association: explaining the different outcomes in Singapore, Taiwan and Korea', in Richard Robison, Mark Beeson, Kanishka Jayasuriya and Hyuk-Rae Kim eds, *Politics and Markets in the Wake of the Asian Crisis* (London and New York: Routledge, 2000), pp.151–168

'The retrocession of Macau and the limitations of the "Hong Kong model"', *Pacific Focus* Vol 15(2000), no 2, pp.49–63

'East Asian Democracy: Progress and Limits', in Larry Diamond and Mark F Plattner, Yun-han Chu and Hung-mao Tien, eds, *Consolidating the Third Wave Democracies: Regional Challenges* (Baltimore: Johns Hopkins University Press, 1997), Vol 2, pp.95–122. Reprinted with permission of the Johns Hopkins University Press.

'Jilin's coastal development strategy: China and Tumen River cooperation', *Asian Survey* Vol 36 (1996), no 11, pp.1086-1101. © 1996 by the Regents of the University of California. Reprinted by permission of the Regents.

'The Rajin-Sonbong Free Trade Zone Experiment: North Korea in pursuit of new international linkages', in Samuel S Kim ed, *North Korean Foreign Policy in the Post-Cold War Era*, (Hong Kong: Oxford University Press, 1998), pp.212-233

James Cotton,
School of Politics and Australian Defence Studies Centre,
University of New South Wales@the Australian Defence Force Academy

INTRODUCTION

The impact across borders of transnational identities, business linkages and even ideas has long been on the agenda of international politics. Such cross-border phenomena have a consistent and sometimes even determinative influence on domestic politics as well as on politics between states. Yet because they can be subversive of accustomed conceptions of sovereignty they are a challenge to the understanding of international politics conceived as the activity of discrete states. This issue was on the research agenda more than thirty years ago.[1] More recently it has been the subject of attempts to generalize regarding the likely success or failure of transnational actors or coalitions with reference to the character of domestic political structures on the one hand, and the extent of institutionalization of those transnational influences on the other.[2] With the rise of the narrative of globalization, it has become perhaps the main focus or premise of international politics with some analysts even developing new terminologies in order to stress the centrality of cross border forces.[3]

The essays in this collection exemplify the diversity and influence and simultaneously the limitations of cross-border phenomena in the Asia Pacific. It should be recalled that this region, from the point of view of formal diplomacy, is the home of the principles of non-interference and respect for sovereignty, as exemplified in the modalities of ASEAN and those other regional organizations (including APEC) that have adopted elements of the 'ASEAN way'. In addition, its governments have articulated suspicions and reservations regarding the impact of westernization and globalization, notably in the 'Asian values' discourse developed in the 1980s. Yet in each of the cases considered in this collection, state policies, inter-state relations and even constitutional forms have been shaped by external and transnational influences. Perhaps the most striking example is the impact of the regional financial crisis that forced reforms upon reluctant political leaderships in the region. This is not to say that such cross-border forces are necessarily overwhelming. To take two examples discussed in this book, a number of the features of Korean democracy reflect the influence of domestic forces as opposed to the characteristics of the Western liberal model from which that democracy was adapted. Similarly the Singapore state has retained a surprising degree of leverage despite its dependence upon international investment and trade.

The Southeast Asian 'haze' crisis of 1997-98 (the subject of chapter 1) was a clear case of the impact of transboundary phenomena, in this case atmospheric pollution. Precisely because ASEAN had made only limited concessions to transnationalism, its mechanisms were inadequate to deal with the problem, and some of the grouping's member countries had to resort to alternative cross-border strategies to mitigate the threat to life and property thus posed. ASEAN's limitations (considered in chapter 2) are the consequence of its central strategy, which has rested upon an elite concord and has been aimed at avoiding cross border pressures that might pose political challenges to those elites. The haze episode and its outcome is illustrative of the more general loss of momentum and consensus experienced by ASEAN from 1997, as the group failed to foster a genuine regional consciousness while it also was slow to adapt to the consequences of its enlargement and to turbulent domestic political dynamics in a number of the member states. These political changes were the product, in important measure, of the regional financial crisis (considered in chapter 3). The crisis demonstrated the power of international finance and also of internationally endorsed development strategies, but the differential outcomes in the region reflected the impact of domestic political structures.

Singapore's character (the subject of chapter 4) reflects its regional and international linkages. The city-state would hardly exist without cross-border flows of finance, commodities and people, and even the formal identity of its citizens (identified by its government alternatively as 'Chinese', 'Indian', or 'Malay') cannot be understood without reference to much wider cross-border communities. Yet these many linkages have been skillfully employed by its political leadership to accord them a role the independence of which belies their reliance upon external resources, financial and ideological alike. Macau shares some of these characteristics, but (as chapter 5 shows) its external dependence is such that its political and economic dynamics are increasingly a response to developments in China. The importation of democracy to East and Southeast Asia has been one of the most important world-historical developments of the last half-century. A broad comparative view (offered in chapter 6) illustrates both the power of this cross-border idea as well as the impact of domestic political cultures on the regimes that have emerged. In this connection, the case of Korea (as discussed in more detail in chapter 7) is especially significant. A prominent example of the 'third wave' of democratization, and one in which power has been passed regularly between different political parties since the presidential elections of 1987, its democracy, whether judged by practice or by citizen sentiment, still clearly manifests important limitations.

The landlocked and disadvantaged Chinese province of Jilin attempted in the era of national reform to use its border position to advantage in order to attract regulatory concessions from the central government and to access international development funds. This strategy (as is shown in chapter 8) enjoyed some degree of success, though its ultimate shortcomings reflected the fact that its international partners were not committed to this approach to the same degree. By opening a small part of its border territory to international investment, in the 1990s North Korea pursued similar objectives, at the same time (as chapter 9 illustrates) treating this expedient as a pilot project for more extensive reform in the economy as a whole. In the event the decision was taken that such cross-border influences were too much of a challenge to the political leadership and the experiment remained contained in the area around Rajin, though it is still having an important impact upon the country's population and especially upon its managerial elite. Australia's engagement with its 'region' (the subject of chapter 10) though it has been sought for economic and security advantage, has also been pursued to shape and influence the national identity, and the precise strategy appropriate for such engagement is still a matter of partisan debate.

What picture of the Asia Pacific emerges from this collection? The cross-border penetration of ideas, organized interests, and financial flows is fundamental to any explanation of the region's dynamics. Fluctuations in the power of these factors suggest that a domestic and regional equilibrium has yet to be reached. The fact that these influences work often outside of formal state and regional structures implies that the degree of institutionalization in the Asia Pacific has yet to take the full measure of cross border forces. However domestic dynamics cannot be discounted as a determinant of policy and state behaviour. In the Asia Pacific region, though borders have become more porous, state power and local identities still resist, shape and modify cross border influences.

NOTES

1 Robert O Keohane and Joseph S Nye eds, *Transnational Relations and World Politics* (Cambridge: Harvard University Press, 1972).

2 Thomas Risse-Kappen ed, *Bringing Transnational Relations Back In. Non-State Actors, Domestic Structures and International Institutions* (Cambridge: Cambridge University Press, 1995).

3 James N Rosenau, *Along the Domestic-Foreign Frontier. Exploring Governance in a Turbulent World* (Cambridge: Cambridge University Press, 1997).

Chapter 1

ASEAN, THE 'HAZE' CRISIS, AND THE FAILURE OF REGIONAL INSTITUTIONS[1]

Though much recent commentary has been devoted to the predicament of ASEAN (Association of Southeast Asian Nations), the problems that have been its focus have been the regional financial crisis, and the internal tensions generated by the enlargement of the membership. These have been serious enough, and their resolution will leave their marks on the organisation. But a further problem, the more serious because it is home-grown, has revealed important failings within the structure of ASEAN. This is the 'haze' of 1997–98.

It is the argument of this chapter that the haze crisis poses a dual challenge for the group. First, conventional ASEAN modalities have proved a severe disappointment. A proliferation of meetings and plans have produced little of consequence. The Indonesian regime was unwilling or unable to put the interest of the neighbourhood ahead of those of its closest associates. The effect on the self-image of the group has been corrosive, and the likelihood that these modalities will fail when tested by a crisis of a different kind has increased. Second, alternative approaches have been the desperate resort of ASEAN elites, a strategy that has had major implications. Prominent in these alternatives has been the positive role accorded to NGOs and trans-national opinion groups. This has posed a challenge to the character of ASEAN, given that a number of regimes within the group have been reluctant to accept the legitimacy of such political activity, and also in light of the fact that the much vaunted accord and consensus of ASEAN has been largely the creature of agreement among in some cases narrow and unrepresentative national elites.

THE SIZE OF THE PROBLEM

Extensive forest and grass fires, leading to smoke pollution as well as a host of losses and costs, some less immediately visible and more lasting, have become regular events in Southeast Asia. With particular atmospheric conditions, this pollution has persisted for long periods, and has become known, somewhat euphemistically, as 'haze'. Previous episodes of the haze have occurred in 1982–83, 1987, 1991, 1994, and again in 2002, but that of 1997–98 was extreme, costly, and in some localities life-threatening.[2]

Something of the size of the problem can be gauged from the areas of forest and other lands burned. In 1982–83, somewhat more than 3.5 million hectares in East Kalimantan alone were ravaged by fires, with perhaps several million more similarly effected in other parts of Indonesia and East Malaysia.[3] With greater attention being paid to environmental problems globally, the various dimensions of the most recent fires have been more accurately determined. In particular, satellite data has been extensively analysed to provide a reasonably comprehensive mapping of the types and extent of terrain damaged by fire.[4] Satellite derived mapping has also been used as a guide to follow up fieldwork, which has sometimes resulted in detailed study of the conditions and causes of the fires in particular localities. Malaysia and Singapore have also recorded and published regular data on the concentration of pollutants in their atmospheres, thus permitting an analysis of the movement and persistence of the haze over time.

Estimates of the actual amount of land effected by fire vary. Official estimates released by the Indonesian government considerably understated the size of the area in question. Independent studies of East Kalimantan indicate that about 4 million hectares of forest and other lands were burned in 1997–98, with the total for Indonesia as well as the Malaysian states of Sarawak and Sabah being as much as 8 million hectares. To put this figure in perspective, this is more than 120 times the size of Singapore, or twice the size of Taiwan. The total area of Indonesia's lands which have been granted, in one form or another, to logging concessionaires stands at about 54 million hectares, so the area burned (though not all forested land) is equivalent to 15% of that area.

While a consistent time-series is not available from Indonesian sites, the degree of pollution caused by the fires can be gauged from measurements made in Malaysia and Singapore. These states employ slightly different forms of measurement (MAPI—Malaysia Air Pollutant Index—and PSI—Pollutants Standard Index—respectively), but both record the presence in the air of pollutants such as sulphur dioxide, oxides of nitrogen, ozone, carbon monoxide and (this being the major cause of the haze phenomenon) particulate matter. A reading of over 100 is judged as 'unhealthy' and in excess of 300 is 'hazardous'. Singapore recorded a PSI of 140 in two days in September 1997 (as compared with a reading of 153 during the haze of October 1994). Peninsula Malaysia was similarly affected. In East Malaysia, however, the situation was a good deal more serious. A peak MPI reading of 849 was recorded in October 1997 for Kuching in Sarawak. When it is recalled that this site was some hundreds of kilometers from the nearest source of the haze, it is clear that readings of over 1000 must have been common in much of Indonesian Kalimantan. Nor was this reading an isolated event. In early April 1998, the index reached 502 in Miri (Sarawak), a state of emergency was declared and schools were closed. Precisely what these figures imply for everyday life can be inferred from the fact that at the height of the haze the inhabitants of Kuching could hardly see more than a few meters even at noonday, and most ordinary social and economic activities came to a halt. In Malaysia 500 MAPI is the level at which an emergency is declared, though it should be recalled that when the National Haze Contingency Plan was first introduced that level was set at 300.

This haze event was costly, though counting the precise dimensions of that cost is not a straightforward task. The destruction of forest and plantation resources can be estimated, and the expense of treating the increased incidence of respiratory and other related illnesses can be measured with some degree of precision. Lost tourist earnings and production can also be estimated. Less easy to determine and thus to evaluate are such items as the ultimate health costs, the possible loss of species (including perhaps the orangutan communities in much of Kalimantan) and the consequences of increased erosion and the deterioration of water supplies used for human consumption. Finally, the ultimate cost to the global environment of the increase in greenhouse gases must also be recognised.

Using a rigorous methodology, the Economy and Environment Program for Southeast Asia (EEPSEA) and the Worldwide Fund for Nature (WWF) prepared an estimate of fire and haze costs for the nations involved. This estimate was presented to the Kuching meeting of ASEAN Environment Ministers in February 1998. The researchers found that the overall cost was US$4.5 billion ($3.1 billion for fire damage, and $1.4 billion for haze costs).[5] This estimate is based upon conservative assumptions—including that the burned area was limited to 5 million hectares—and does not incorporate the final toll of loss and damage for 1998, nor does it attempt to compute the longer-term health costs, so the actual figure is likely to be somewhat larger. Already some work has been done on the more generalised effects of haze events, which suggests that some climate change—and its associated costs—might be expected to eventuate.[6] Further, while it does include a small amount for biodiversity loss, it would be difficult, for example, to put a figure on the devastation of the unique environment of the Kutai National Park in East Kalimantan, much of which was burned in early 1998. It should be recalled that some of the costs were tangible and immediate, including the loss in September 1997 of an Indonesian airliner with 234 passengers and crew, in conditions of low visibility due to the haze. An estimate calculated at the end of 1998 suggested that Sarawak alone experienced agricultural losses of 51 million *ringgit* ($13.4 million) as a result of the haze in 1997.[7]

THE CAUSES OF THE PROBLEM

The causes of the haze have increasingly become a matter of dispute between governments, forestry interests, and conservationists.[8] There is general agreement that an occurrence of the El Niño Seasonal Oscillation (ENSO) event produces the dry conditions which make fires in normally moist rainforest and former rainforest terrain possible. While there is some evidence that fires have occurred periodically even in the remote past, in more recent times unprecedented levels of human activity have been a major factor in fire outbreaks. For some time, those connected with large-scale timber extraction have ascribed the major cause to the practice of swidden agriculture, which in dry years has led to deliberately set small fires spreading out of control. Study of the problem, and especially the evidence that came to light as a result of the most recent fires, has shifted the blame from forest dwelling populations practicing simple agricultural techniques to the activities of large commercial concerns.

Both forestry and oil palm producers and production techniques play a role in outbreaks of fire. The granting of extensive timber 'concessions' and the poor policing of regulations regarding mandatory selective logging and provisions for reforestation give little incentive to adhere to sound conservation or fire prevention policies. Rather than careful logging of selected plots, extensive areas are opened rapidly with only the best and largest trees felled. Considerable damage to the forest cover and remaining trees results, and timber debris litters the forest floor. Reduced and disrupted forest canopy exaggerates the drying of the forest in seasons with low rainfall, rendering the outbreak of fires more likely.

On occasion, logged areas are then converted to timber or oil palm plantations. Such conversion requires the land to be cleared, and burning is the cheapest and easiest method to achieve this result. The establishment of oil plantations from previously forested areas, a program which has received extensive government support in Indonesia, has therefore also been a factor in the production of smoke pollution. Again, the land must be stripped of vegetation, and while a method of clearing without burning has been tested successfully in Malaysia, it is more expensive and involves the use of machinery.[9] The clearing of land through logging has also been linked to trans-migration programs that require deforested areas to settle new immigrants. The establishing of large pulp mills in East Kalimantan before the plantations intended to supply them had matured was a further factor in the subsequent fires. The result was timber foraging over wide areas which later figured prominently in the 1997 disaster.[10] In all, Indonesia's commitment to what now is obviously an unsustainable exploitation of its timber resources was a major factor in the environmental crisis.[11]

The draining of peat swamps for rice cultivation—most notoriously in the one million hectare project in Central Kalimantan—has been an additional human activity that has contributed to the fire problem.[12] Dried peat burns easily, and as the fires sometimes extend to deposits deep underground, rainfall does not always extinguish them. Quite apart from the exacerbation of the haze that results, peat deposits are an exceptionally good form of carbon sink, and the overall contribution to the production of greenhouse gases from peat fires in Indonesia has been estimated as being as large as all the pollution produced by motor vehicles in Europe.[13] Correspondingly, the smoke produced from peat fires contains the highest concentration of pollutants, though the Indonesian government did not acknowledge the contribution of these fires during the crisis of 1997–98.

Field studies of areas in which fires were extensive indicate that the land most susceptible to burning was degraded forest that had already been logged. There were also instances of fires set to clear land for plantations spreading beyond the plots in question. A consideration of the causes of the fires must therefore focus on human activity. Preliminary studies with this focus have indicated that the appearance of logging, palm and timber plantation activity, and related road building and industrial construction in the more remote regions of such places as Kalimantan all help to set in motion a potentially destructive social dynamic.[14] Often title to land is vague in communities where the once prevailing pattern of communal tenure is at an uncertain stage of dissolution, and disputes arise between those who wish to benefit from cooperating with the new economic order and those who resist its encroachment. Fire becomes a weapon of dispossession, or an expression of envy, or a lever for compensation, as much as a method of land clearance. Many logging companies use sub-contractors or even 'illegal' loggers who have little interest in fire prevention, and such companies devote few if any resources to fire-fighting capability. But the fact that this dynamic has been unleashed can only be understood with reference to the management of forest resources.

MANAGING RESOURCES

The rights to exploit much of Indonesia's forest resources, and also those of East Malaysia, have been granted to private companies and individuals. But this exploitation is conducted within what appears at first glance to be a densely structured regulatory regime.

In Indonesia which is the major focus of this text, a number of state agencies have been involved in forest management.[15] Unfortunately not all of these agencies have acted in concert, and even where they have, state policy capacity has been weak due to the presence of other important actors in formal and informal policy making. Generally speaking, the Environment Minister and the Forestry Minister have endeavoured to restrain production, and to encourage sustainable development of Indonesia's timber resources. In 1994 the Forestry Minister announced that over the next five years, annual timber production would be reduced to 22.5 million cubic meters. This was regarded as a sustainable harvest, and well short of the levels of production then prevailing, of between 36 million and 44 million cubic meters (the latter figure an estimate from NGOs which includes timber which is felled illegally).[16] However, under the seventh five year development plan (Repelita VII) which covers the period to March 2003, annual timber production is set at 57.17 million cubic meters, 24.8 million cubic meters of this from 'natural' and 'conversion' forest.[17]

However, the Environment Minister heads a 'State' ministry that has insufficient powers and resources to secure compliance in the provinces, where it lacks local branches. Although Indonesia did establish an environmental agency with potential to exercise real power in the regions—BAPEDAL (*Badan Pengendalian Dampak Lingkungan*), in 1990—its role has yet to be properly institutionalised.[18] During the crisis of 1997, the environmental authorities, under the leadership of the then Environment Minister Sarwono Kusumaatmaja, sought to enforce regulations that, since 1995, had categorically prohibited the use of fire to clear land. The penalties for ignoring this law were increased in 1997, and the authorities were empowered to seize the assets of companies ignoring the ban. Forestry Minister Jamaludin Suryohadikusumo revoked the logging licences of 176 concessionaires, including Kiani Lestari (owned by Bob Hasan, a close associate of then President Soeharto), during the haze crisis of late 1997. On 4 October, many of these licences were restored, and the minister later went on record to assert that the chief cause of the fire problem was not human error or policy failure but El Niño.[19] The Environment Minister then passed the comment that enforcing the nation's laws in parts of Kalimantan was as difficult as policing the 'Wild West'.

In practice, provincial governments have played a much greater part in the administration—and in the avoidance—of national regulations on forestry and on fire prevention. Until the decentralization reforms of 2000, provincial governors were nominated by the central government in Jakarta, and were often individuals from outside the area in question. They were not accountable to local assemblies that in any case had few powers. Provincial authorities waived regulations, and even ignored directives from the Jakarta bureaucracies when it suited them. In East Kalimantan it was as a consequence of the development occasioned by the timber boom of the 1970s that local elites were eclipsed by economic and political outsiders.[20]

But in the Indonesian context, private individuals have played a greater role in establishing policy settings. The term 'private' is used advisedly, since their position was a result of important, albeit informal, relationships with Soeharto and key members of his regime, including his family.

Approximately 60 million hectares of timber resources are held by about 500 concessionaires, who have been given logging rights (HPH—*Hak Pengusahaan Hutan*) to designated forestland. These concessionaires, who include some businesses associated with the military, were granted their holdings—directly or indirectly by the President—in the years after 1967, and enjoy the right to log the land in question for 20 years. Until the fall of Soeharto in 1998, a small number of major businesses controlled the bulk of these HPH concessions. The biggest single concession is still held by Prajogo Pangestu (Phang Djun Phen), a Kalimantan Chinese, whose Barito Pacific Group controls about 5.5 million hectares of forest, as well as one of the world's largest pulp mills, located in Sumatra.[21] Suharto's eldest daughter, Siti Hardijanti Rukmana, was a partner in a number of Barito Pacific's business concerns.

The archetype of the regime associate was Mohamad 'Bob' Hasan (The Kian Seng) who held in his own right around 1.6 million hectares of timber concessions, but who was the most important figure in the business by virtue of his dominance of the various industry associations in Indonesia. Hasan had been a close associate of Soeharto since the 1950s, later serving as a partner in the Nusamba (*Nusantara Ampera Bhakti*) business group with Soeharto's son, Sigit Harjojudanto, in which Soeharto family foundations also participated. Hasan's timber interests began when he became the local partner (with a 10% interest) in PT Georgia Pacific in the early 1970s to exploit a timber concession in

Kalimantan. He later acquired the controlling ownership of the company, which was re-named PT Kiani Lestari, and became part of Hasan's Kalimanis group. By the 1980s his business interests had expanded into almost every area of Indonesian industry, and he served as a key administrator of the plethora of 'philanthropic' foundations into which Soeharto chose to place his money.[22]

Since 1981, when Indonesia announced the banning of exports of raw timber, a measure fully implemented by the beginning of 1985, the government's policies helped establish plywood and paper production as the most important forest derived products. In particular, the Indonesian plywood cartel has dominated the world market for this form of processed timber, with marketing policies driving other competitors from the scene. At this time Hasan expanded his business interests to include plywood manufacture and marketing.

'Private' organisations play a crucial role in the timber industry. As early as 1974, Bob Hasan appreciated the leverage that a place in such organisations would give him, and formed the Indonesian Timber Society (*Masyarakat Peryayuan Indonesia*—MPI) with himself as Chair. This strategy was repeated in the plywood industry. Apkindo (*Asosiasi Produsen Kayu Lapis Indonesia*—the Indonesian Wood Panel Association) grew to control the granting of export licences to plywood manufacturers and to set production quotas for domestic producers, as well as to dominate the transport of plywood to and distribution within major markets, notably Japan. Apkindo charged producers a range of fees for development and marketing. These controls and finances, and the fact that Indonesia produces around 70% of all the plywood sold in the international market, made the organisation a major actor in the nation's export trade. It was dominated, however, by Bob Hasan, who managed it laregly as a personal fiefdom until it was dismantled after pressure from the IMF in 1998. Hasan endeavored to replicate in the other sectors of the timber industry, his domination of the plywood business. He became chairman of the Indonesian Sawmillers Association and also the Indonesian Furniture Industry Association.

Forestry and palm plantations are intimately linked. Many of the actors and regulations are the same. Land acquired originally for the extraction of timber has often been transformed into oil plantations. Many of the owners of major timber companies also have extensive interests in the production and processing of palm oil. As with the conversion of degraded forestland to plantation timber, the establishment of a plantation requires that the land first be cleared, and fire is by far the cheapest method. Just as the Indonesian government gave a major impetus in earlier days to forestry exports, so more recently palm plantations have become a national priority. The area of land devoted to oil palms doubled (to 2.5 million hectares) between 1990 and 1997, and government plans to increase the total area to 5.5 million hectares by the early twenty-first century require a very high continuing rate of conversion.

The situation in East Malaysia is not much different, though the absolute area of forestland is proportionately smaller, and the timber generally of poorer quality. The power to grant logging concessions in Sarawak is in the gift of the state's Chief Minister (since 1981), Datuk Patinggi Taib Mahmud, who is also Forestry Minister. Due to a split in the ruling elite in 1987, details of the holders of concessions were published in the press in Sarawak, which demonstrated that political associates, family members and friends of the Chief Minister were the most important concessionaires.[23] These include the Environment Minister, Datuk Amar James Wong, whose company, Limbang Trading, controls over 100,000 hectares of concessions. These timber holdings are often exploited by milling companies, with the nominal owners deriving an income from rent. Timber is a vital component of the Sarawak and Sabah economies, accounting for the largest single export item for each at around 30% of overall exports.[24] The Malaysian tax regime encourages timber exploitation since the states have the power to tax this sector (unlike petroleum, the bulk of the taxes on which are collected by the federal government). In Sabah, where 2.7 million hectares of the 3.3 million hectares have been designated for commercial use, similar circumstances are to be found. The rate of deforestation through the 1980s was so high that in 1990 the granting of licences for milling timber or producing plywood or veneer was suspended indefinitely, and timber production is now in marked decline.[25] Nevertheless, around 500,000 hectares of forest or former forestland was devastated in fires which broke out in early 1998 in Sabah.

TESTING THE PATRIMONIAL THESIS

So far, defective forestry practices in a policy environment in which private individuals and interests under the patronage of Soeharto had the upper hand, would appear to account for Indonesia's woeful record on fire prevention.[26] This interpretation of the dynamics of policy making is supported by evidence that industry money collected by the government was made available for private purposes. In Indonesia, all logging concessionaires must pay a timber tax. This tax, called the Reforestation Fund (Dana Reboisasi: DR), is composed of a levy of (on average) $16 a cubic metre on all raw timber logged. It has been established that Hasan was given presidential approval for a Rp 250 billion (then $100 million) low interest loan to fund the construction of his massive scale Kiani Kertas pulp mill, the operations of which, of course, were bound to lead to the very reverse of reforestation.[27] There is evidence that regulations were waived to the advantage of Hasan's business. As has been noted, in an attempt to discipline the logging industry, Forestry Minister Jamaludin Suryohadikusumo revoked the licences of many concessionaires, including Hasan's Kiani Lestari, during the haze crisis of late 1997. Hasan's licence was very quickly restored even though local reports indicated that his concerns had ignored the prevailing regulations prohibiting the use of fire in land clearing.[28]

The fact that Hasan's power, having reached its zenith in the final days of the Soeharto regime when he assumed the office of Minister of Trade and Industry, began to disappear once Soeharto resigned the presidency again supports the patrimonial hypothesis. Within months, reform groups within Hasan's industry organisations contested his leadership and management, the state intervened to seize his assets after he failed to follow bank restructuring requiremements, and his expenditure of industry levies was scrutinised.

A movement called MPI Reformasi emerged to challenge Hasan's dominance of the timber industry. His companies lost forest concessions after disputes regarding title and land use. His business empire then suffered debilitating blow after blow. He fell foul of banking laws when it was shown that bank emergency relief funds went—via the bank of which he was co-proprietor, Bank Umum Nasional (BUN)—to his timber business, rather than being used to restore the bank's creditworthiness. After the Indonesian Bank Restructuring Agency became aware that *Rp* 150 trillion ($24 billion) Bank Indonesia loans were directed to debt-ridden PT Kiani Kertas, and BUN was unable to repay the loan, the Agency assumed control of BUN assets.[29] The conditions of the IMF restructuring program, which required a consolidation of bank debt, then forced Hasan to sell much of his plywood and timber empire, including the PT Kiani Kertas mill in Kalimantan.[30] His other holdings, including his interests in the Freeport mining operation and in the Astra group also came under threat.

The legal system, having long functioned to legitimise the power of the ruling elite, then began to deliver judgments against Hasan and his interests. In North Sumatra, thirteen youth organisations were successful in mounting a court case against Hasan's Indonesian Forest Business Association (APHI), claiming that the magnate had burned forests without any concern for the environment. The judgement of the court was that Hasan be required to pay compensation to these organisations totaling *Rp* 50 billion.[31] He was eventually sentenced to a term in gaol for financial malfeasance, though not directly for mismanagement and corruption in connection with his timber interests.

If it is the case that the control of the timber industry is best understood with reference to the patrimonial model, or as Dauvergne argues, the 'patron-client model', then the 'cause' of the haze problem may be identified in those terms. Timber concessionaires may be seen as the holders of benefices from the ruler, a form of transaction that generates complementary power, though at the expense of the general population. On this view, the expense involved initially entailed depriving the indigenes of the use and enjoyment of the forest, and ordinary citizenry of any revenues or income from the timber trade, while creating an extra-legal sphere beyond the reach of normal state regulation. The predatory forestry practices that arose in these circumstances then generated additional expenses, in the form of the haze and of environmental degradation.

But such an approach requires some reinterpretation, as the Weberian assumption that the corollaries of modernisation, bureaucratic rationality and the market, are necessarily corrosive of the patrimonial impulse has been challenged in the Indonesian case.[32] The development of bureaucratic rationality actually gave Hasan and those like him enhanced power, since they were able to dominate industry organisations from which they stood to benefit financially, just as they were able to frame state regulations to accord to their activities a veneer of legitimacy. Far from engagement with the world economy requiring greater discipline and acceptance of market priorities, these concessionaires were able to exploit their dominance of the export sector to derive additional finances. The characterisation of the New Order state offered by Robison, which centres on 'a pact of domination ... between the politico-bureaucrats who dominate the state apparatus and the leading elements of the capital-owning classes based upon a complex conjuncture of interests'[33] captures the mixed sources of power of the forestry magnates. However, Robison's contention, in 1988, that 'the state's autonomy and its power to determine the structure of capital ownership and investment through regulation and allocation of resources has been diminished, as has the power of officials to appropriate the authority and resources of public office'[34] was, at best, premature. In the ten years following the time those words were written, the Soeharto regime engaged in a prolonged and ultimately fatal campaign of plunder which saw the property and control of courtiers and cronies reach new heights.

A further modification is required to the patron-client model in this instance. This is clearly the logic that is at work, since Bob Hasan would neither have held the concessions, nor controlled the market, nor received special finance if he had not received highly favourable treatment from President Soeharto. Moreover, as Michael Ross contends, the Indonesian case shows that it is no accident that potential resource rents are most imperfectly captured by such a patronage state.[35] But to describe the situation simply as one dominated by patron-client relations is to miss a major aspect of the Indonesian situation.

As William Ascher and Michael Ross further point out, the arrangement whereby Chinese clients are granted by Soeharto the use of extensive timber concessions does not conform to the usual patron-client model.[36] Though these individuals may be wealthy, their support is not so apparently crucial to the regime, in the way that the support of military clients was vital in the years immediately after Soeharto's assumption of power. A historical view of the timber sector shows, however, that in the 1970s many of the concession holders were originally companies associated with the military. These largely vacated the industry in the 1980s, with the ban on unprocessed log exports (which was announced in 1981 and came into full effect at the beginning of 1985) and the movement by timber interests to downstream processing which required significant new investments. They were replaced by Chinese business interests.

Why did Soeharto need these clients? They appeared to play several roles. First, they acted to host business activity on the part of members of the Soeharto family. Bob Hasan, for example, was associated in various business ventures with three of Soeharto's children, functioned as manager of the International Timber Corporation of Indonesia on their behalf, and had a major role in the creation of the Nusamba business group which managed many of the interests of the Soeharto family foundations. This hosting sometimes took the form of subsidising or even rescuing failed Soeharto business and 'charitable' ventures. Second, they were used to advance industrialisation projects with 'nationalist' ends, often contrary to their own immediate material interests. The ban on raw timber exports, for example, though it artificially lowered the price of timber inputs, required significant investments in wood and pulp processing while wiping out previously handsome export earnings. Chinese capital was also a significant component in investments to create a comprehensive petrochemicals industry. Their dominance of this sector gave Soeharto control over a significant source of 'off-budget' funding, which allowed him thus to pursue programs sometimes contrary to the policies of his own technocrats. And ethnic Chinese clients were chosen, partly because they had the capital or business expertise, but also because they had limited attachment to the generality of the population, and thus would never become alternative sources of power. To pursue this analysis, the 'haze' was therefore the outcome of logging concessions and plantation agriculture that were themselves aspects of patronage politics.

Moving from the overall analysis of the Indonesian system to the obstacles that arose to control the fires which were the immediate source of the haze in 1997, policy paralysis and/or lack of state capacity were both in evidence. Environment and forestry officials and cabinet members sought in vain to have prohibitions on burning enforced; their efforts were undermined by the president, and government reshuffles then removed those individuals who had acknowledged that the state had not behaved in accordance with its formal-legal duty. The character and limitations of state capacity in the late industrialising state has been a major theme of the literature.[37] Donald Crone's view of the sources of state capacity appears to be borne out by the Indonesian case:

> .. the capacities of states vary with the structure of political support and the means of political control available to a state's elite. Narrow, authoritarian regimes tend to be coercive and controlled by powerful interests, which detracts from their states' capacities to promote economic and political goals. Moderately broad-based regimes, by contrast, provide a greater degree of flexibility and political capacity with which state elites can manage economic and political challenges.[38]

The haze may therefore be attributed both to the New Order's original patrimonial impulse, as well as to the specific use by the elite of the bureaucratic instruments that came into their hands as a result of the pursuit of modernisation, which compromised and undermined the rational-legal capacity of the state to deal with the problem. It may also be attributed to the regime's development priorities, which required a free hand to be given to the business activities of the chosen clients. With regard to regional cooperation, what is clear is that the protection of these interests, or perhaps their power of veto over effective policy innovation, was more important than the effective realisation of what had become by the end of 1997 the increasingly desperate demands of ASEAN elites and publics alike. President Soeharto's public apology for the haze in September 1997 was not matched by action. Indonesia, the pivotal actor in ASEAN, when forced to chose between regime solidarity and regional concern took the former option. This failure to take any real initiative condemned the many attendant examples of ASEAN diplomacy to irrelevance.

ASEAN Cooperation and the Haze

This regime dynamic within the core state of ASEAN has had the most profound implications for regional order. In effect, domestic priorities have prevailed over the needs of the region, with drastic consequences for cooperation between the states of Southeast Asia and for mutual confidence and security. ASEAN cooperation on the environment has a history of over twenty years, being initiated by the 'ASEAN Environment Program I' of 1977.[39] The standing of environmental issues was enhanced when occasional group gatherings of specialists on the issue were upgraded to annual meetings of the ASEAN Senior Officials on the Environment (ASOEN) in 1989. In June 1990, the ASEAN Ministers on the Environment endorsed a document which became known as the Kuala Lumpur Accord on the Environment and Development, and which enunciated a common stand, that could be described as generally 'pro-development', on the relationship between these two issues.

Since that time, ASEAN's approach has changed markedly. In the early days, governments and government nominated specialists were regarded as the chief—or only—relevant actors. In the Strategic Plan of Action on the Environment, adopted in April 1994, however, ASEAN's implicit policy community was significantly broadened. The Plan notes that 'ASOEN in general should establish mechanisms that will motivate, educate, train and build capacities especially among the major groups identified in [the UNCED's] Agenda 21'.[40] Now the latter explicitly includes NGOs and indigenous people, and as such considers the task of 'capacity building' in developing states should include their contribution.[41] Given the record of disputed and uncertain legitimacy that has been accorded to NGOs in most ASEAN nations, and also bearing in mind that forestry proceeds often at the cost of indigenous land rights in Indonesia and Malaysia, this is a noteworthy shift.

But ASEAN's sensitivity to environmental concerns is uneven. Thus the Plan also includes a reference to the Singapore Resolution of 1992 which enjoined 'joint regional action to counter the anti-tropical timber campaign launched by environmental NGOs and governments in the more developed countries to stop the importation of tropical timber.'[42]

Though 'transboundary pollution' was considered in the 1990 document, the Indonesian forest fires of 1994 prompted ASEAN to adopt measures specifically designed to meet this problem, in the form of the 'ASEAN Cooperation Plan on Transboundary Pollution', considered at an ASEAN Ministerial Meeting on the Environment convened in Kuching in October 1994. The first 'programme area' identified relates to 'regional haze incidents', and the strategy outlined to deal with these incidents emphasises fire fighting capability (including early warning of fires) and the prohibition of burning during dry periods. Longer term, 'zero-burning practices' and 'awareness building efforts to eliminate the use of fire in land clearing activities through economically sound and environmentally friendly methods in agriculture' are also recommended.[43] What is noteworthy in this document is the avoidance of any mention of the promotion of forest conservation or protection as a means of minimising the generation of smoke. Following from this agreement, a 'Haze Technical Task Force' was established by ASOEN in

1995, with the aim of sharing information on fire prevention and containment, including making available satellite data on actual fires.

But even though ASEAN had focused on the haze problem, the mechanisms established moved ponderously. However, the crisis of 1997 mobilised ASOEN to meet three times in the year. Senior official agreed a regional division of labour in November, with Singapore taking the lead in the monitoring of fire hazards, Malaysia concentrating on fire prevention, and Indonesia dealing with fire fighting. In addition, a ministerial level meeting in December 1997 adopted a 'Regional Haze Action Plan' which focused squarely on the problem. This identified three objectives—to develop better management and enforcement so as to prevent fires, to establish cooperative mechanisms to monitor fires, and to build fire-fighting capability. The first appeared to address the difficult question of internal regulations and national policies, but the approach taken was to request that each nation formulate a 'National Plan' (RHAP) in these areas, with an emphasis upon strict controls on burning.

These plans were reviewed in 1998, though by that time the financial crisis had come to deflect and absorb crucial government energies. At this stage, the frequent convening of meetings on the haze had brought home to all the nations in the region the full dimensions of the problem. Perhaps felicitously, the meeting of ASEAN environment ministers held in Brunei in April, which declared that RHAP was now in operation, was conducted in severe haze conditions, with the PSI level standing at over 400 in the extremely hazardous range.[44] So serious were the fires in East Kalimantan that the ministers concluded that nothing could be done about them, though this decision was not well publicised within ASEAN.[45] Three days after the meeting the airport at Bandar Seri Begawan was closed to traffic as a result. Confronted with a PSI of over 500, authorities in neighbouring Miri in Sarawak were forced to close all schools. Nor were regional expedients the only devices considered at this time. On 12 December 1997, Malaysia and Indonesia signed a bi-lateral memorandum of understanding for joint efforts at disaster relief, including the haze.

As part of the 'Hanoi Plan of Action' adopted at the sixth informal summit in December 1998, the ASEAN states agreed to take all necessary steps to protect the environment, declaring (in article 6.1) the following objective:

> Fully implement the ASEAN Cooperation Plan on Transboundary Pollution with particular emphasis on the Regional Haze Action Plan by the year 2001.

But the proliferation of plans and acronyms, though it has led to enhanced contact between officials and experts from all the ASEAN nations, did not materially influence the situation on the ground. Reviewing the record of ASEAN cooperation on the issue, Simon Tay's judgement must be regarded as definitive: 'ASEAN has to date been unable to supplement failures by Indonesia to address the South East Asian fires.'[46]

INTERNATIONAL ORGANISATIONS, NGOS AND THE HAZE

As the haze crisis developed, ASEAN turned to various international and foreign institutions for aid, advice, and funding. And as the crisis became more serious, domestic publics were progressively drawn into policy-making circles in the hope that they would have an impact.

In 1991 a workshop sponsored by the German government produced a draft of a 'Long-term Integrated Fire Management System'. GTZ (Deutsche Gesellschaft fur Technische Zusammenarbeit), the international development consultancy funded by the German government, then established the Integrated Forest Fire Management Project (IFFM) in East Kalimantan, which has worked on the fire problem from 1994.[47] In April 1998 the Global Environment Facility (GEF) allocated US$6.75 million to assist the Indonesian fire-fighting effort. Participation by the United Nations Environment Program (UNEP) in an ASEAN workshop in May 1998 led to a grant from UNEP of US$850,000 to the GEF to support a fire prevention project in the region, mostly dedicated to providing 'early warning' data. UNEP also took responsibility for raising a fund of US$10 million to support a regional fire-fighting effort, though international donors proved unresponsive. At the same time, the Asian Development Bank pledged US$1 million specifically to Indonesia, and a further US$1 million to ASEAN as a group, for regional technical assistance (RETA) in preventing and mitigating the haze. Bilateral assistance from twelve nations included US$4 million from the United States, as well as aid from Australia, Canada and Japan. Significantly, the workshop which considered implementing these schemes placed on record that fact that 'incipient partnerships between the ADB's ASEAN-RETA with a Singapore-based legal environmental NGO'[48] were developing. Indeed, the seriousness of the crisis led ASEAN to entertain offers of help from almost any quarter, including the World Wide Fund for Nature (WWF), and a range of forestry conservation organisations, notable among them the Centre for International Forestry Research (CIFOR) and the International Centre for Research in Agroforestry (ICRAF).

Domestic interests were also mobilising to confront the haze problem. The Indonesian state has long existed in an uneasy relationship with NGOs.

Summarising the situation in the 1980s, Robert Cribb came to the following judgment:

> Most environmentalist groups ... occupy a terrain of fluctuating size between being banned and being compulsorily incorporated into government-sponsored structures in which they would lose all freedom of action.[49]

Regarding some environmental issues, especially land tenure, NGOs have supported the rights of individuals and communities against the state and powerful interests.[50] In respect of some aspects of environmental protection, however, there have been instances of state partnerships with NGOs and international groups with the objective of conserving resources and natural habitats. Thus SKEPHI, the Indonesian Network for Forest Conservation (*Sekretariat Kerjasama Pelestarian Hutan Indonesia*), having long served as a vocal critic of government policy went into several partnerships with the government, supporting for example community-based forest conservation in the Mentawi Islands, and became a participant in dialogues on a range of environmental issues.[51] The Indonesia Environment Network, WALHI (*Wahana Lingkungan Hidup Indonesia*), an umbrella group for a number of NGOs, and the most important of the local civic actors, gained a reputation for balancing advocacy and analysis in the 1980s. During the closing years of the Soeharto regime, however, it became more inclined to contest aspects of government policy, developing a strong critique of the costs incurred by the Freeport mining operation in Irian Jaya. Something of a watershed was crossed when WALHI filed a suit in a state administrative court seeking to invalidate a presidential decree that diverted *Rp* 400 billion (then $175 million) from the state reforestation fund to the nation's failing aircraft industry, then the fief of Science and Technology Minister B J Habibie. Although the court ruled that WALHI could not bring the suit, and Habibie promised to return the funds with interest, from that time the government's record especially in forestry management was the subject of trenchant criticism.

International actors have also become involved with environmental issues in Indonesia. The World-Wide Fund for Nature (WWF) has been assisting the Indonesian government in the management of 17 of its 32 national parks (including the over 1.4 million hectare Kayan Mentarang Nature Reserve in East Kalimantan)[52], and has therefore enjoyed a degree of prominence and influence in Jakarta, sometimes even generating some envy amongst domestic NGOs. A measure of the role of the WWF can be gained form the fact that it drafted the Indonesian National Biodiversity Action Plan in 1991 for the government, and in late 1995 signed a 'Letter of Intent to Cooperate' with the Indonesian Ministry of

Environment to produce an assessment of Indonesian compliance with the requirements of the Global Biodiversity Convention, to which Indonesia is a signatory.

The events of 1997 brought many of these interests together. Assisted by information and support from the international players, local groups—the most active of which was WALHI—pressured the government to police its own regulations. Activists in Kalimantan and elsewhere exposed the more flagrant violators and also took the lead in delivering immediate relief measures, including the distribution of face masks and first aid for respiratory complaints. In the words of a military participant in fire-relief operations:

> ... a small number of local intelligentsia, informal native leaders, NGO activists, religious groups, and youth groups initiated a number of direct actions on their own, dismayed that local and national authorities, and particularly the Armed Forces, were reluctant and half-hearted in their response to the crisis. Their actions often generated a sense of solidarity and served to establish a network of concerned, active citizens. These networks succeeded in gathering and distributing relief aid.[53]

Widespread dissatisfaction with the crony dominated structure of the timber industry and the environmental disaster it engendered was then a factor in the ouster of Soeharto in 1998.

ASEAN Modalities under Challenge

There is an intensive and inconclusive debate on the character of ASEAN, but most commentators accept that it came into existence and has persisted for a mix of security and economic reasons. To address issues in these crucial areas, its internal modalities have developed from the premise that Southeast Asian nations should solve their own problems in their own way. The governments of the region should practice mutual solidarity, and policy between them should be coordinated using the complex network of personal relationships built up over a generation of quiet and informal diplomacy. The key actors in this web have traditionally been governing elites and senior officials and experts. For a long period, NGOs were regarded as having no major part in the ASEAN policy community, and participation by international organisations and trans-national NGOs was seen as illegitimate. International regimes—aside from those pertaining to trade—were held to be of limited relevance for the region. ASEAN's many reservations on the applicability of the global human rights regime, as was expressed in the Bangkok Declaration of 1993, may be taken here as emblematic.[54]

The position of the Singapore government on 'civil society' has long been critical. Interest groups, provided they conform to the Societies Act, may be constituted, but any overtly 'political' activity is held to be out of bounds. As Chua Beng-Huat points out, this prevents an autonomous civil sphere from developing:

> Civic voluntary associations, quintessential institutions of civil society, are barred by the [Societies] Act from making political statements beyond the interests of their respectively defined constituencies, under threat of being deregistered. The Act effectively suppresses the commonplace activity of a civil society in which voluntary associations establish their solidarity by publicly sympathising with each other's causes.[55]

Interest articulation outside established and licensed channels is therefore held to be illegitimate. The extent to which this practice undermines the claims of Singapore to be a democracy is a matter of debate, but there is no doubt that it is a distinctive and prominent feature of the political system. In recent times, an enhanced role for civil, or 'civic' society has been mooted by intellectuals and political figures, though as yet with little practical result. In Malaysia, similar constraints exist on the manifestations of civil society, though at times of political upheaval, these have sometimes been ignored.[56] However, it is noteworthy that in November 1997 the then Education Minister, Najib Tun Razak, banned academics from making comments on the haze on the grounds that this tarnished the nation's image abroad.[57] In April 1998 the Information Minister, Mohamed Rahmat, admonished a local television station for using the term 'haze', rather than reporting what should have described as 'low-cloud, dew and smoke'.[58] These examples illustrate that the Malaysian government is unwilling to permit free discourse in an untrammeled civic space on a national problem of this magnitude.

Indeed, the 'Asian values' discourse arose in part to counter the claims of such agencies and regimes. The Asian values paradigm represented state-society relations as following a distinctive 'non-Western' path in the region, with interest groups subsumed within a broad social consensus, and governments enjoying pre-eminent prestige and discharging their role in the manner of a trustee.[59]

As has been shown, the haze problem has both security and economic dimensions. The short term costs of the haze have been the subject of many estimates, but whatever the precise dimensions, the impact on production, resource depletion, bio-diversity loss, tourism, and health, as well as the opportunity cost of financing fire prevention and extinguishing measures, has been to generate immense costs. Ultimately these costs will have to be paid beyond Southeast Asia, given the impact the haze is likely to have on global climate. The security dimensions have been both direct and indirect, striking at the economic foundations of military power as well as weakening regional accord. It would not be an overstatement to maintain that the haze has been Southeast Asia's biggest internal challenge if not since the era of 'confrontation' then since Vietnam's invasion of Cambodia in 1979. While the 1997 financial crisis had a greater impact, its causes were partly external, and increasingly it is viewed as a product of the globalisation of finance. Although Peter Dauvergne has argued persuasively that Japan's 'ecological shadow' has encouraged, and even financed, the forestry practices that have been a major cause of the problem, this is nevertheless a secondary or 'pull' factor.[60]

The haze has posed a challenge to every aspect of ASEAN's character and modalities. Mutual solidarity on the part of governments and a preference for indirect diplomacy have collapsed in the face of the seriousness of the problem. Action plans and ministerial meetings did not prove efficacious, with the Indonesian government incapable of policing its own regulations. A sign of the shift in policy could be seen in the endorsement, at the Fourth ASEAN Ministerial Meeting on the haze held in Singapore on 19 June 1998, of non-official participation in dealing with the issue. In the words of the final communique:

> The Ministers ... welcomed the increasing role of the Non-Government Organisations and the private sector in regional, national and local efforts to combat, prevent and mitigate fires. To this end, the Ministers welcomed regular dialogue between NGOs and the ASOEN Senior Officials on the forest fires and haze matters.[61]

At the 1998 summit of foreign ministers, the group openly debated, albeit without success, a more interventionist approach to its common concerns. Meanwhile, in desperation, Singapore and Malaysia provided directly information and resources to NGOs, and sought assistance from international organisations in the hope that the former would change conditions on the ground, and the latter would provide the impetus to move opinion in Jakarta.

In a very significant development, the Centre for Remote Imaging, Sensing and Processing (CRISP) at the National University of Singapore began to publish on the internet satellite imagery which provided ineluctable evidence of the dimensions and location of the fires in Indonesia. Previously CRISP had performed analysis of satellite imagery that had been passed to the Ministry of the Environment in Singapore, who had made this available from time to time to their opposite numbers in Indonesia. The fact that CRISP were permitted to go public using the internet was a calculated strategy. As Garry Rodan has demonstrated, the Singapore government is very sensitive to the political impact of information propagated by way of the internet.[62] The decision, therefore, was clearly intended to have an effect on opinion within Indonesia, and was thus an implicit departure from the ASEAN policy of refraining from intervening in the internal affairs of member states. The orchestration of NGO and interest group pressure on Indonesia was taken a stage further with the convening of the Singapore Environment Council (SEC) 'Policy Dialogue on the South-east Asian Forest Fires' in June 1998. The choice of this vehicle indicated that the Singapore government had become thoroughly exasperated with Indonesian inaction. The SEC is an example of an entity labeled in the citystate a GONGO—'near-state non-government organisation'—and the meeting was chaired by Ambassador Tommy Koh.[63]

Simon Tay's judgement on the international dimensions of the problem is instructive:

> If the ASEAN Action Plan is not a solution in itself, it may still be significant for the legitimacy and urgency it gives to assistance from outside ASEAN—from other countries and international organizations.[64]

It could be argued that the actual relationship between these two was the reverse of that posited above—the appeal to international organisations may have been launched in the hope that this would motivate key Indonesian actors to follow a plan that, to that point, had been largely an empty document. The strategy of using the doctrine of state liability for trans-boundary damage and harms, a strategy advocated by Singapore's former Ambassador to Washington, Tommy Koh, himself a champion in former times of the discourse of 'Asian values', represents little less than a sea-change in ASEAN, especially in light of the fact that he openly charged 'logging companies and palm oil plantations' with responsibility for the greater bulk of the fires.[65] Although the sources of the haze within Indonesia are 'private' concerns, nevertheless it is arguable that the state's failure to police and enforce its own regulations renders the latter culpable.

Meanwhile, in the report on the lessons of the fires produced by the State Ministry for the Environment, in association with the United Nations Development Program (UNDP), NGOs occupy centre stage. The major contribution of NGOs during 1997 in fund raising, networking and sharing vital information, is recorded. Further, the solution proposed to deal with future fire crises is to form a new public-private agency involving NGOs and local stake holders which will empower the communities most affected or threatened by fire to take the necessary preventive steps free from interference from the state and from private interests.[66]

The acceptance, indeed the endorsement, of the positive role of NGOs poses an additional problem for the newly enlarged ASEAN. The group now incorporates states in which civil society is either under-developed (as is the case in Laos) or states dominated by elites who contest or reject outright the legitimacy of autonomous agencies in civil society (as is the case in Vietnam and Myanmar and to an extent in Cambodia,). If ASEAN modalities are to be modified to embrace NGOs as essential actors in the domestic and regional policy community, a significant divide will emerge between the old and new ASEAN states. The established members will then be faced with the decision either to seek to bridge that divide by fostering civil society, and risk alienating the ruling elites in the new member states, or to accept that for an indefinite (but likely prolonged) period, the organisation will observe different rules for different members and thus be less than fully effective.

Commentators on ASEAN are generally in agreement that the group faces a range of new challenges that are testing the structures and even the rationale of the group. Even before the financial crisis, expansion to incorporate economic and social systems—first Vietnam, then Myanmar, Laos and Cambodia—at quite a different level of development and with distinctive priorities, while attempting to take the lead role—through the ASEAN Regional Forum—in developing Asia wide security discourse, and simultaneously committing to ever more ambitious economic liberalisation objectives—both with the ASEAN Free Trade Area (AFTA) and through APEC—would have tested the most resilient institutions.[67] The financial crisis has further complicated this agenda. However the fact that the haze was a locally produced problem, ASEAN structures already existed to deal with it, and previous 'haze incidents' had alerted key actors to the need to take strong measures, but in the event ASEAN cooperation was found wanting, has been a salutary reminder of the limitations of regional consciousness. This precedent may even indicate that regarding other issues of good governance, ASEAN will need both to affirm a more critical approach to domestic policy making, and also act to foster and empower civil society especially in those member nations in which it enjoys little autonomy.

In June 2002 Environment Ministers took the step of signing a formal treaty stating regional and national obligations to deal with the causes of the haze. The preventive measures specified include those identified in 1995 and again in 1997 as the most effective, notably policies of 'zero burning'. It is noteworthy also that the document enjoins the state parties to practice the management of their natural resources in 'an ecologically sound and sustainable manner', and involve 'local communities, non-government organizations, farmers and private enterprises' in discharging this responsibility.[68] It remains to be seen whether this agreement will have any real effect on the problem, though it is surely extremely significant that such diplomatic weight should be brought to bear in order to find a solution.

Conclusions

The recurrence of haze in 2002 was an indication that the institutional shortcomings exposed by the events of 1997–98 had not been addressed. The fall of Soeharto damaged the fortunes and power of many of his cronies, and especially Bob Hasan. But most of the structures identified above remain in place. In addition, the Indonesian state continued to experience policy incapacity, partly as a result of divided leadership, and partly due to shortage of government revenues with the failure of the economy to recover the ground lost during the regional economic crisis. Indeed, the crisis exacerbated the problem, since the economic downturn forced many individuals and companies to adopt even more predatory and often illegal approaches to the forests in order to remain solvent or secure an income. [69] Neither has ASEAN resolved the contradiction between its commitment to major trans-boundary problems such as the haze, and its reluctance to interfere in the internal affairs of its members.

Notes

1 I am obliged to the Institute of Southeast Asian Studies, Singapore, for the use of the Library, and Priscilla Hon, Mari Pangestu, Tubagus Feridhanusetyawan, Stuart Davies, Simon Tay, Soo Chin Liew, and Ooi Giok Ling, for sharing the results of their work with me. Thanks are due to Sue Moss for research assistance.

2 MNS Science and Conservation Unit, 'The Haze Thing', *Malaysian Naturalist* vol.51(1997), no.2, 18–21.

3 Cynthia Mackie, 'The Lessons Behind East Kalimantan's Forest Fires', *Borneo Research Bulletin* vol.16(1984), no.2, 63–74; Nengah Wirawan, 'The Hazard of Fire', in Harold Brookfield and Yvonne Byron eds, *South-East Asia's Environmental Future. The Search for Sustainability* (Tokyo: United Nations University Press, 1993), 242–260.

4 Satellite analysis is based upon the interpretation of data from four separate systems: Florian Siegert and Anja A Hoffmann, 'Evaluation of the 1998 Forest Fires in East-Kalimantan (Indonesia) using multitemporal ERS-2 SAR Images and NOAA-AVHRR data', <http://www.smd.mega.net.id/iffm/n&r0.htm> (accessed

30 November 1998); Douglas O Fuller and Michele Fulk, 'Satellite Remore Sensing of the 1997–98 Fires in Indonesia: Data, Methods, and Future Perspectives', available from the WWF, Indonesia site, <http://www.wwf.or.id/forest.html> (accessed 22 December 1998).

5 EEPSEA/WWF, 'The Indonesian Fires and Haze of 1997: The Economic Toll', <http://www.wwf.or.id/forest.html>, accessed 22 December 1998; Priscilla M L Hon, 'Singapore', in David Glover and Timothy Jessup eds, *Indonesia's Fires and Haze. The Cost of Catastrophe* (Singapore: ISEAS, 1999), 51–85.

6 Janet Nichol, 'Bioclimatic impacts of the 1994 smoke haze event in Southeast Asia', *Atmospheric Environment* vol.31(1997), no.8, 1209–1219.

7 'Sarawak crop losses amount to $22 million', *The Straits Times*, 2 December 1998.

8 Paul K Gellert, 'A Brief History and Analysis of Indonesia's Fire Crisis', *Indonesia* vol.65(April 1998), 63–85; Peter Dauvergne, 'The Political Economy of Indonesia's 1997 Forest Fires', *Australian Journal of International Affairs* Vol.52(1998), no.1, 13–17; Andrew P Vayda, 'Finding Causes of the 1997–98 Indonesian Forest Fires. Problems and Possibilities', (WWF – Indonesia Report, July 1998), <http://www.wwf.or.id/forest.html>, accessed 22 December 1998.

9 On oil plantation agriculture and the fires, see: Lesley Potter and Justin Lee, 'Oil Palm in Indonesia: its role in forest conversion and the fires of 1997/98' (WWF – Indonesia Report, December 1998), <http://www.wwf.or.id/oilpalm.htm>, accessed 22 December 1998; Eric Wakker, 'Forest Fires and the Expansion of Indonesia's Oil Palm Plantations', (WWF – Indonesia Report, July 1998), <http://www.wwf.or.id/ERICOILP.html>, accessed 22 December 1998.

10 Jeff Sayer (Centre for International Forestry Research, Indonesia), 'Fires: Symptoms or Cause of Natural Resource Degradation in SE Asia', paper presented at Singapore Environment Council, *Policy Dialogue on the South-East Asian* Fires, 4 June 1998.

11 Lesley Potter, 'The Onslaught on the Forests in South-East Asia', in Harold Brookfield and Yvonne Byron eds, *South-East Asia's Environmental Future. The Search for Sustainability*, 103–123; Lesley Potter, 'Forest Degradation, Deforestation, and Reforestation in Kalimantan', in Christine Padoch and Nancy L Peluson eds, *Borneo in Transition. People, Forests, Conservation and Development* (Kuala Lumpur: Oxford University Press, 1996), 13–40.

12 'Politics and peat: The One million hectare sawah project', *Inside Indonesia* vol.48(October-December 1996).

13 James Schweithelm/WWF Indonesia, 'The Fire this time. An overview of Indonesia's forest fires in 1997/98', <http://smd/mega.net.id/iffm/First.html>, accessed 7 December 1998, section 3.2, 1

14 Christian Gonner, 'Conflicts and Fire Causes in a Sub-District of Kutai, East-Kalimantan, Indonesia', <http://smd.mega.net.id/iffm/Fire_Causes.html>, accessed 30 November 1998; Ludwig Schindler, 'The Indonesian Fires and SE

Asean Haze 1997/98. Review, Damages, Causes and Necessary Steps', Indonesia', <http://smd.mega.net.id/iffm/SIN-Paper.html>, accessed 30 November 1998.

15 A Hadi Pramono and Abdon Nababan, 'Pushing the Limit: the status of forest resources', *Environesia* vol.6(1992), no.1–2, 7–9; Charles V Barber, *Project on Environmental Scarcities, State Capacity, and Civil Violence. The Case Study of Indonesia* (Cambridge MA: American Academy of Arts and Sciences, 1997), 49–53.

16 On these estimates, see Peter Dauvergne, *Shadows in the Forest. Japan and the Politics of Timber in Southeast Asia* (Cambridge: MIT Press, 1997), 73.

17 Walid Badawi, Thomas Walsh, Hira Jhamtani eds, *Forest and Land Fires in Indonesia. Impacts, Factors and Evaluation* (Jakarta: State Ministry for the Environment/UNDP, 1998), vol.2, 7–8.

18 'BAPEDAL: Indonesia's New Environmental Control Agency', *Environesia* vol.4(1990), no.3, 12.

19 *Inside Indonesia* Digest no. 42, 4 October 1997; Gerry van Klinken, 'Taking on the timber tycoons', *Inside Indonesia* vol.53(January-March 1998).

20 Burhan Magenda, *East Kalimantan. The Decline of a Commercial Aristocracy* (Ithaca: Cornell Modern Indonesia Project #70, 1991), ch.6.

21 Adam Schwarz and Jonathan Friedland, 'Green Fingers: Indonesia's Prajogo proves that money grows on trees', *Far Eastern Economic Review*, 12 March 1992, 42; *The Jakarta Post* 16 July 1998, 1. For an overview of concession holdings in Indonesia, see Michael L Ross, *Timber Booms and Institutional Breakdown in Southeast Asia* (Cambridge: Cambridge University Press, 2001), 184–5.

22 Reuters Business Briefing: *Indonesian Commercial Newsletter,* 29 June 1998; Christopher M Barr, 'Bob Hasan, the rise of Apkindo, and the shifting dynamics of Control in Indonesia's Timber Sector', *Indonesia* vol.65(April 1998), 1–36.

23 S C Chin et al, *Logging against the natives of Sarawak,* second edn (Kuala Lumpur: Insan, 1994), 5–9, 73–4.

24 Wee Chong Hui, *Sabah and Sarawak in the Malaysian Economy* (Kuala Lumpur: S Abdul Majeed/INSAN, 1994), chapter 4.

25 Murtedza Mohamed and Ti Teow Chuan, 'Managing ASEAN'S Forests. Deforestation in Sabah' in Maria Seda ed, *Environmental Management in ASEAN. Perspectives on Critical Regional Issues* (Singapore: Institute of Southeast Asian Studies, 1993), 111–140.

26 For an overview of theoretical approaches to political power in Indonesia, see: Andrew MacIntyre, *Business and Politics in Indonesia* (Sydney: Allen and Unwin, 1990), ch.2.

27 *Inside Indonesia*, Digest no 46, 8 Dec 1997.

28 *Inside Indonesia,* Digest no 42, 4 October 1997.

29 *Asian Wall Street Journal*, 21 October 1998, 2.

30 *Asian Wall Street Journal*, 10 November 1998, 1.

31 *The Straits Times* 20 June 1998.

[32] Writing in 1979, an influential exponent of the neo-patrimonial interpretation concluded that 'Indonesia's apparently patrimonial political structures have been built on non-patrimonial foundations, with the result that patrimonial-style stability is not likely to endure': Harold Crouch, 'Patrimonialism and Military Rule in Indonesia', *World Politics* vol.31(1979), no.4, 587.

[33] Richard Robison, 'Authoritarian States, Capital-Owning Classes, and the Politics of Newly Industrializing Countries: The Case of Indonesia', *World Politics* vol.41(1988–89), no.1, 55.

[34] Richard Robison, 'Authoritarian States', 73.

[35] Michael L Ross, *Timber Booms and Institutional Breakdown in Southeast Asia*, 36–40.

[36] William Ascher, 'From Oil to Timber: the political economy of off-budget development financing in Indonesia', *Indonesia* vol.65(April 1998), 37–61; Christopher M Barr, 'Bob Hasan, the rise of Apkindo, and the shifting dynamics of control in Indonesia's timber sector'.

[37] Frederic C Deyo ed, *The Political Economy of the New Asian Industrialism* (Ithaca: Cornell University Press, 1987), especially ch.8; Stephan Haggard, *Pathways from the Periphery. The Politics of Growth in the Newly Industrializing Countries* (Ithaca: Cornell University Press, 1990), ch.2.

[38] Donald K Crone, 'State, Social Elites, and Government Capacity in Southeast Asia', *World Politics* vol.40(1987–88), no.2, 254.

[39] ASEAN policy is discussed in: Mari Pangestu and Mubariq Ahmad, 'ASEAN Regional Cooperation on Haze', (Jakarta: CSIS, unpublished paper, 1997); Simon Tay, 'What Should Be Done About the Haze', *The Indonesian Quarterly* vol.26(1998), no.2, 99–117.

[40] *ASEAN Strategic Plan of Action on the Environment* (Jakarta: ASEAN Secretariat, July 1994), 9.

[41] <http://www.igc.apc.org/habitat/agenda21/index.html>, accessed 7 December, 1988.

[42] *ASEAN Strategic Plan of Action on the Environment* (Jakarta: ASEAN Secretariat, July 1994), 16.

[43] *ASEAN Cooperation Plan on Transboundary Pollution* (Jakarta: ASEAN Secretariat, November 1995), 4.

[44] 'Stopping new fires is top priority', *The Straits Times* April 5 1998; 'Brunei Shuts Smog-Shrouded Airport', *The Straits Times* 8 April 1998.

[45] 'Let fires burn in Indonesia's E Kalimantan – ASEAN', *Reuters*, April 4, 1998.

[46] Simon Tay, 'What Should Be Done About the Haze', *The Indonesian Quarterly* vol. 26(1998), no.2, 110.

[47] The IFFM maintains a web-site cataloguing their activities: <http://smd.mega.net.id/iffm/>

[48] 'Vanguard ASEAN-ADB Initiative to Design, Implement and Monitor Regional Collaborative Programme to tackle transboundary Haze', <http://www.aseansec.org/news/reta.htm>, accessed 2 June 1998.

49 Robert Cribb, *The Politics of Environmental Protection in Indonesia* (Clayton: Monash University, Centre for SE Asian Studies, Working Paper #48, 1988), 34.

50 Philip J Eldridge, *Non-Government Organizations and Democratic Participation in Indonesia* (Kuala Lumpur: Oxford University Press, 1995), chapter 7; Bernard Eccleston and David Potter, 'Environmental NGOs and different political contexts in South-East Asia: Malaysia, Indonesia and Vietnam', in Michael J G Parnwell and Raymond L Bryant eds, *Environmental Change in South-East Asia. People, Politics and Sustainable Development* (London: Routledge, 1996), 49–66.

51 Margot Cohen, 'Environment in Asia. Indonesia: Cautious Cooperation', *Far Eastern Economic Review* 16 November 1995, p.67; Colin MacAndrews, 'Politics of the Environment in Indonesia', *Asian Survey* vol.34(1994), no.4, 369–80.

52 For details of the WWF program in Indonesia, see: <http://www.panda.org/resources/inthefield/lop/indonesia.htm>, (accessed 31.12.98).

53 Major Djuanda, 'Indonesian Armed Forces and the Management of Forest Fires', *East-West Center Working Papers*, Environment Series, no.49 (Honolulu: East-West Center, December, 1998), 9.

54 James T H Tang ed, *Human Rights and International Relation in the Asia Pacific* (London: Pinter, 1995).

55 Beng-Huat Chua, *Communitarian Ideology and Democracy in Singapore* (London: Routledge, 1995), 205.

56 James Jesudason, 'Statist Democracy and the Limits to Civil Society in Malaysia', *Journal of Commonwealth and Comparative Politics* vol.33(1995), no.3, 335–356; William F Case, 'Can the "Halfway House" Stand? Semidemocracy and Elite Theory in Three Southeast Asian Countries', *Comparative Politics* vol.28(1996), no.4, 437–64.

57 'Gagging academics who speak about haze "against freedom of speech"', *The Straits Times*, 13 November 1997.

58 'Don't blow up fire problem, media warned', *The Straits Times* 21 April 1998.

59 Diane K. Mauzy, 'The human rights and "Asian values" debate in Southeast Asia: trying to clarify the key issues', *The Pacific Review*, Vol.10 (1997), no.2, 210–236.

60 Peter Dauvergne, *Shadows in the Forest. Japan and the Politics of Timber in Southeast Asia.*

61 'Joint Press Statement, Fourth ASEAN Ministerial Meeting on Haze', <http://www.aseansec.org/function/prhaze4.htm>, accessed 20 July 1998.

62 Garry Rodan, 'The Internet and Political Control in Singapore', *Political Science Quarterly* vol.113(1998), no.1, 63–89. The provision by CRISP of satellite imagery on the internet was discussed by its Director, Professor Lim Hock, during his presentation, 'Monitoring of Land and Forest Fires by Remote Sensing' at the Singapore SEC dialogue. See also, Soo Chin Liew et al, 'A Study of the 1997 Forest Fires in South East Asia using SPOT Quicklook Mosaics', paper presented at the 1998 International Geoscience and Remote Sensing Symposium, 6–10 July,

1998, Seattle. International NGOs also began publicising such satellite derived material in 1997.

63 On the GONGO mode of organisation, see Ooi Giok Ling and Gillian Koh, 'State-Society Synergies: New Stakes, New Partnership', in Arun Mahizhnan and Lee Tsao Yuan, *Singapore. Re-Engineering Success* (Singapore: Oxford University Press/Institute of Policy Studies, 1998), 99. The SEC was established by the National Council on the Environment, and more than half of its funding is provided by the Singapore government: *Singapore Environment Council, Annual Review 1997* (Singapore: SEC, 1998). On the SEC dialogue, see 'NGOs want to be at Asean meet on haze', *The Straits Times* 8 June 1998; 'Asean must fight pollution across borders', *The Straits Times* 18 June 1998.

64 Simon Tay, 'South East Asian Forest Fires: Haze over ASEAN and International Environmental Law', *Review of European Community and International Environmental Law* vol.7(1998), no.2, 205.

65 Tommy Koh, 'Introductory Remarks', The Singapore Environment Lecture, Singapore Environment Council, Singapore, 4 June 1998. Professor Koh also recommends that interested parties 'mobilise public opinion' to condemn the forestry companies responsible.

66 Walid Badawi, Thomas Walsh, Hira Jhamtani eds, *Forest and Land Fires in Indonesia. Impacts, Factors and Evaluation*, vol.1, 174–6, vol.2, 72–6.

67 Mari Pangestu, 'The Future of ASEAN', *The Indonesian Quarterly* vol.25(1997) no.4, pp.362–81; Leszek Buszynski, 'ASEAN's New Challenges', *Pacific Affairs* vol.70(1997–98), no.4, 555–577 .

68 'ASEAN Agreement on Transboundary Haze Pollution', <http://www.aseansec.org/view.asp?/file=/function/hazeagr2002.htm>, accessed 17 June 2002.

69 Peter Dauvergne, *Loggers and Degradation in the Asia-Pacific. Corporations and Environmental Management* (Cambridge: Cambridge University Press, 2001), 83–103.

Chapter 2

ASEAN: A CONSTRUCTIVIST OR AN ELITE COMMUNITY?

ASEAN (the Association of Southeast Asian Nations) has been in existence for thirty-five years. Neither an economic community nor a defence alliance, bound by designedly vague modalities, it prospered in the local circumstances of the Cold War but survived their demise, and grew to incorporate all of geographic Southeast Asia (save East Timor) by 1999. Now a grouping of decidedly disparate states, its progress has been impaired by political turmoil in its core state, Indonesia, but it nevertheless survives and indeed continues to provide the main focus of regionalism in East Asia, most recently manifest in the 'ASEAN plus 3' (ASEAN plus China, Japan and South Korea) concept. In publications over more than a decade, Amitav Acharya has striven to make sense of the ambiguities and contradictions of ASEAN. In two works that will prove of considerable interest to Asia Pacific area specialists and especially to students of comparative security studies, he has gathered his ideas to present, respectively, an historical and a systematic overview of this topic.

The Quest for Identity[1] offers an historical survey of the concept of Southeast Asian regionalism, most recently manifest in the formation and eventual enlargement of ASEAN. Adopting a generally chronological approach, the book begins with a review of some conceptions of regional identity that pre-dated European colonialism, passes to the complex interaction of nationalism, decolonisation and the impact of the Cold War that at first prevented a more comprehensive regionalism from developing, and then discusses the 'new regional consciousness' that appeared in the 1960s. After the false start of the Association of Southeast Asia—ASA—in 1961, the foundation of ASEAN in 1967 is explained both as a response to regional apprehensions about communism and as an attempt to coordinate economic and social development across the nations concerned. Despite the absence of specific security goals, such concerns then sustained the organization and deepened the cooperation of its members. Aimed at an undergraduate or advanced student audience, this work favours a 'constructivist' approach to the subject, though is does not dwell overmuch on issues of theory but concentrates on historical and thematic issues. It can be firmly recommended for survey courses on Southeast Asian politics and international relations.

Constructing a Security Community in Southeast Asia[2] is altogether a more ambitious and focused work, and one that takes a more rigorous approach to its subject. The book is devoted to the formation and development of ASEAN from its inception in 1967 to the realization of 'one Southeast Asia' with the final enlargement of the group in 1999. While it incorporates a detailed and useful chronological discussion of the group's fortunes, it is a book that develops a specific argument employing an explicit international relations methodology. The argument is that ASEAN is a 'nascent security community', that is, a group of states that in their behaviour towards each other have set aside the threat or use of force in favour of 'a long-term habit of peaceful interaction'.[3] Neither an alliance nor a collective security arrangement, a security community depends, on Acharya's view, upon shared 'norms' of behaviour founded upon mutual trust.

The idea of a security community was originally developed by Karl Deutsch in connection with the states of Western Europe and the North Atlantic, and taken up more recently by Emanuel Adler and Michael Barnett, as well as by Peter Katzenstein and others.[4] It is now associated with a 'constructivist' approach, and this methodology is explicitly adopted in this book. Constructivism focuses upon the understandings that are prior to and constitutive of action. Applied to this topic, a constructivist would hold that a security community has come into being to the extent that the 'socialisation' of its members has been effective in producing an inter-subjective and common identity and thus awareness of 'a convergence of interests'.

Acharya claims that this methodology is superior to other analytical approaches to the issue. Realists would not be able to accept the diminution of sovereignty entailed in the formation of a security community but which nevertheless, in the case of ASEAN, is in prospect. Liberal institutionalists would recognize the effectiveness of ASEAN in reducing transaction costs and facilitating cooperation towards shared objectives but they would not regard the norms of inter-state behaviour that are emerging as anything other than utility maximizing. By contrast, constructivism offers a 'more qualitatively deeper view of how institutions may affect and transform state interests and behaviour' (22).

Acharya is not the first to propose the use of this concept to account for the character of ASEAN. As he notes, Richard Mansbach as early as 1977 suggested this characterization of ASEAN (157), and in 1986 one of the group's leading thinkers, Dr Noordin Sopiee, specifically invoked Deutsch in referring to ASEAN as an incipient 'pluralistic security community' (128). However this work is the first monograph devoted to an exposition of this approach.

The book proceeds by considering the evolution of interstate norms in Southeast Asia; ASEAN's role in the resolution of the Cambodia problem; the enlargement of the group to incorporate Vietnam, then Myanmar/Burma and Laos, and finally Cambodia; the issues that have confronted the group in the post-Cold War period; and ASEAN's position in the wider security multi-lateralism that has emerged in the region.

The definitive statement of ASEAN's norms of conduct was incorporated in the Treaty of Amity and Cooperation signed in Bali in 1976. They are mutual respect for sovereignty, the right of states to be free of external coercion, a prohibition on intervention in the internal affairs of other states, the settlement of disputes by peaceful means and the renunciation of the threat of force. The existence of a tangle of territorial disputes and of various security alignments with external states (notably Malaysia and Singapore with the UK, Australia and New Zealand, and also the Philippines and Thailand with the United States) on the part of the original ASEAN six prompted what was in effect an attempt to institutionalize the status quo. The incomplete realization of the ZOPFAN (Zone of Peace, Freedom and Neutrality) concept endorsed by ASEAN's leaders in 1971 illustrated the difficulties of moving beyond that position. Nevertheless, Acharya argues that these norms, collectively termed by some later commentators as 'the ASEAN way' and characterized by consultation, consensus and an absence of formal structures, while they possessed recognizable underpinnings in the regional culture led over time to a process of 'incremental socialisation' (71). The chapters that follow, consistent with a constructivist view, attempt to show that that, as these norms became more widely affirmed, state conceptions and thus behaviour altered.

On the Cambodia issue, Acharya regards the Vietnamese invasion of Cambodia as having posed a crucial test for the group and its modalities:

> Not only did ASEAN see Vietnam's action as a blatant violation of its norms, but the Cambodia conflict also tested intra-ASEAN relations, thereby threatening its emerging culture of unity and consensus. Differences among ASEAN members as to how to deal with the conflict challenged ASEAN's professed role in the peaceful settlement of regional disputes without interference by outside powers. (80)

Although the process was prolonged, ASEAN was undoubtedly a player in the final settlement that emerged in the Paris Agreement of 1991. But ASEAN practice contradicted its affirmation of principle, as Acharya admits. While 'ASEAN presented the Vietnamese invasion as a gross violation of the principle of non-intervention in the internal affairs of states as well as the principle of non-use of force' (98), in fact ASEAN acted as 'a subregional political, if not military, alliance against Hanoi in concert with China' (97) in seeking a resolution to the problem. So far ASEAN's performance hardly exemplified a deepening and consistent affirmation of the group's declared norms. This author is inclined to see its activities here as conforming to those typical of a more conventional alliance of states, an analysis shared by Michael Leifer who characterized the group as a 'diplomatic community'.[5]

The 1992 ASEAN summit adopted the Singapore Declaration that opened the way to the extension of ASEAN membership to Indochina. As a consequence, Vietnam gained formal admission in 1995. While this was to be a major step towards the realization of the 'one Southeast Asia' objective, as Acharya notes the motives of the states concerned were decidedly mixed. Thailand's anticipation of the objectives enunciated in the Declaration clearly showed that Bangkok sought the economic benefits that would flow from the commercial domination of the entire 'golden peninsula'. For their part, the rulers of Vietnam were able to join with ASEAN in their opposition to the application of Western human rights standards to their society, and also found membership a means of balancing the influence of the major powers.

This pattern was repeated in the case of Myanmar, where prospective membership was a much more difficult and controversial issue and one that tested the limits of the doctrine of non-interference. In the years prior to Myanmar's formal admission, ASEAN refused to join the international quarantine that the United States, Australia and other countries sought to impose on Yangon, in favour of a policy of 'constructive engagement'. Acharya traces the origins of this doctrine to the rapprochement between Myanmar's military rulers and the government of Thailand that was marked by the visit of the Thai Army Commander, Chaovalit Yongchaiyut, to Yangon in December 1988. Despite the refusal by the SLORC (State Law and Order Restoration Council) regime to recognize the result of the democratic elections in Myanmar of May 1990, commercial and security cooperation between the two states was not disrupted. In attempted rebuttal of Western criticism that Thailand was therefore abetting the oppression of a whole country, the ASEAN doctrine of 'constructive engagement' emerged. As Acharya explains it,

> constructive engagement was ... moulded in the belief that the possibility of regional implications stemming from the crisis in Myanmar was a Southeast Asian issue to be handled by the regional countries themselves. The Western call to isolate Myanmar and punish it with sanctions was therefore a challenge to ASEAN's doctrine of both non-interference and regional autonomy. (110)

In the event, Myanmar became a full member of ASEAN in 1997. Again, more conventional diplomatic objectives were in evidence in that balancing the growing strategic influence of China provided an additional reason for ASEAN's elites to further extend the group's membership. Nevertheless, Myanmar's appalling human rights record led, as Acharya explains, to visible strains in applying the principle of non-interference in relations with such a regime. The attempt to include Cambodia in the same year, which was aborted by Prime Minister Hun Sen's *coup* and regarding which ASEAN's attempt to mediate was embarrassingly rebuffed, led Anwar Ibrahim, then Malaysian Deputy Prime Minister, to call for a new approach embodying 'constructive intervention' in the affairs of member states. It was not clear, however, how much if at all this would have modified the original doctrine of non-interference, and in the event Anwar did not remain in office long enough for the policy to be tested. Despite claims that the entry of new members required them to accept the 'regional code of conduct', it is difficult not to conclude that the most significant outcome of the enlargement episode was the realization of the proposition that 'ASEAN's expansion may enhance regime security in new members' (122).

In the post-Cold War era, despite ASEAN's long experience of regional confidence building, the group's norms were challenged by a series of bi-lateral disputes on territorial and other issues. The uncoordinated and sometimes competitive acquisition of technologically advanced weaponry by member states led commentators to assert that the region was experiencing an arms race. It is Acharya's view that ASEAN has continued to make little progress towards the realisation of a 'defence community', that is, to move from common norms on conflict avoidance and dispute resolution forward to actual military cooperation and integration. Such defence cooperation as has developed is bilateral, rather than multilateral. Even some standard confidence building measures are lacking, including the fact that '[t]he level of transparency in the defence budgets and policies of ASEAN states has continued to be low' (141). Acharya explains this state of affairs as follows:

> Three reasons explain why ASEAN has never seriously contemplated adopting a collective defence posture. First, the ASEAN states continue to

> see threat-oriented cooperation as unduly provocative to potential adversaries (Vietnam in the past, China now). Second, such cooperation has been seen as of limited value given the weak self-defence capabilities of individual ASEAN members and their consequent dependence on external security assistance. Third, despite the proliferation of bilateral ties, the degree of standardization of equipment and interoperability among ASEAN armed forces was, and remains, limited. (151)

Perhaps the biggest security challenge faced by ASEAN was the territorial dispute with China on sovereignty over the Spratly Islands and adjoining seabed. In Acharya's discussion of this issue he notes that the ASEAN states, having affirmed in a Declaration of 1992 a common position on the need to settle the status of the region peacefully, have sought to convince China to affirm a congruent policy. But the results have not been encouraging, and most recently some states have been preparing 'to move closer to China's position of seeking bilateral solutions to the dispute' (136). Acharya is right to suggest that China seeks to provoke 'a display of disunity' (136) from ASEAN regarding the Spratlys. But he does not deal with the foundation for such disunity that is the incapacity of the ASEAN states to resolve even amongst themselves their mutually conflicting claims to various parts of the South China Sea.

ASEAN also faced new economic challenges in the 1990s. Despite measures taken in 1977, the intensity of intra-regional trade remained weak. In 1992 in an attempt to achieve closer economic cooperation, the goal of an ASEAN Free Trade Area (AFTA) was proclaimed, the deadline for which was subsequently set, for the more advanced economies, for 2003. Regional micro-cooperation schemes were also adopted. This new focus on economic issues undoubtedly was a response to the rival economic regionalism (from 1989) of APEC, a point Acharya does not mention. Throughout, though ASEAN has been devoted since its inception to economic and development cooperation, programs in this area have been dogged by the problem of weak institutionalization. Although prompted by ASEAN's inability to respond effectively to the regional financial crisis some common reporting and surveillance agencies have been established, no actual mechanisms for sanctions exist if group members do not adhere to agreed plans. In an example not considered by Acharya, if, as seems likely, the AFTA targets for 2002/3 are not achieved, there will be no means beyond peer pressure and informal diplomacy to resolve the problem. And the jealousies and rivalries that Acharya recognizes to have emerged from the SIJORI (Singapore-Johor-Riau) 'growth triangle' experiment are an indication that ASEAN's transition from a security to an economic community is most uncertain.

The strains produced by the regional economic crisis, and the difficulties posed by the membership of Myanmar provoked the revisiting of the internal debate over constructive intervention. Thai Foreign Minister Surin Pitsuwan proposed replacing the principle of non-intervention with the concept of 'flexible engagement', a proposal that elicited some support from the leadership of the Philippines. Other members were less receptive to this idea, and though the impotent response to the regional 'haze' crisis of 1997–98 exemplified the limitations of the existing modalities[6], in 1998 ASEAN's policy makers resolved to move no further than adopt a new lexicon, that of 'enhanced interaction', to describe what amounted to no change of policy. Acharya argues that differential development in the group's domestic political systems is at the root of these tensions:

> The ASEAN 'consensus' on human rights and democracy, widely perceived to be a justification for authoritarian rule in the region, has ... unravelled. As their societies democratised further, Thailand and the Philippines have come closer to a 'universalistic' understanding of human rights and democracy .... It is therefore no coincidence that the two most open societies in ASEAN, Thailand and the Philippines, are also the strongest advocates of a more interventionist ASEAN, while Vietnam and Burma, the two least democratic systems ... remain most opposed to rethinking non-interference.(155)

It is something of a paradox that at the same time that internal disparities were straining ASEAN's coherence, in the wider region the group was becoming regarded as a model for building multi-lateral security concord. Aware that ASEAN should take the initiative lest its existing and accustomed form of cooperation be eclipsed, the 1994 ASEAN Regional Forum, though a response to calls from outside the group for a wider security community, in effect evolved out of the ASEAN post-ministerial process. The latter involved ASEAN Foreign Ministers meeting informally each year with a group of 'dialogue partners' that had grown over the years to include most of the important Asia Pacific countries with the exception of Russia and China. With its foundations in ASEAN, the Regional Forum adopted modalities congruent with those of the original group. While the agreed work program outlines a progressive agenda of confidence building, preventive diplomacy, and conflict resolution (the last later altered, as a result of Chinese sensibilities, to 'elaboration of approaches to conflicts') the Forum has not developed any effective mechanisms for the realization of these aims. Acharya does not address the issue of the lack of a 'decision making' process in the Regional Forum, but this is surely a vital point. A 'president's statement' concludes each full session, but this has no binding force and represents merely the host foreign minister's view of the proceedings. How such an agenda, and especially its second and third items, might be advanced in the absence of decision-making mechanisms is a moot point.

In the light of the fact, as Acharya notes, that the Forum has made no real contribution to the resolution of the region's most serious problems, the Korean nuclear issue and the South China Sea dispute (setting side altogether the Taiwan question), what does the Regional Forum add to the security architecture of the Asia Pacific? Against the argument of Michael Leifer that the successful operation of the Regional Forum depends solely upon the prior existence of a stable balance of power[7], Acharya develops the view that it functions as a supplement to rather than replacement for balance of power policies. But usage may enhance its standing, so that in the long run 'the ARF may even enable states to transcend the balance of power approach' (184). For the present, however, 'ASEAN countries have been obliged to reconcile their enthusiastic promotion of the ARF with a quiet adherence to the mechanisms of a balance of power system' (185).

In his conclusions, Acharya is cautious on the degree of success that ASEAN can claim in the building of a security community. On the one hand, 'one Southeast Asia' has been realized, the peaceful settlement of intra-mural disputes has become the norm, and external actors have recognized the existence of an ASEAN identity. To this extent, ASEAN might be seen as a 'nascent security community' (208). On the other, tensions and differences within the group especially as a result of enlargement, and the failure of leadership elites to win the endorsement of emerging civil societies and respond effectively to such new issues as human rights and environmental problems, have compromised ASEAN's coherence. Responding to these problems will require modification of those very norms that have defined and regulated the group.

Overall, Acharya's account of ASEAN's evolution in *Constructing a Security Community in Southeast Asia* is faithful to the facts and is indeed enlightening on many aspects of ASEAN's history. But the book is also a particular argument about the group's character using a specific methodology. These require further assessment. We will first examine the analysis before offering some comments on the appropriateness of the methodology.

Accepting the claims that Acharya makes for a constructivist approach, does he successfully and comprehensively characterize the emergence and transformation of ASEAN? The ASEAN norms, their meaning and evolution, are the centerpiece of Acharya's book. In this context, recall Acharya's analysis of ASEAN's role regarding Cambodia. He argues that despite Vietnam and Cambodia not being members of the group, Vietnam's intervention challenged

ASEAN's norms. The countries concerned were regarded as part of the Southeast Asian region, the threat and use of force characterised Vietnamese policy, and the guerilla struggle that resulted was an encouragement to great power involvement, as was evident in the roles of China, the United States and Soviet Russia. The last point denied the group's strong desire for regional solutions to regional problems.

Now consider the role of these norms in the case of Myanmar. Acharya acknowledges the difficulties for the ASEAN norms posed by policies towards Myanmar both before and after 1997, but he fails to address the issue posed by the fact that government in Yangon was notorious for the wars it waged against members of its own ethnic populations. As the policy of 'constructive engagement' came into operation and the ASEAN leaders pondered Myanmar's entry, Yangon was expanding its armed forces to almost half a million combatants, and these forces became engaged in increasingly bloody conflicts with Kachin, Karen, Mon, Shan and other ethnic armies while they also continued to repress (often using deadly force) domestic political dissidents. In the arming of these combatants China played a major role, though Singapore was a source for some advanced weaponry. The origins of these conflicts could be traced, as was well known in the ASEAN capitals, in the first instance to the failure of the (then) Union of Burma government to keep to agreements to observe and protect the rights of the border nationalities, and in the second instance to the denial of the results of the democratic elections of 1990. *Prima facie*, Myanmar would seem to have been involved in a sustained and blatant use of force that encouraged the involvement of a major power in the affairs of the region. The incorporation of Myanmar into ASEAN would thus appear to have been a complete denial of the norms that are the central feature of Acharya's analytic framework.

There is a more contemporary challenge to those norms. At the time of this writing some 30,000 Indonesian troops are stationed in the province of Aceh and the killing of independence activists there is a daily occurrence. Over the past four years, thousands of citizens have been killed in conflicts in Maluku, Kalimantan and especially Irian Jaya/West Papua in which the security or military have been implicated. The position of the ASEAN countries has been (for quite self-evident reasons) merely to reaffirm their commitment to Indonesia's integral status. Once again the norms seem not to have the fundamental status that Acharya's account holds them to be.

At this point it might be objected that these issues are the internal affairs of states and that the non-intervention principle has thus been operative. This argument is unsatisfactory at least to the extent that it assumes non-intervention should necessarily apply even though the means to settle the problems concerned are far from peaceful. In any situation where more than one norm or rule applies, there must be some ordering of the norms in a serial or hierarchic manner, or some decision procedure to assess the relevance of the different norms. In ASEAN's case these are lacking, a point that Acharya does not consider.

But there is a further case where even this objection is clearly not valid. On the question of the most signal use of force in the region, that of East Timor, the book is strangely and indeed inexcusably silent. Acharya does mention East Timor but only in passing, in relation to the international reaction to the Dili massacre of 1991, and to ASEAN's inadequate response to the crisis of 1999. He also notes, without further comment, the action taken by the governments of Malaysia and the Philippines to obstruct meetings convened by NGOs in their capitals on the East Timor question. Yet on any reading Indonesia's annexation of East Timor involved the sustained use of aggressive force and the systematic violation of the human rights of the population of the territory. Indonesia had no title or claim to the territory and its invasion of 7 December 1975 was a blatant intervention in pursuit of conquest. Even if the independence declaration made in East Timor on 28 November 1975 is disregarded, then under international law and according to the United Nations the territory remained under Portuguese administrative authority pending an act of self-determination. In addition, Indonesia's actions violated the intent of ZOPFAN. The East Timor venture led to the nation's military dependence upon the United States, the very further entanglement with foreign powers that the group sought to reject.

Now the reasons for the group's avoidance of this conflict, and indeed their steadfast support at the United Nations and elsewhere for the Indonesian position are clear enough.[8] But if ASEAN's concern with the Cambodia issue represents a partial undermining of the ASEAN norms, its complete lack of concern with East Timor until 12 September 1999 must be interpreted as an even greater denial. Acharya's avoidance of any consideration of this omission is almost as serious a flaw as that manifest in ASEAN's tendentious observance of its erstwhile 'norms'. Once again, a more conventional diplomatic analysis would make much more sense of ASEAN's behaviour.

We will now turn to the methodological claim on which the book is founded, namely that its constructivist approach facilitates a 'qualitatively deeper' analysis of the phenomena in question. This claim is difficult to evaluate conclusively in a single chapter, since to an extent it requires some allusion to alternative methodologies.

Acharya's constructivist approach focuses on the shared identity that emerges from internalizing common norms. It is arguable that such a focus may miss the possibility that from its inception the ASEAN founders were coming together in part to achieve economic goals for which cooperation was a *means*. It may be correct to maintain, as Acharya does, that economic cooperation was part of a much larger project of cognitive community building. However this is a proposition for which some evidence must be adduced. But if Acharya is allowed his point that security questions are at the heart of ASEAN, and if it is further assumed that the means used to address those questions consist in the propagation of inter-subjective norms, then the question of *whose* security requires elaboration.

Acharya uses Deutsch's expression, 'we feeling' on many occasions to describe his understanding of the sense of community that is being constructed in ASEAN. Who is the 'we' at issue? Now on this question there is some confusion in the position taken by constructivists. In a piece quoted by Acharya from a book that also contains a chapter from his pen (and from which much of the text of the present book's conclusion is drawn) Emanuel Adler and Michael Barnett relate the concept of a security community to a collection of *states*, but also extend the notion to a community of *peoples*. But it would seem that a consolidated community would depend upon widespread popular affirmation:

> States remain 'free agents', acting on the basis of their own preferences, as long as these preferences are cognitively framed by the shared understanding of the community. Therefore, while people remain nationals of their respective states, they also become 'citizens' of the community.[9]

Indeed, Adler and Barnett concur that strong civil societies and thus liberal democratic polities are more likely to develop the shared transnational culture that is essential for the existence of a mature security community. Nevertheless, other bases are possible for such a community, including, with specific reference to Southeast Asia, 'a shared developmentalist ideology'.[10]

Who are the members of Acharya's community? From *Constructing a Security Community in Southeast Asia* it would seem that it is essentially the political leaderships of the states in question:

> the idea of regional cooperation and community building, including mutual responsiveness and socialisation, remains narrowly confined to the intergovernmental level in ASEAN. This kind of regionalism does not necessarily translate into cooperation or development of 'we feeling' at the societal level ... (207)

From the constructivist perspective, then, ASEAN would seem to be a community exclusively of elites and thus a community only in the thinnest of senses. If this point is agreed, then the question of the reasons for the construction of such community arises.

In *Constructing a Security Community in Southeast Asia* the approach taken is to argue that the ASEAN sense of community has been built to avoid war and conflict, and this is a self-evident good. But is this the whole story, or even its most important part? At the very least, a consideration of alternative hypotheses would be in order. Though it has been noted above that ASEAN membership serves to 'enhance regime security' (122), to deal comprehensively with this issue some reference must be made to Acharya's other book. Many passages (perhaps amounting to as much as 20 pages) that appear in *The Quest for Identity. International Relations of Southeast Asia*, can also be found, sometimes with slight emendations, in *Constructing a Security Community in Southeast Asia*. Indeed, material in both books is freely drawn from Acharya's earlier articles and chapters (though none of this borrowing is specifically acknowledged). This is hardly remarkable in the age of the word processor. But a passage only found in *The Quest for Identity* most clearly depicts Acharya's view of the real end of the ASEAN 'community':

> In the case of Myanmar, ASEAN was instrumental in resisting Western calls for sanctions against the military regime and pushing for a policy of 'constructive engagement'. Similarly Vietnam was allowed to join ASEAN despite its communist political structure. These confirmed the nature of Southeast Asian regionalism as an elite-driven process in which human rights and democracy did not figure. Despite its claims to be based on broad historical, cultural and societal ties, the drive for regionalism to a large extent reflected the need of the post-colonial elite to ensure regime survival. The definition of what constituted the region, and who was to be included and excluded were determined by the political and security interests of states, with non-state actors playing a rather marginal role.[11]

Two points require some emendation in this passage. First, Acharya's final reference to 'states' is clearly to 'state elites' since members of non-state entities are also in the ordinary language sense parts of states. Second, the expression 'a marginal role' is an understatement, since in Myanmar, Vietnam and Laos non-state actors are illegal entities. However the drift of the argument is clear. ASEAN was created for the end of keeping particular elites in power. Conflict avoidance, and especially ensuring that neighbouring states did not support cross-border subversion or separatism, was a means rather than an end. As Acharya shows ASEAN is now under challenge from the NGO sector, but that challenge has yet to make a real difference to its functioning.

Now would a constructivist be equipped to notice such a feature? Constructivism's prejudice appears to be in favour of extensive communities, with limited communities being regarded as popular communities under (hopeful) construction, hence Acharya's use of the term 'nascent'. If, as Acharya acknowledges elsewhere, ASEAN has essentially been a community of, by and for elites, then there is nothing nascent about it and (in light of the longevity of many Southeast Asian regimes) it has done its job very well over a considerable time span. In short Acharya's methodology seems to have obstructed his enquiry, though his account has been at least partially retrieved by his very close acquaintance with ASEAN's record and history. It is for the virtues of the latter that Acharya's work is of interest.

NOTES

1 Amitav Acharya, *The Quest for Identity. International Relations of Southeast Asia* (Singapore: Oxford University Press, 2000).

2 Amitav Acharya, *Constructing a Security Community in Southeast Asia. ASEAN and the problem of regional order* (London: Routledge, 2001).

3 Amitav Acharya, *Constructing a Security Community in Southeast Asia*, 1. In this chapter all subsequent page references unless otherwise noted are to this book.

4 Karl W. Deutsch et al., *Political Community and the North Atlantic area: international organization in the light of historical experience* (Princeton: Princeton University Press, 1957); Emanuel Adler and Michael Barnett eds., *Security Communities* (Cambridge: Cambridge University Press, 1998); Peter J. Katzenstein ed., *The culture of national security: norms and identity in world politics* (New York: Columbia University Press, 1996).

5 Michael Leifer, "The ASEAN peace process: a category mistake", *The Pacific Review* 12, no. 1 (1999), 30.

6 James Cotton, "ASEAN and the Southeast Asian 'haze': challenging the prevailing modes of regional engagement", *Pacific Affairs* 72, no 2 (1999), 331–51.

7 Michael Leifer, *The ASEAN Regional Forum*, International Institute for Strategic Studies, Adelphi Paper 302 (Oxford: Oxford University Press/International Institute for Strategic Studies, 1996), 58.

8 Sonny Inbaraj, *East Timor. Blood and Tears in ASEAN* (Chiangmai: Silkworm Books, 1995).

9 Emanuel Adler and Michael Barnett eds., *Security Communities*, 37. This passage incorporates a quotation from an earlier article by Adler.

10 Emanuel Adler and Michael Barnett eds., *Security Communities*, 40.

[11] Amitav Acharya, *The Quest for Identity. International Relations of Southeast Asia* (Singapore: Oxford University Press, 2000), 140.

Chapter 3

DOMESTIC AND INTERNATIONAL ASPECTS OF THE REGIONAL FINANCIAL CRISIS

Explanations of the regional financial crisis incorporate, according to varying degrees of emphasis, domestic, regional and global factors. Weak financial institutions and government-business collusion made Asian economies susceptible to capital flight, but this flight would not have occurred so rapidly without the global financial system that was a product of the new information technologies of the 1990s. And it is likely that a number of countries were affected almost simultaneously because investors took the decision that economic weakness was in part a region wide characteristic.

This chapter is concerned with the question of the differing performance during the crisis of countries across the region. The interplay of domestic and international forces is central to any explanation of the capacity of countries such as Singapore and Taiwan to evade the full consequences of those forces that brought South Korea, Thailand and Indonesia to the point of requesting international assistance. This chapter will focus on the more mature economies in the region—Singapore, Taiwan and South Korea.

The Asian financial crisis can be attributed in part to the 'enterprise association' model of governance pursued in East and Southeast Asia. As a consequence, business has served governmentally defined ends, the independence of the social sphere has been stymied, and autonomous legal institutions have been slow to develop. Although this model has conditioned important policies pursued in Singapore and Taiwan, other influences have mitigated—though unintentionally—its worst effects. In Singapore the élites have seen the importance for international financial credibility of the rule of law as it applies in many areas of commerce; the desire to limit for political ends the development of a powerful local bourgeoisie has encouraged it to keep the country particularly open to the activities of trans-national corporations (TNCs). In Taiwan, the division (before the mid 1980s) of politics and business which reflected the divide between 'mainlanders' and 'Taiwanese', and the institutionalised resourcing of the ruling KMT by the state, along with the 'Taiwanese' (and thus potentially autonomous) character of most political and social movements, modified the business-government nexus. Comparison with Korea illustrates the different outcomes where analogous factors do not operate.

THE IMPACT OF THE CRISIS

The impact of the regional crisis upon South Korea was severe. Seoul was forced to appeal to the IMF for emergency credit, and after negotiation received a $57 billion aid package with stringent conditions attached. Official statistics recorded that 7.5% of the Korean workforce were unemployed by July 1998.[1] Given the traditional reluctance of Korean workers to admit that they have no work, and also the understating of female unemployment, this figure was correctly regarded as conservative. Labour disputes erupted across the country, with the Hyundai auto manufacturing plant at Ulsan closed for a six week period after it was occupied with workers threatened with retrenchment. The economy contracted at the rate of 5.3% in the first half of the year, and the overall performance for 1998 was minus 6.5%.

Within days of the IMF rescue package being negotiated in 1997, the three presidential candidates then campaigning publicly pledged to obey its conditions. With the presidential contest decided, the new administration observed that pledge. Korea's political leadership was outspoken on the causes of the crisis. These amounted, in the words of President Kim Dae-jung, to 'past government failures', and especially 'collusive links between companies and politicians'.[2] Officials responsible for the management of economic policy under the preceding Kim Young-sam administration were questioned in the legislature, and the former president himself narrowly escaped being called to account for his failure to deal with a crisis the portents of which (as the record shows) some members of his administration had recognised in the first half of 1997.

The prescription for reform adopted by the Kim Dae-jung administration was a combination of 'democracy and a free market economy', though the degree of government regulation which the reforms entailed were reminiscent of the powers exercised by the US administrators of Japan during the era of *zaibatsu* dissolution. The Financial Supervisory Commission, which had oversight of the government's reform of the financial sector, required the merger of five debt-encumbered banks into five healthier institutions. The Korea Asset Management Corporation formulated a plan whereby the five largest *chaebol* would divest themselves of some of their interests and swap a range of their assets in order to concentrate on core activities—Hyundai on auto manufacturing and ship building, Samsung on electronics and microchips, and so on. At the same time, the pervasive but highly opaque practice of sub-divisions of the conglomerates standing surety for each other's debts was outlawed. This second stage of the government's program was less than fully successful, with some groups reluctant to surrender control of major components of their longterm industrial strategies. There were even some contrary developments. The government having temporarily assumed the debt of the bankrupt Kia group, the concern was then auctioned to Hyundai, increasing the latter's debt and at a time when it possessed surplus production capacity. However, government plans to privatise major public enterprises, including POSCO (Pohang Iron and Steel Corporation) and KEPCO (Korea Electric Power Corporation) were successfully pursued.

By contrast, it is striking that in this period neither Singapore nor Taiwan suffered such dislocation and loss of confidence. Nevertheless, they were still vulnerable to some of its effects. In 1998 the growth rates of both nations slumped, with Taiwan's growth falling to 4.8%, and Singapore slipping into recession in the second half of the year. But they did not suffer to anything close to the same degree from the initial contagion of the currency crisis. Monetary values are a good indicator. In the first and most devastating year of the crisis (1 July 1997 to 30 June 1998), while South Korea's currency had depreciated by 34.1% (against the US$), the Singapore dollar had declined by 16.5%, and Taiwan's currency by 23.7%. With low levels of foreign denominated debt, international relief was not required by Singapore or Taiwan. Though their stock markets suffered a general lowering of prices, and unemployment increased, none of these developments were so severe as to trigger social protests and political instability. They appeared to have weathered the storm, though given their very strong linkages to the economy of the People's Republic of China, the fact that the *renminbi* was not devalued (despite some fears of this eventuality) was a major factor.

While Kim Dae-jung blamed the ineptitude of his predecessor, and the engrained corrupt practices that are the legacy of a generation of authoritarianism, the leaderships in both Singapore and Taiwan claimed by contrast that their good fortune was the result of sound governance. There are some grounds for these latter claims. Both have been committed for some time to progressive but cautious liberalisation in their financial sectors. Government policy has led to the pursuit of objectives that in the 1990s increasingly distinguished these systems from others in the region. Both have maintained large reserves, and overall foreign debt has not been significant. Inflation has been kept low, and both governments have run current account surpluses. Gross national savings have usually exceeded investment, with the consequence that capital formation has been on the basis of local rather than external funds. Attention has also been paid to policy sequencing. In most of Southeast Asia, financial and industrial markets were opened at the same time, while in Taiwan they were opened in sequence, with a sound industrial basis laid first.

Nevertheless, the governments in Singapore and Taiwan introduced policy changes to cope with the new and more adverse climate. On June 30 1998, Singapore's Finance Minister, Richard Hu, announced a SING$2 billion extra-Budget package to stimulate the economy, at the same time conceding that the region's economic troubles were expected to have a major impact on the city-state.[3] The package included measures to lower business costs, bring forward public construction projects to stimulate local demand, and offer a boost to the collapsing property market by halting government sales of land. Altogether, these measures resulted in a budget deficit of SING$7.3 billion, the first since the slowdown of the mid-1980s. At the same time it became apparent that the nation's growth had now slowed to the point that a contraction in the economy was inevitable, thus demonstrating that earlier estimates of 3.5% growth were excessively optimistic.

The cause of this slowdown can be traced directly to the Asian economic turmoil. Singapore's trade volume declined by about 5% in 1998. This was due largely to the poor performance of most regional economies. Vital markets in Malaysia, Japan, Hong Kong and South Korea for consumer and capital goods contracted, and with Indonesia still in free fall, transportation was also seriously affected. Nor were there any prospects of tourism rescuing the national revenues, with the number of tourist arrivals diminishing by about 20% in 1998.

Longer term, further steps in the continued slow liberalization of banking and financial services were likely, but in a nation which has prided itself for tight regulation and fiscal rectitude, more radical expedients were not adopted. Using measures last resorted to in 1986, a specially formed Committee on Singapore's Competitiveness recommended in November 1998 pay cuts of 5–8% and other economy measures. Nevertheless, the exposure of Singapore's banks to Indonesia may yet generate additional uncertainties. While cushioned by the absence of sovereign debt and in possession of large foreign reserves, Singapore's open economy remains uniquely vulnerable to the regional and international climate.

The response in Taiwan was similar.[4] In 1998, Taiwan's exports to Asian markets fell by around 25%. As these markets customarily account for half of all exports, this had a significant dampening effect on the economy. Unlike in Japan, Taiwan's domestic demand remained relatively buoyant. The government announced its intention to boost this demand further, by bringing forward some major infrastructure projects, including the North-South high speed railway.[5] The government also remained strict in its insistence that not only all banks but all financial institutions should satisfy the 8% Bank of International Settlements capital-adequacy ratio. There were clear signals that the government was prepared again to intervene in the stockmarket if necessary to boost confidence, just as was done during the 1996 missile crisis. Having already experienced a property speculation boom that caused a drastic fall in the stockmarket in 1990, policy makers had some prior experience of the problems seen in other economies. Taiwan's biggest concern was the prospect of a currency devaluation in the People's Republic of China (and Hong Kong), given the island's appreciable surplus in trade with the mainland. If this happened, the Chinese market would contract, with fewer funds available for imports. Though a few Taiwan companies with joint ventures on the mainland would have benefited from cheaper costs, especially labour, the overall effect would have been strongly negative. Fortunately Beijing's policy makers did not take this decision. With the particular structure of its industrial capacity, Taiwan continues to find it difficult to diversify its trade to cushion such effects, as much of its business is with TNCs.

While there is little doubt that policy made a difference, and there is therefore some basis for the claim that Singapore and Taiwan have enjoyed unusually good governance while Korea has not, the fact that these former systems have been characterised by differences in *institutional capacity* is less noticed or analysed.[6] The fact that these differences exist is itself a puzzle, given that there are some grounds for viewing these systems as members of a particular group, the Asian NICs/NIEs (Newly Industrialised Countries/Economies). The pursuit of this issue requires an excursus first into theory, and then into the particularities of these political and economic systems so that their superior performance by comparison with Korea can be fully assessed.

THE POLITICS OF ENTERPRISE ASSOCIATION

The argument of this chapter, in brief, is that these three systems have all been constructed according to the same impulse and with the same model, that of the 'development state', in mind. All three states actively pursued extensive external linkages at a time when the global environment was especially favourable for such a strategy. The characteristics of this model were at the center of the regional crisis of 1997–98. In most of the NICs and would-be NICs, what was once strength by the mid-1990s had become weakness. But particular contingencies in the trajectory of Singapore and Taiwan, though the result of other factors, served to protect them from the worst of the regional contagion. Without these contingencies, Korea suffered its full force.

Singapore, Taiwan, and South Korea are all members of the genus, 'Asian industrialising/development state.' Theorising this state is clearly beyond the scope of this chapter, yet it is a topic that must be considered. While there is an extensive literature on this subject, there is a good deal of disagreement as to how these states may be characterised, or indeed whether a single characterisation is entirely appropriate. There is some agreement, however, on the distinctiveness of the policies and institutions of these states; accounts differ regarding what scope there has been for state autonomy, and precisely what constraints and opportunities have been imposed by their positions in the world system and by the timing they have chosen for their programs of rapid modernisation. It is generally accepted that the earlier examples—Korea and Singapore especially—were presented with unusual advantages by virtue of their security and market linkages with the dominant Cold War order in the Pacific. They were able to make effective use of their circumstances for a variety of reasons, including as a result of contingent historical and cultural factors.

The success and example of these systems shifted the focus of development studies from Latin America to East Asia. By the early 1980s, the experience of the Asian NICs came to be regarded as something of a model, not merely for the Asia Pacific region but worldwide. This model was emulated by policy makers in the next tier of Asian development states (in Southeast Asia), which phenomenon encouraged at the same time financial institutions to invest in their markets on the assumption that they would exhibit a similar trajectory and present renewed possibilities for profit.

Meanwhile, the historical moment that had brought forth this model had passed, surpassed no less by democratisation within these systems than by globalisation without. Democratisation has fundamentally transformed the political character of Taiwan and South Korea (though not Singapore) over the past decade. Nevertheless, the policies and attitudes that had served the 'trading states' of East Asia so well had become sufficiently part of the social and political fabric that they could not be readily abandoned, even in those instances where their inappropriateness was recognised.

A 'trading', 'development', or 'industrialising' state is clearly a state of a particular type. Theorising this type requires analysis more abstract than the approach usually taken, which generally rests upon a specification of the policies, institutions, and international linkages of one or several of these states.[7] The position taken here will be to advance the view that many of the characteristics and policies of these states are best understood by regarding them as examples of 'enterprise association'. Enterprise association can be considered as a *purpose governed community*. Such a community is to be distinguished from a 'civil association', which is a body of individuals governed by rules (legal, moral, conventional) that regulate their conduct *but which is not committed to any particular or identified purpose.*[8] 'Enterprise' is here understood as an undertaking: an actual enterprise association may pursue irrational or unattainable goals, such as racial purity or socialism, rather than a goal such as rapid economic growth. *The purpose of the enterprise in this instance is the national equivalent of market share.* To use Cerny's characterisation, the states in question have sought to become 'competition states'. These states sought, at least avowedly[9], to follow a pattern of development that would lead them to become major trading entities, mastering the technologies necessary to produce ever greater number of manufactures of ever greater sophistication for world consumption.[10]

The (comparative) 'success' of Japan and Korea in this project suggests that it is a legitimate or at least a recognisable national strategy. As to its attractiveness or viability as a strategy, it is surely remarkable that the post-revolutionary Chinese state, having pursued with extraordinary assiduity the goal of socialism, should have exchanged this, by degrees after 1979, with the goal of market share. This exchange, indeed, was accompanied by conscious attempts to replicate the Asian NIC experience in China. But it is important to grasp both what is entailed and what is excluded by such a strategy.

First, what is entailed. Clearly there are degrees of commitment to a goal, and some societies are better at mobilising to such an end than others. Yet if the goal really is accorded supreme or overriding importance, then institutions or policies will only be judged as good as their service to this end, and institutions and policies which serve other goals or are consistent with other—perhaps multifarious—purposes will not be established or fostered, or may even be abandoned or their functions abridged. A legislature, for example, will only be as good as its role in building national market share. If it does not make that end its prime business, it may find its operations sidelined (as in Korea in the period 1961–71) or subverted (as in Korea from 1972 to 1987). Civil servants may be required to be trained to sensitize themselves to their new responsibilities (as in the operations of Singapore's Political Study Centre after 1959), and if traditional bureaucratic offices do not discharge these responsibilities effectively, new agencies might be established (like the Economic Planning Council in Taiwan) to take the lead. Banks and bankers, newspapers and journalists, alike will be expected to serve the national purpose, and business, its owners and managers must serve as the shock troops and standard bearers of the nation's advance into the world market. In short, the dominant motif of an enterprise association is *managerialism*.

As to what is excluded, it follows that both those institutions and practices that do not accord with these goals, *as well as those social institutions and practices that are not defined in terms of particular ends* will be extirpated, modified, or stultified. Thus trades unions, by definition organisations devoted to the amelioration of the conditions of their members, were corporatised in the original NICs, their leaders often drafted into cabinets, with their functions to be cheerleaders for government 'productivity' campaigns and the like. Further, a space was not allowed to develop for those many human associations that can exist for both limited and also for uncertain purposes. To the present, the provisions of the 'Societies Act' in Malaysia and *a fortioiri* in Singapore control and constrain most manifestations of interest aggregation and expression. The Lion City must be the only mature economy in which the prime minister's office appoints the leadership of the university students' society, and in which a government minister regulates the peak environmental pressure group, the Singapore Environment Council.

A more insidious process diverted or frustrated those practices from which no certain outcome could be expected. The rule of law is perhaps the supreme example of a practice that serves no end except to extend, interpret and maintain those rules that construct the network of obligations and rights owned or carried by one person in relation to others. This rule is indifferent to overriding national purpose as such, and may well find against an interfering or regimenting state. For this reason, neither legal personnel nor institutions were allowed to function without state interference or control in the original NICs. During the high tide of authoritarianism in Korea in the 1970s, even justices were incarcerated when they resisted the bidding of the political leadership. The question of judicial independence is still a matter of debate in Singapore.

To recapitulate, the creation of an enterprise association can be seen at least as a recognisably coherent national project. But by travelling on one road, others are left untraversed. In pursuit of national market share, the Asian NICs neglected civil society, jeopardized the rule of law, stymied social debate, and sought to control the flow of information across national borders. The business sphere was made reliant upon government, and bureaucracy became a political tool. The social and policy consequences of this pattern were those features most frequently identified by analysts and critics of the 'Asian model'.

Businesses were often allowed to enjoy local monopolies for particular goods or other forms of protection. Access to development finance bred habits of dependence, and rather than focus upon viable commercial strategies, enterprises pursued gigantism or the sure rewards that would come from captive markets. Further, as it appeared that businesses in receipt of such funds enjoyed a form of sovereign guarantee, foreign investors did not exercise the caution that should have been due when lending to them or engaging in joint ventures. With the supreme policy objective being market share, independent controls on financial institutions were actually discouraged, on the grounds that these would obstruct that policy. It was not the business of banks to maintain liquidity levels or control debt, but to support the national purpose. Korean banks, for example, were required to disperse a proportion of their funds in the form of 'policy loans' to exporting conglomerates. When, under international pressure, Asian financial systems began to liberalise, they did so hastily without the experience or institutions necessary for the property scrutiny and control of those systems.

Even if these mechanisms could have functioned free of corruption, it is clear that the trajectory of these economies could only be maintained as long as external conditions held. If corruption and malfeasance developed, then funds that might have been put to productive purposes would instead be diverted for selfish ends. In this situation, the fact that the state was an enterprise association almost guaranteed that there would be very little check on such phenomena. An active civil sphere and an inquiring and independent media, both of which might have exposed and shamed corrupters, and mobilised countervailing political power, were lacking. And the legal system, which might have prescribed controls and punishments, was instead framed by and subordinated to the same national ends.[11]

The outcomes in the various systems concerned varied considerably, due to the operation of (sometimes, contingent) factors. Where the individuals in control of policy were genuinely committed to the national objective, and where they had the talent and support to envision the necessary social and economic programs, impressive and (possibly) lasting results could be achieved.

Aside from timing and sequence, cultural and institutional limitations could deflect the avowed national purpose, or lead to attempts to combine development with personal enrichment, or the fulfillment of other policy goals. While the role of Indonesia's Soeharto family is illustrative of all these limitations and failings; the restraint of the Lee family in Singapore and the Chiang dynasty in Taiwan (though partly a consequence of other factors) demonstrates the full range of possible outcomes, functional and dysfunctional. Even in the Korean case, while it was Park Chung-hee's proud and truthful boast that he would die without significant property of his own, both his immediate successors Chun Doo-hwan and Roh Tae-woo became notorious for the immense sums they were able to divert to their own purposes. The emergence of *bumiputera* 'cronyism' in Malaysia, with the consequent distortion of business priorities, was the result of attempting to achieve increases in national market share while also pursuing policies with an avowed ethnic dimension.[12]

In this congeries of structural and political relations can be seen the seeds of the crisis of 1997. For the seeds to grow, of course, they had to receive nutrients, and this was in the form of indiscriminate finance and 'hot money' that flowed in ever-greater quantities into the Asia Pacific especially in the years 1993–1997. To understand why this money was available is to ask another set of questions, relating mostly to the international system.[13]

Briefly, in the years in question, massive amounts of international capital, often in the form of short-term loans and portfolio investments originating from pension and hedge funds, flowed into the Asia Pacific economies. Rapid growth in the region, weak performance in Western Europe (outside Britain) and Japan, and the quest of international investors to diversify their portfolios following the 1995 Mexico crisis all impelled this trend. As this money encountered many limitations on foreign ownership, rather than being channeled into productive undertakings, it found its way into speculative concerns, including stock and property. The prices of the latter inflated, and deficits grew in the current accounts of many of the regional economies. In particular, short-term dollar or yen denominated debt accumulated far too rapidly.[14] Cheap money sourced from Japan was often re-loaned to enterprises and individuals at higher rates of return, which was a profitable operation so long as the domestic currency retained its value, permitting the original borrowers to repay interest and principal in dollars or yen.

Meanwhile in Japan, the erstwhile power-house of the regional economy, the investment of surplus funds in real estate had become an engrained habit, a habit which was copied especially in Korea during the real estate boom of the 1980s. While it was recognised that real estate was not generally a productive asset, years of inflating real estate values led investors and banks to assume that it would always yield a generous return. This assumption was transferred to investments in Asia.

This system unraveled when doubts emerged that the loans advanced would be repaid. The first clear danger signals were seen with the collapse of the Hanbo conglomerate in Korea in January 1997, although because Korea had traditionally relied much less on foreign borrowings (a pattern which changed markedly following Korea's entry into the OECD) the markets were slow to apply this lesson to Southeast Asia. Once the international market began to doubt the ability of the borrowers to repay, credit disappeared and money flowed in the opposite direction. This caused exchange rates to fall, and stock prices and property values followed. The first noticeable manifestation of this syndrome occurred in Thailand. A liquidity crisis developed, and social unrest put regimes across the region under pressure. As the financial crisis became a currency crisis, falling currency values eroded the capacity of borrowers to repay their loans. Once the Thai government ceased defending the currency, the crisis spilled over to other systems, especially Korea and Indonesia, where institutions and policy were similarly tested by the market. The crisis had a regional dimension as much because of the interlinkages of investments and trade between the systems as because there was a *perception* that they exhibited similar characteristics and problems.

Benedict Anderson and other commentators have been correct to point to the wider regional and global context in which the whole NIC phenomenon has been located.[15] An estimate of the precise impact of these factors is difficult. However, the variable impact of the crisis, as can be illustrated from the Taiwan and Singapore cases, and also the varying policy responses of the systems—with Korea requiring support from the IMF, and Malaysia escaping the need for such a bailout through a temporary quarantine of its currency market—indicate that there has been some room for policy initiative on the part of the individual nations. At best, therefore, these factors comprise a broad context.

At this point, one generalisation can be advanced. The outcome of the crisis was the consequence of that very lack of autonomous social institutions that had once been the strength of the development state. Without civil society, trust and transparency, that is, crucial institutional and policy capacity, formerly close business-government relations degenerated into corruption and malfeasance. The winds of globalisation then caused the Asian development states to falter at the next stage of their trajectory. But if this analysis of the Asian crisis is accurate, it ought to have been similarly manifest as much in Singapore and Taiwan as in Korea. The reasons why the former escaped the worst effects of the crisis will now be considered.

THE CONTINGENCIES OF DOMESTIC POLITICAL STRATEGY

At first glance, Singapore and Taiwan exhibit both *policy* and *structural* differences when compared with Korea. Spokesmen from their governments were quick to draw attention to the former, as proof of their good governance. While there are some grounds to such claims, the structural differences have received less attention. These have led to some insulation of these systems from the difficulties in the region, in a manner that will be described. Their existence, however, has had less to do with economic management, but a great deal more to do with the specific governmental characteristics of systems that, by any standard, are unusual and devoted to idiosyncratic (though not unsuccessful) political aims.

It can be readily demonstrated that both Singapore and Taiwan have been as much committed to the 'enterprise association' model as Korea or any of the other NICs in the region.[16] Both have pursued rapid growth through programs of Export Oriented Industrialisation, and both have relied upon bureaucratic instruments to superintend this commitment to growth. During the high tide of the NIC model, both sought to corporatise labour and other interests, subordinate the legal process to the wider national purpose, and restrain the critical functions of the media. The leaderships of the two political systems were equally adept at depicting their environments as hostile and unforgiving, and thus representing dedication to the national purpose as necessary to survival. However, due largely to its more compact size and higher level of development, Singapore's capacity to complete this project was greater.

Further, the means used by the Kuomintang until the mid-1980s to deter its political opponents have no parallel in Singapore, where an event analogous to the Kaohsiung incident of 1979 (as opposed to other instances of public disorder) never occurred. Thus, whereas detention without trial has been used in both systems to impede dissidents, the political murders in Taiwan and abroad which made the Kuomintang notorious and feared in the 1970s and early 1980s were unique.

Nevertheless, particular circumstances and inheritances required the modification of the typical enterprise association model in its application to Singapore and Taiwan. Regarding the city-state, developmentalism was modified in several important ways as a response to Singapore's circumstances. At this point it can be seen that the pursuit of international linkages has had powerful domestic consequences.

From the beginnings of Singapore's industrialisation, the decision was taken to facilitate wherever possible the operation of TNCs in the city-state. This was done for a range of reasons. With little domestic market and limited capital of its own, Singapore's prosperity ultimately depended upon investments that would turn to good account its labour supply, along with its regional location and already established entrepot status. In attracting TNCs the Lee government used all the familiar devices of the enterprise association model, with the Economic Development Board supervising the undertaking in the classic manner of the 'bureaucratic commanding agency'.[17] It is significant that in this development, nothing more than a subordinate status was envisioned for local capital. Lee and his associates were professionals, intellectuals and labour leaders with few organic linkages with the domestic bourgeoisie; their Fabian sympathies caused them to distrust a business sector which, in time and after modernisation had run something of its course, might in any case provide rival candidates for political power.[18] By attracting TNCs, therefore, domestic capital was also kept in its place.

In time, as the best brains and resources of the city-state were absorbed into the bureaucracy, bureaucratic modes of problem identification and management became pervasive. When it was decided that the time had come to stimulate local entrepreneurship and overseas investment, state instrumentalities took on the tasks of financing, encouraging, and organising these activities. Thus were developed the policy instruments whereby small companies can now turn to financial packages sponsored by the Productivity and Standards Board and the Economic Development Board, while businesses engaged in what are deemed sunrise industries, including computers and bio-technology, may also gain support from the National Computer Board and the National Science and Technology Board.[19]

Singapore's overseas investments, especially in such locations as the Singapore-Johor-Riau 'Growth Triangle' and the 'Suzhhou Industrial Park/Singapore-Suzhou Township' in China have been orchestrated by concerted government action. In the latter, for example, government orchestrated funds assisted in the construction of a school and a medical clinic, along with roads, lighting and sewers, the very items that are last on the list in most other 'development' areas in China.[20] While most of these activities appear free from obvious corruption—though the delights of Suzhou help explain why young Singaporean trade officials are so keen to be seconded there[21]—the consequence for Singapore capitalism has been to make its entrepreneurs much less flexible and more risk averse than their counterparts elsewhere in Southeast Asia. There are clearly some grounds for the argument that Singapore's continued growth in the last decade was the result of devoting an ever-higher concentration of resources to its industries rather than achieving higher levels of human productivity.[22]

If the state has been omnipresent, how has corruption and bureaucratic malfeasance been avoided? The People's Action Party regime recognised early that international business would not regard Singapore as a profitable field of investment without the protections for contracts, property, and labour controls that were to be found in the system of law which had been bequeathed to the island by the British. The government was careful, accordingly, to retain those elements of this system which fulfilled significant commercial purposes. Only a section of the legal territory was thus quarantined. The subordination of other aspects of the law to government fiat is a commonplace of commentaries on Singapore's contemporary history, down to the dissolution of the Law Society when its leadership expressed reservations on the use of the law to muzzle political debate.[23] At the same time, it was recognised also that corruption was one of the greatest obstacles to the smooth and predictable functioning of international business in the region. Lee's leadership was especially fierce in disciplining official venality of any kind, and closeness to the regime was never any guarantee of immunity. Indeed, so successful has this aspect of the PAP program been that presently many of the city-state's assets are guaranteed only by the *esprit de corps* of the elite civil service who superintend the various holding companies which own and control them. Accordingly, Vennewald points out that without Lee's commanding presence and single minded devotion to these principles, Singapore may eventually find that the absence of institutional checks—for example, the activities of government holding companies cannot be scrutinised in any critical sense by parliament—will be a hostage to fortune in the post-Lee era.[24] Already the merger in 1998 of two major government instrumentalities—Singapore Technologies and Sembawang—if it had occurred in a system where there was greater transparency and where private capital was involved, might have been described as a bailout.[25]

'Corruption', of course, is a value-laden term. There is some room for the contention that the very high salaries paid to politicians and officials in Singapore, though a preventive against the temptations of malfeasance in one sense, comprise an irregular reward in another. It is surely noteworthy that the president and prime minister receive higher salaries than their counterparts in Washington and Paris. Further, the veiled activities of the Singapore Government Investment Corporation in Myanmar, exposed in 1996 by the investigations of foreign media and an issue the subject of energetic official rebuttals, might also entail corruption.[26] Both Lee Hsien Loong and Lee Kuan Yew serve on the executive board of the Singapore GIC (Government Investment Corporation), for which service they receive rewards and perquisites which are not a matter of public record. The business of the Singapore GIC is to invest the money of taxpayers, though because its conduct cannot be investigated by parliament or any independent body, the facts of this case cannot be independently determined.

The pattern of industrialisation in Taiwan was also influenced by local regime and political factors. Until the prospects of unification with the mainland faded in the late 1970s, the island was governed as a 'model province'. In order to ensure that they had no political rivals, and especially given the popular rising of February 1947, the KMT government acted to remove the influence of the landowning class. Their property was converted to bonds, many of which funded investments in industry. The Kuomintang then turned their attention to fostering industrialisation. Initially the government's response was to enter enterprise directly, but in the 1960s it was decided that attracting trans-national capital would be a better strategy. Investment rules were liberalised, and in 1966 the Kaohsiung EPZ (Export Processing Zone) was established. The 'bureaucratic commanding agency' which oversaw these policies was the Council for International Economic Cooperation, from 1973 the Economic Planning Council, and from 1978 the Council for Economic Planning and Development.[27] This investment encouraged Taiwanese SMEs (Small and Medium Sized Enterprises) to develop linkages with US and Japanese companies as junior partners and component providers.

However, because Kuomintang rule was envisioned as 'temporary', the mainlander leadership left actual participation in commerce to others. Indeed, this division of labour may be interpreted as an implicit compact with the local population, which functioned with some effectiveness until at least the mid-1970s. The post-1949 Republic of China may be conceptualised as a superstructural imposition on Taiwan society. This feature was reinforced through to the 1960s by virtue of its function as a distributor of externally derived largesse, mostly civil and military aid from the United States. Corrupt linkages with business were minimised, unlike in the Korea and Malaysia cases,[28] by the expedient of giving the ruling party direct and generous (but concealed) access to government funding.

The Kuomintang government's isolation from the general population of Taiwan was mirrored by its international position. The regime became committed to a policy of large and portable reserves. This reflected the experience of ruinous inflation which dealt a fatal blow to the Kuomintang's credibility on the China mainland in the 1940s, in the handling of which the young Chiang Ching-kuo had a large personal responsibility, as well as the regime's longer term goals. At the same time, Taiwan was slow to open its financial system given the volatility of domestic opinion and international confidence as a consequence of the continued problem of recognition and identity that plagued 'The Republic of China'. The lack of convertibility of the NT$ has insulated it from some of the region's troubles.

As it was such, it did not develop strong linkages with the local entrepreneurs. Its funds often came from elsewhere (China's transplanted reserves, US support), and it was content—having denied them effective political power—to concede to the Taiwan elite a key role in the business sphere provided they did not contest the mainlander monopoly of political power. Without government largesse, and in the absence of a government policy of fostering large conglomerates with special finance, Taiwan's SME sector was much stronger and more competitive.

The choice of SMEs, in addition to direct TNC participation, as the best vehicles for industrialisation had important implications for Taiwan's vulnerability to the regional turmoil of 1997–98.[29] Taiwan's SMEs, being modestly capitalised, were never able to attract significant finance from abroad. Unlike many Southeast Asian businesses, they have thus never built up US$ or *yen* denominated debt, the repayment of which so crippled the Thai and Indonesian business sectors. These SMEs being smaller, they have generally been conducted upon more prudential financial bases, not being highly leveraged (like business in Korea and Indonesia) and often being supported by informal and family finance.[30] In addition, the bursting of Taipei's stockmarket bubble in 1989–90 made domestic and international investors more cautious, and led to a tighter regime of financial controls guaranteeing bank liquidity and restricting the size of loans made for the purposes of real estate purchase. Cautious progressive financial liberalisation was then pursued, with the opening of the bond market and parts of the banking sectors in 1991.

In the analysis of industry policy, the comparison with Korea is instructive.[31] After 1961, the Park Chung-hee government fostered large conglomerates as their chosen vehicle for industrialisation. This was because Korea sought to emulate and rival Japan, while escaping the integration of Korean business into Japanese production networks that would have been the result had Korea relied upon small and medium sized enterprises. In complementary fashion, in many industrial sectors, barriers were placed in the way of foreign direct investment. This policy was, at best, a mixed success, and its legacy was to exacerbate the problems encountered in 1997. Taiwan escaped such a legacy. The Chiangs were not hostile to the trend towards symbiosis with Japan. The integration of Taiwanese companies into production networks dominated by Japanese or, to a lesser extent US, companies is the pattern of this era.[32] Unlike the policy makers in Seoul, they saw no need to develop 'national' industrial champions—or foster 'national' capitalists—since their sojourn on Taiwan was only to be temporary, and in any case the business sphere was an area mostly left to native Taiwanese (and some émigré Shanghai capitalists) to dominate. Government guaranteed finance was therefore, as a rule, unnecessary. This had the further effect that business-government-bureaucracy relations developed without the extensive personal networks and corruption encountered in Korea.

The mainlander/Kuomintang predominance in the political and governmental commanding heights left it exposed, once the failure of the original project of the Party removed its longstanding rationale.[33] On the one hand, the neglect of the business area left the mainlanders without the extensive network of linkages that would have given them an alternative purchase in Taiwan society. On the other hand, under the leadership of Chiang Ching-kuo, the Kuomintang became committed to a policy of 'Taiwanisation' in an attempt to absorb (and even represent) the new social forces unleashed by democratisation. By the end of the 1980s, significant portions of the Party had been successfully colonised by its erstwhile subjects. There was then a noticeable increase in the levels of corruption and crime, but these were dealt with—at least to some extent—through the exposure of malefactors in the media, and the classic expedient of electing members of the counter-elite to positions that made them responsible for dealing with these problems. It is no accident that the voters in Taipei City and Taoyuan County turned to the opposition Democratic Progressive Party (DPP) to remedy the decline in social order. Democracy also led to the development of further transparency specifically in the financial sector. In the era of KMT dominance, prior to around 1990, there were some instances of politically connected businesses receiving concessionary finance. Such 'cronyism' has now disappeared due to the political scrutiny such measures would receive.

In the Korean case, comparable limitations upon the operation of the logic of enterprise association are hard to identify. Industrial champions were fostered to serve patriotic purposes in a contest that was played out upon an economic field. The policy instruments and business-bureaucratic links that evolved became the most important institutional features of the Korean political economy. The movement towards democratisation, which made a major breakthrough when competitive presidential elections were convened in 1987, led to the liberalisation of many spheres of life. The legal system began to develop the power and the confidence to regulate itself free of government interference, trades unionists and their leaders progressively dismantled the corporatist controls of the authoritarian era,[34] and non-government organisations emerged to occupy parts of the new civic space.[35]

Liberalisation did not have an immediate effect, however, on the economic sphere. Instead, the already strong regional and personal basis of political factionalism was given an additional filip with the advent of the highly monetised politics of the Roh Tae-woo and Kim Young-sam administrations.[36] To an extent, this was even an objective of government policy, with Roh Tae-woo channeling campaign funds to the rival democratic champions, Kim Young-sam and Kim Dae-jung, in the confident expectation that they would compete with each other in the electoral contest of 1987, thereby delivering him the presidential office. The policy linkages which had been one of the most important features of Korea heretofore took on a new aspect. The major conglomerates all sought to buy political influence with the new parties and representatives, and as three decades of policy had made them economic actors who dwarfed all others, they had the resources to accomplish this end. Money flowed freely, as the record now shows, with Roh Tae-woo in his time in office accumulating more than US$200 million in political funds. However, they extracted a price, in the form of contracts and especially concessionary loans. As state—that is, bureaucratic—direction of finance was a major aspect of the Korean model, this was easy to organise. Any oversight that the new democratic institutions might have exercised was deflected by political payments. With many players now crowding around the trough, and the patriotic foundations of the old policy now lost in the era of 'globalisation' (*segyehwa*), less viable operators also bought influence and were rewarded with loans.

The ineffective and divided administration struggled with *chaebol* and labour reform and measures to introduce greater transparency into the banking and financial sectors. In the event, the reforms in the latter were the undoing of Kim Young-sam's credibility since they exposed corruption involving his own family, but not before the Hanbo conglomerate had been brought to bankruptcy, thus initiating in 1997 the slide into insolvency of many of Korea's economic institutions. A measure of the dimensions of the problem can be gained through the Hanbo case. With 300 billion *won* of assets, Hanbo was able to borrow 5 trillion *won* in order to finance a new steel production facility, when there was already an excess in the national market and at a time of declining world steel prices. Democratisation eventually allowed the political leadership of Korea to catch up with the need to reform the nation's political economy, but its slow response was a costly failure.[37]

Nevertheless, if there have been important differences between Taiwan and Singapore, they have shared one major characteristic which has also had a parallel in the Korea case. While this argument should not be overextended, the impact of 'development shocks' on both systems should not be neglected.[38] When the People's Republic of China staged extensive military maneuvers during the 1996 presidential elections, the still contended nature of Taiwan's polity was highlighted. The semi-official public contacts between Taipei and Beijing initiated in 1992 did not prevent a serious security crisis in the Taiwan Straits in 1996–97, and the 1998 official paper on China's defence policy made it plain that China does not exclude the use of force in the pursuit of the objective of 'unification' with Taiwan. It can be argued that there is a widespread awareness in Taiwan that treating the state as a private resource to be exploited will weaken a system still, in a sense, under siege from external forces. The 1998 Malaysia-Singapore railway war was only a further installment in a lengthy series of crises and altercations (including differences on rival accounts of their separation in 1965, port facilities, transport links, customs procedures, crime, media stereotypes, security cooperation and even water supplies) that have long served to remind Singaporeans of their economic and geo-strategic vulnerability. To be sure, this vulnerability has been exploited by the ruling party, but it has helped to constrain the inclination to corruption. South Korea's security anxieties, manifest most dramatically in 1998 in the test by North Korea of what may be the prototype of a long range multi-stage missile, have been a continuous presence in Korean social and political affairs for five decades. This factor is clearly contingent, and therefore difficult to appropriate to any theoretical approach to state structure, but it has played its part in all three cases nonetheless.

ENTERPRISE ASSOCIATION AND THE OUTLOOK FOR SINGAPORE, TAIWAN AND KOREA

The crisis forced a re-evaluation across Asia of the long-term viability of the particular form of enterprise association seen in the region. In some of the systems, including Korea and Thailand (at least until the advent of the Thaksin administration in 2001), further liberalisation was the order of the day. Yet it would be wrong to conclude that this will be the preferred path in every case. In Malaysia the espousal of the notion that the financial crisis was largely a result of a foreign conspiracy to blight the country's progress to fully developed status—a position made explicit in the public musings of the Prime Minister—produced rather different policy and political outcomes.[39] If widespread and even nation-threatening disorder results in Indonesia, where recovery from the crisis is as yet only partial, similar consequences may yet follow. In Indonesia and Malaysia the penetration of foreign capital has always been regarded with some suspicion, and the extension of this attitude would have profound effects for the trajectory of both. Even in Korea, where official commitment towards liberalisation and transparency appears unequivocal, the popular roots of such commitment are shallow. It should be recalled that at the beginning of the IMF rescue mission to

Korea, (then) presidential candidate Kim Dae-jung initially criticised the program as yet another example of foreign interference, giving voice not only to his own long held views,[40] but to those of many of his countrymen. Attempts to sell failing enterprises—including major banks and the auto production arm of Daewoo—to foreign bidders evoked strong nationalist resistance. By contrast, the comparative robustness of the prevailing economic and social models in Taiwan and Singapore was taken as a signal that no major innovations were required.

It has been the argument of this chapter that Singapore and Taiwan, while examples of enterprise association, escaped a more severe dose of the regional affliction because of contingent structural features in their political economy. These include the separation of politics and business, mirroring the 'Taiwanese'-'mainlander' divide in Taiwan, and in Singapore the strategy of reliance on trans-national capital managed by a closed élite with few linkages to the local bourgeoisie. To adopt a severely summary view, these features have led to the incorporation of limited liberalisation in the first, and limited pluralisation in the second. Their relative good fortune may lead to an acceptance of the view that the fundamentals of their respective policies have been sound. In Korea, however, though liberalisation and pluralisation have made significant strides since 1987, until the crisis of 1997 this only had a limited effect on the nation's industrial structure and was also frustrated by the growth of corrupt money politics. The response in Korea has therefore been to pursue a radical break with the past, though the success of this departure has yet to be seen.

NOTES

1. Unless otherwise indicated, data cited in this paper is from the following sources: <http://www.singstat.gov.sg/> (Singapore); <http://www.nso.go.kr/eindex.html> (Korea); <http://www.dgbasey.gov.tw/english/dgbas_e0.htm> (Taiwan).
2. Kim Dae-jung, 'Economic Reform in Korea: Establishment of a Democratic Market Economy', Address at Stanford University, June 12 1998, *Korea and World Affairs* Vol. 22(1998), no.2, 279–83.
3. Ravi Velloor, '\$2b boost for economy', *The Straits Times* 30 June, 1998.
4. Vincent C Siew, 'Taiwan Weathers the Asian Financial Crisis', *Industry of Free China* 88(1998), no 6, 65–69; Steve Ruey-Long Chen, Director General, Board of Foreign Trade, Taipei, 'Taiwan and the Asian Financial Crisis', seminar, Australian National University, 11 May 1998; interview with Jeremy S C Chen, Council for Economic Planning and Development, Taipei, 13 July 1998.

5 Interview with Taiwan Finance Minister, Paul Chiu Cheng-hsiung, *South China Morning Post*, 6 July 1998: <http://www.scmp.com/news/special/AsiaChallenge/>, accessed 10 August, 1998.

6 On institutional capacity, see David C Kang, 'South Korean and Taiwanese development and the new institutional economics', *International Organization* Vol. 49(1995), 555–87.

7 There is an extensive and ever growing literature on this topic. Influential examples include: F C Deyo ed, *The Political Economy of the New Asian Industrialism* (Ithaca: Cornell UP, 1987); Thomas B Gold, *State and Society in the Taiwan Miracle* (Armonk: M E Sharpe, 1986); Robert Wade, *Governing the Market: Economic Theory and the Role of Government in East Asian Industrialization* (Princeton: Princeton UP, 1990); Stephan Haggard, *Pathways from the Periphery: the politics of growth in the newly industrializing countries* (Ithaca: Cornell UP, 1992); Ezra F Vogel, *The Four Little Dragons. The Spread of Industrialization in East Asia* (Cambridge: Harvard UP, 1991).

8 Michael Oakeshott, *On Human Conduct* (Oxford: Clarendon Press, 1975), ch 2. Cerny has recognised the applicability of 'enterprise association' in theorising the tasks of the modern state in the era of late modernity: see Philip G Cerny, 'Paradoxes of the Competition State: The Dynamics of Political Globalization', *Government and Opposition* Vol 32 (1997), 251–274.

9 This qualification is important, since to some degree some of the leaders of the Southeast Asian states sought to combine this objective with kleptocracy.

10 One of the most succinct analyses of states driven by market share is: Richard Rosecrance, *The Rise of the Trading State. Commerce and Conquest in the Modern World* (New York: Basic Books, 1986).

11 Other features could be added to this (illustrative) listing. It is important to note that the downside of the Asian development model was noticed long before the crisis of 1997. For examples, consult: James Clad, *Behind the Myth. Business, Money and Power in Southeast Asia* (London: Grafton, 1991); Kunio Yoshihara, *The Rise of Ersatz Capitalism in South-east Asia* (Singapore: Oxford U P, 1988); Walden Bello and Stephanie Rosenfeld, *Dragons in Distress. Asia's Miracle Economies in Crisis* (San Francisco: Food First, 1990).

12 Peter Searle, *The Riddle of Malaysian Capitalism. Rent-seekers or real capitalists?* (Honolulu: University of Hawaii Press, 1998).

13 The Asia Society, *Asia at a Crossroads*, http://www.asiasociety.org/publications/epg.html; Dan Biers ed, *Crash of 97. How the Financial Crisis is Reshaping Asia* (Hong Kong: Review Publishing, 1998); Ranjit Gill, *Asia Under Siege. How the Asian Miracle Went Wrong* (Singapore: Epic Management, 1998). The sources in the Roubini homepage are the biggest archive of relevant material: http://www.stern.nyu.edu/~nroubini/asia/AsiaHomepage.html.

14 'Charting the Crisis', *Asiaweek* 17 July 1998, 41.

15 Benedict Anderson, 'From Miracle to Crash' *London Review of Books*, Vol. 20(1998), no. 20.

16 The following points are drawn from the considerable literature on the two systems, including: Thomas B Gold, *State and Society in the Taiwan Miracle* (Armonk: M E Sharpe, 1986), Garry Rodan, *The Political Economy of Singapore's Industrialization: National State and International Capital* (London: Macmillan, 1989), Murray A Rubinstein ed, *The Other Taiwan. 1945 to the Present* (Armonk: M E Sharpe, 1994).

17 On the EDB, see Linda Lim, *The Political Economy of a City-State. Government-made Singapore* (Singapore: Oxford University Press, 1998).

18 See James Cotton, 'Interpreting Singapore: class or power?', *The Pacific Review* Vol. 8 (1995), 558–63.

19 Ben Dolven, 'Pay Before You Play', *Far Eastern Economic Review* 6 August 1998, 16.

20 China-Singapore Suzhou Industrial Park Development Co Ltd, *Singapore-Suzhou Township* (Singapore, 1995). It is ironic that Chinese entrepreneurship has undermined this project, with a more competitive Park, the 'Suzhou New District' opening under local government auspices next door. The sewers are undoubtedly inferior, but the labor is cheaper. See 'Why one park is better than two in Suzhou', *The Sunday Times* 14 December 1997, 18–19. Ultimately the Singapore sponsored entity could not compete, and a majority interest was acquired by its local competitor in 2001.

21 Interview with China-Singapore Suzhou Industrial Park Development Company officials, seconded from Singapore EDB, 26 October 1995, Suzhou.

22 Paul Krugman, 'The Myth of Asia's Miracle', <http://web.mit.edu/krugman/www /myth.html>; see also Darren McDermott, 'Singapore Swing: Krugman Was Right. Stung by a Professor, the Island Starts an Efficiency Drive', *The Wall Street Journal*, 23 October 1996: <http://www.stern.nyu.edu/~nroubini/asia/Growth KrugmanSingaporeWSJ1096.htm>, accessed 10 August 1998.

23 Francis T Seow, *To Catch a Tartar. A Dissident in Lee Kuan Yew's Prison* (New Haven: Yale University, Southeast Asia Studies Monograph #42, 1994), Christopher Tremewan, *The Political Economy of Social Control in Singapore* (London: Macmillan, 1994); Tang Liang Hong homepage: <http://www.ozemail. com.au/~tangtalk/.>

24 W Vennewald, *Technocrats in the state enterprise system of Singapore* (Murdoch University, Asia Research Centre, Working Paper #32, 1994).

25 Ben Dolven, 'Who Said Bailout?', *Far Eastern Economic Review*, 11 June 1998, 62.

26 Mike Carey, 'Singapore Sling' (SBS Dateline, 12 October 1996); Singapore Government Press Release: <http://www.gov.sg/mita/pressrelease/archives/ 96110402.htm>, accessed 14 November 1996.

27 Robert Wade, *Governing the Market. Economic Theory and the Role of Government in East Asian Industrialization* (Princeton: Princeton UP, 1990), ch.7.

28 James Cotton and H A V Kim, 'The new rich and the new middle class in South Korea: the rise and fall of the "golf republic"', in Richard Robison and David S G

Goodman eds, *The New Rich in Asia* (London: Routledge, 1996), 185–203; Edmund T Gomez and Jomo K S, *Malaysia's Political Economy. Politics, Patronage and Profits* (Cambridge: Cambridge U P, 1997).

29 Ho-Ching Wei and Chris Christodoulou, 'The Changing Relationship Between the Taiwanese Government and Small and Medium-sized Enterprises', *Asian Studies Review* Vol. 22 (1988), 239–60.

30 Susan Greenhalgh, 'Families and Networks in Taiwan's Economic Development', in Edwin A Winckler and Susan Greenhalgh eds, *Contending Approaches to the Political Economy of Taiwan* (Armonk: M E Sharpe, 1988), 224–45.

31 Cheng Tun-jen, 'Political Regimes and Development Strategies: South Korea and Taiwan', in G Gereffi and D Wyman eds, *Manufacturing Miracles: Paths of Industrialization in Latin America and East Asia* (Princeton: Princeton UP, 1990), 139–78.

32 Mitchell Bernard, 'The Post-Plaza Political Economy of Taiwanese-Japanese Relations', *The Pacific Review* Vol. 4 (1991), 358–367.

33 Linda Chao and Ramon H Myers, *The First Chinese Democracy. Political Life in the Republic of China on Taiwan* (Baltimore: John Hopkins U P, 1998).

34 Jongryn Mo, 'Political Learning and Democratic Consolidation: Korean Industrial Relations, 1987–1992', *Comparative Political Studies* Vol. 29 (1996), 290–311.

35 Su-Hoon Lee, 'Transitional Politics of Korea, 1987–1992: Activation of Civil Society', *Pacific Affairs* Vol. 66 (1993), 351–67.

36 James Cotton and H A V Kim, 'The new rich and the new middle class in South Korea: the rise and fall of the "golf republic"', 185–203.

37 Jongryn Mo and Chung-in Moon, 'Democracy and the Korean Economic Crisis', NAPSNet Forum #15, <http://www.nautilus.org/napsnet/fora/15A_Mo&Moon.html>, accessed 3/19/98.

38 Stephan Haggard, *Pathways from the Periphery. The Politics of Growth in the Newly Industrializing Countries* (Ithaca: Cornell UP, 1990).

39 Lim Kok Wing et al, *Hidden Agenda* (Petaling Jaya: Limkokwing Integrated, 1998); M V Pandiyan, 'Globalisation "a means, not an end"', *The Star* 29 July 1998: <http://www.jaring.my/~star/current/29vpgl.html>, accessed 30 July 1998.

40 Kim Dae-jung, *Mass-Participatory Economy. A Democratic Alternative for Korea* (Boston: University Press of America, 1985).

Chapter 4

THE SINGAPORE IDENTITY: DOMESTIC AND GLOBAL INFLUENCES

The master discourses in social science are class, state, society and nation/ethnicity. While all four have featured in analyses of Singapore, there is a clear tendency for the policy and perspective of the state to predominate. Consequently, most recent literature on Singapore's identity has been concerned with one of three relationships: that between state and class, that between state and society, and that between state and ethnicity. This chapter reviews some examples of that literature, illustrating the proposition that in general the state is the central phenomenon therein.[1] While state-centred discourse is the foundation for much social scientific work on Singapore, however, this chapter finds further that, while the state is ineluctably part of any analysis, there is insufficient attempt to disaggregate or investigate the state itself. Singapore's identity revolves around the state as an active and shaping influence, but the mechanisms of that influence are particularly obscure. And this obscurity persists despite the fact that Singapore is crucially dependent upon regional and global linkages.

STATE AND CLASS

This section compares two recent works on Singapore, by Christopher Tremewan and Francis Seow respectively. Both focus upon recent developments in the city-state, but while the first endeavours to develop a hypothesis regarding state-class relations, the second is a personal memoir, though one which provides much information about political dynamics and elite perspectives.

The main task of Tremewan's book[2] is to recount (largely on the basis of the secondary literature) the record of regime policy in four major areas, public housing, education, political institutions, and the legal regime. The argument here is that with respect to policies in each of these areas, the objective of social control has been paramount. And this social control has been exercised by and for a particular class.

Tremewan begins with the assertion that social control in Singapore has never before been viewed in so systematic or comprehensive a fashion, but given the author's references to such authorities as Deyo, Rodan, Salaff, Bello and others[3], it would have been more accurate to have said that this book's central thesis was to state this argument in a particularly strong form. This is not to disagree that there is not a lot of evidence for this position, nor that Tremewan marshals it well, showing a very good familiarity with his subject. It is surely remarkable, to take an example drawn from one of his main areas of concern, that in 1968 the Singapore government owned some 26% of the land area of the city-state, whereas now it owns more than 75%, and is empowered to acquire land without restriction (usually recompensing owners at well below market value). The consequence has been that some 85% of the population has come (or been forced) to live in publicly provided housing, which has then afforded the government a vast range of controls to oversee, constrain and restrict everyday life in Singapore. And this power has been used specifically for political purposes, as was demonstrated in 1985, when the government stated that it would give priority to the upgrading and improvement of housing estates which were in PAP (ruling People's Action Party) constituencies. To a large extent, this story has already been told—and Tremewan's account relies significantly on the work of Linda Lim and several others[4]. The originality of this approach lies, rather, in its insistence that virtually all major policy initiatives in these areas have had the implicit objective of enhancing the regime's capacity for social control.

But control for what purpose? Tremewan now parts company with the bulk of the secondary literature that he employs to offer a different view of the citystate (or, to be strictly correct, an updating of the interpretations offered by Buchanan and also by Caldwell[5]). For Tremewan is determined to see all of these phenomena through the prism of class. He takes for granted the heuristic value of this approach from the outset; and thus contradictory developments are never considered and alternative explanations are never canvassed. The problems with such an approach to a system of the Asian Newly Industrialising Country (NIC) type are, however, well known. Tremewan shows little awareness of them, though he does list items in his bibliography that analyse the difficulties of dealing with the NIC state as an emanation of a class, and of linking its policies to particular class interests and strategies (domestic and trans-national) when it often seems to act with a surprising degree of autonomy.

Setting this major shortcoming aside, how, then, does Tremewan show that the 'Lee faction' (as former Prime Minister Lee Kuan Yew and his associates are labelled) is a creature, surrogate, or agent of Singapore's capitalist class? Here there is a good deal of room for serious and original social science research on Singapore. Lee's background, his class outlook and prejudices, his recruitment of particular later generation leaders and his fostering of a range of policies are all worth examining from the point of view of this hypothesis. Much of the material of the book touches on these themes, but tangentially, since it is never thought worthwhile to test this hypothesis. Tremewan then compounds his difficulties by offering several different accounts of his untested but crucial hypothesis, that is, his assertion regarding the class standing of the Lee faction. Initially, Lee is described as transforming the PAP 'from an anti-imperialist party of the Chinese lower class to a party of the small, pro-British, English-speaking capitalist class.' Later, however, we have the statement that 'the lack of a strong domestic capitalist class had opened a route to power for the Lee faction of the PAP', which immediately raises the (unanswered) question, how did the weakness of Lee's class base facilitate his rise to power, rather than constitute an impediment to be overcome? Further in the book we have the statement, 'unlike other NICs where a local capitalist class had emerged with real political power to protect its interests, the PAP could ignore the demands of its local capitalist class as well as the working class'. This would suggest that the PAP is not an agency of local capitalism, and indeed possesses extraordinary autonomy in its policies and strategies. This latter interpretation is finally confirmed where it is observed that 'The PAP-state ... has been characterised by its autonomy from local class forces'.[6] We have come a long way from the categorical statement at the opening of the book that the system of social control in Singapore is maintained by 'the relationship between the Singapore capitalist class, represented by the PAP-state, and foreign capital' whose interests are served by the economic transformation policies pursued from the 1960s onwards.

The author's approach similarly falters when he attempts to account for the emergence from the 1980s of new forms of political opposition (of which Francis Seow—of whom more later—might be regarded as representative). What has been the basis for this new opposition? Tremewan presents a good account of the ways in which particular government policies have alienated sections of the population—Malay speakers, graduate women, workers on low pay—but cannot develop a consistent class approach towards the development of this opposition. Thus, 'the rise of local capital and the growth of a middle class concentrated in the service sector has confronted the PAP-state with a challenge from within its own class. The PAP-state faces the danger of a democratically inclined fraction of the capitalist class building an electoral alliance with elements of a resentful working class'.[7] Here middle and capitalist class are conflated, and a political alliance crossing class boundaries is deemed possible. Once again, Tremewan appears incapable of operationalising his hypothesis consistently.

The expression 'PAP-state', by which Tremewan means the organisational core or the key personnel and offices of the Singapore regime, conceals more problems than it solves. There have been important tensions within the party, some of which are exposed in the later sections of the book (which neglects, however, to discuss the split between former President and PAP elder Devan Nair and Lee). Tremewan himself notes that the party went into a state of somnolescence in the 1970s with the vanquishing of its political rivals, to be revived in the 1980s when new political opposition arose. The present difficulties the system is experiencing in the transition to the post-Lee Kuan Yew era may yet see the party split or redefine its role. Here it can be suggested that while Tremewan argues that the introduction of a powerful elected presidency has been aimed at providing the Lee faction with veto powers should a significant number of opposition members enter parliament, its function may actually be to provide a political redoubt should PAP unity fail. At any rate, this expression does have the advantage of suggesting that the commanding presence of the Singapore political system has consisted in a group of individuals wielding bureaucratic and organisational power towards ends that they have themselves defined.

The central difficulty of this account now becomes apparent. Why have these various engines of social control been created? If politics is reduced to matters of class, then the answer would seem to be, to build capitalism in Singapore for the benefit of the capitalist class. But to insist upon this answer is, in fact, to miss the point of much of Singapore's modern experience. The mechanisms of social control have been invented for a number of purposes, including the economic transformation goals that are so much discussed in the conventional literature. But latterly especially, the pre-eminent end and goal has been to keep Lee and his chosen successors in power. This has involved some remarkable contortions, as old threats have subsided and new rivals have emerged. One has only to consider the events of 1986–88, when the agents of an alleged Marxist conspiracy were detained without trial under legislation which was simultaneously employed to imprison the lawyer acting upon their behalf on the grounds that he was an agent of a plot hatched in the US Embassy. The aim of the latter was allegedly to encourage professionals to run against the ruling party in the next elections. It is straining comprehension, to say the least, to interpret these developments as the emanation of class forces, but very easy to understand them as the result of Lee's determination to brook no rivals on the political stage. This interpretation is supported by the fact that the lawyer in question, Francis Seow, had bested the Prime Minister in a televised inquiry into the activities of the Law Society, the executive of which had the temerity to comment (as was permitted and even enjoined by their then charter) on the coherence of forthcoming government legislation. From the point of view of the capitalist class, of course, Lee Kuan Yew is utterly dispensable, depending upon whether he performs what is perceived as a class mission or not, whereas from the point of view of the Lee political machine, he is the only utterly necessary element in the whole political ensemble. Tremewan's book, then, performs a useful function in cataloguing with such precision and comprehensiveness the social control mechanisms that have been developed in Singapore, but seeks the ultimate grounds for the existence of these mechanisms in an untested and finally incoherent hypothesis which deflects his inquiry from taking what would have been a more promising direction. The answers to at least some of these questions are to be found in the memoir by Francis Seow,[8] which, along with Chan Heng Chee's work on the ruling party, James Minchin's biography of Lee Kuan Yew, and Philip Jeyaretnam's fiction, joins the still small shelf of essential readings on the city-state and its identity.[9]

The circumstances of Seow's rise to notoriety have already been mentioned. His account of his imprisonment and interrogation at the hands of the Internal Security Department comprises half of his memoir, and is both intriguing and insightful. It should be recalled that under Singapore's Internal Security Act, individuals may be detained for an indefinite period with no justification being necessary beyond a statement of grounds of detention which is not itself justiciable. In the statement released by the Ministry of Home Affairs regarding Seow's case it is asserted that he had made himself 'a willing party to acts of interference in Singapore's internal affairs by representatives of a foreign power which would undermine the integrity of the political system'.[10] Despite all the powers at its disposal, the seizure of Seow's papers and business records (subsequently passed on to the taxation authorities for a stringent personal tax audit), and the cooperation of his bankers in Malaysia and Thailand (but not in Hong Kong, though with respect to his accounts there Seow gave his consent for them to be made available to the authorities), what could be established by the Internal Security Department (ISD) was only that he had been encouraged in sporadic contacts with US officials to stand as a parliamentary candidate. No trace of American funding or orchestration of Seow's entry into politics could be found.

Now Seow's political ambitions by themselves could not be regarded as subversive—after all, the ruling party in Singapore has long validated its control of government by besting other parties in electoral contests—but they could be represented as subversive if he was an agent or surrogate for a foreign power. Had the power in question been Marxist (even in 1988 when these events occurred), it is conceivable that encouragement by such a power could be represented as threatening to Singapore's integrity. But the power was the United States, a country whose security and economic stake in the stability of Singapore was second to none. Moreover, Seow's American friends evidently did nothing of a material nature to influence his conduct.

What, then, was the real reason for Seow's detention? One of two possibilities is suggested by Seow's story. He regards his defence of the Law Society against the Prime Minister, and his subsequent decision to act as a solicitor for the alleged Marxist conspirators detained in 1987, as actions which so aroused the ire of Lee Kuan Yew that the latter consequently became determined to destroy him. But it is also clear that having attracted public attention by his opposition to Lee in an encounter before a parliamentary Select Committee which was given television coverage, Seow had gained a degree of popular credibility which may well have led the ruling party to seek to dissuade him from entering politics. Ironically, Seow's experience seems to have strengthened his views, and he went on to contest the elections of 1988 (with two other members of the opposition in a 'Group Representation Constituency'), and with 49.1% of the vote, came within a hair's breadth of winning. Seow was then able to claim a seat as a 'non-constituency member', a position open, under Singapore law, to the closest runner-up in the election. In a particularly shabby episode, the convening of the parliament was delayed until he was found in breach of the law in the aforementioned taxation audit, fined, and as a consequence disqualified to become a representative. By this time, however, he was in exile in the United States.

The value of this memoir lies not least in the fact that its author was no radical or malcontent. He was decidedly a representative of the Singaporean elite. As a member of the staff of the Attorney-General's chambers, in the very small legal community of the time, Seow had prosecuted a case before then judge (and later sole opposition MP) J. B. Jeyaretnam in 1957, a case in which Lee Kuan Yew appeared as defence counsel. Seow's path crossed Lee's a number of times, and he rose to become Solicitor-General (and to receive a public decoration in recognition of his services) before entering private practice in 1970. What is surely striking in his case is the apparent carelessness with which the regime alienates institutions and individuals who would seem to be its natural supporters, a point underlined by the fact that former President Devan Nair contributed a foreword to the book. Which point returns us to Tremewan's argument. Whichever factor was uppermost in the minds of those who imprisoned Seow, it is straining credibility to interpret their actions as having any reference to class or class roles. Explaining these events would seem to have a much greater and immediate connection with the struggle by the city-state's founder and guiding intelligence to retain political power in his twilight years. In short, they would seem to be inexplicable without reference to the dynamics and personnel of the state.

STATE AND SOCIETY

States do not act in a vacuum, however, nor without the resources (intellectual as well as material) provided by a given society. In the Singapore case, how might the limitations and requirements imposed by the society on the state be conceptualised?

The authors of two important and well-known works on Singapore sociology are in agreement that the role of the state has been crucial in constructing and reconstructing the society, though with sociological consequences that have not always been to the liking of the architects, and which have therefore been a factor in the adjustment and recension of policy.[11] They also agree that while the People's Action Party has many achievements in nation building to its credit, its rule is at something of a crossroads in that without a diminution of the government's aspiration to control the behaviour of the citizenry, the latter will never assume the full duties of citizenship and thus the polity will not mature. While Michael Hill and Lian Kwen Fee do not fully consider the impact such a development might have upon the structures and mechanisms they describe, Beng-Huat Chua develops his argument further by proposing a communitarian alternative to the liberal democratic model which Singapore's democratisers and critics often regard as the only alternative to the present system. Both books may (ironically) be criticised for concentrating upon the state but neglecting politics, and thus failing to take the measure of the obstacles to the reassertion of society that they anticipate.

At one level, the volume by Hill and Lian is a comprehensive survey of social policy: citizenship and nationality, education and language, housing, the family, and 'parapolitics' are all surveyed. The authors are well informed, and the making and remaking (and sometimes unmaking) of policy in these areas is carefully described and analysed. There are some particular objections that could be levelled at their account of the intermediating para-political institutions—Residents' Committees, Citizens' Consultative Committees, the People's Association—that are the subject of chapter 7, but these objections are almost articulated in their own description. As the authors candidly observe, while they have the appearance of 'mediating structures ... partly because they are closely identified with the PAP their effectiveness has been limited'.[12] In this connection it is surely significant, though it is nowhere mentioned in the book, that around 40% of the individuals in the society in which these institutions (coordinated by the Prime Minister's Office) function support opposition candidates in parliamentary elections.

At another level, however, the authors are mounting an explicit argument about the specific nature and character of Singapore's nation building experience, one that they describe as consisting in the pursuit of 'a national identity grounded in rational and pragmatic values'.[13] Such a pursuit is to be distinguished from the two other paths open, on their view, to new nations: the attempt on the one hand to construct a 'regressive' identity (based upon a reconstructed historical past), and on the other to realise a comprehensive and 'progressive' vision (founded upon a socialist or utopian programme). Now rationality, pragmatism, and a rejection of ideology are certainly claimed by the regime for itself and its record But on further inspection, many of the rational and pragmatic (and 'meritocratic') policies discussed in this book would seem to have both 'regressive' and 'utopian' elements. The government's decision to construct a 'Chinese' identity for the many dialect and lineage groups in 77% of Singapore's population involved the learning of a language which was a foreign tongue to most of the dialect speaking individuals concerned (though it was the original language of the high culture from which their forbears had sprung). The artifice involved is underlined by the fact that the earlier policy had been to promote Malay as the main language of the island, not only because this would ease integration with Malaysia and Indonesia but also because this was the language of communication often used by different dialect groups between each other. The progressive or utopian aspect of the government's program was reflected in the fact that while representative institutions were adapted to the needs of the city-state, it was assumed that they would function more or less indefinitely without generating an organised political opposition, which when it then appeared had to be confronted with ad hoc and shifting stratagems.

Hill and Lian do seek, however, to depict the Singapore regime as cognisant of the need to attend to public responses to their policies. This awareness, 'in contrast with the "topdown" approach of the corporatist model' conforms instead to what they call a 'Return to Sender' logic. On their account, 'this is a process in which the definition of citizen vis-a-vis the state has to be repeatedly renegotiated.'[14]

> The political leadership "educates" its population into identities appropriate to its political agenda; but these identities take on an autonomy which cannot always be anticipated—and may well be unintended—so that the elite then has to readdress them. In the case of Singapore, political discourse has been articulated and encoded in such a visible fashion that the logic of the Return to Sender process is strikingly revealed.[15]

From the many examples of policy which they subject to analysis, it is not clear whether they are saying anything more than that in such an arrangement, policies handed down by the regime have both unintended and unforeseen consequences, and also incoherences and inconsistencies. These are bound to be pointed out by the citizenry, either in their behaviour or articulated explicitly; the policies may then be recast or withdrawn. A good example (discussed in chapter 8) is the decision that it was important for social cohesion for the state to propagate 'religious knowledge', which became a feature of the school curriculum in 1984, but which was withdrawn in 1989 when the regime discovered that the promotion of religion might lead to the development of alternative or even anti-regime loyalties. But these and other examples are quite consistent with the corporatist model, since corporatist policies similarly require constant adjustment and management.

Despite (or as a result of) the Return to Sender' phenomenon, it is Hill and Lian's contention that the 'overtly paternalistic and interventionist policies of the PAP government ... have over the years reduced the social and political space within which Singaporeans are allowed to operate.' Many critics regard this interventionism as anachronistic, and even government spokesmen have expressed the need to create a 'civic society' to allow for greater creativity and individual and group responsibility. On this issue, Hill and Lian are in agreement that the amount of 'political space' the regime is prepared to 'concede' is crucial for the future direction of the city-state.[16] They regard this as both the most important item on the present political agenda, and a necessity if Singaporeans are to assume all the duties and responsibilities consistent with a civic republican conception of the polity. On this issue at least, they are in agreement with the author of another text devoted to many of the same issues.

Chua Beng-Huat's account of the construction of Singapore is generally sound and never less than insightful. The ruling party and its leadership rejected 'race' and 'class' in favour of 'nation', pursuing first mere 'survival' and then 'pragmatism' as the successive watchwords of their policies. While the party's overall record as manager of national economic construction is one of the success stories of recent decades, Chua considers the public housing programme to have been especially effective.[17] In the city-state, more than 85% of the population now live in public sector flats, and many have now become owner-occupiers. By 'delivering the goods' the state has avoided the politicisation of a major welfare provision, despite some inequities and the use by the government of the fact that most of the citizenry must live in state housing to impose a range of political and social controls. In the bulk of the text, however, there is a sharper edge to Chua's critique, and as he covers much of the same policy ground as Hill and Lian, their contrasting perspectives are worthy of detailed complementary study.

As well as being a work of analysis, this book also possesses a prescriptive dimension. However, the author's prognosis and recommendation for the future of Singapore's 'communitarian' democracy, intriguing as it is, is nevertheless in some doubt, since it is not clear whether the state is capable or would wish to respond to the demands and problems which Chua detects in recent events. Indeed, while there are numerous references (averaging around one per page) to the PAP—it is an agency which makes policy, reacts to criticism, anticipates problems, and possesses vision—this most crucial entity is neither explored nor deconstructed.

According to Chua's argument, fundamental changes occurred in Singapore at the beginning of the 1980s. The regime found itself having to deal with a more critical and demanding public. Mere 'pragmatism' was found to be an insufficient basis for rule, and generated its own incoherences. The response of the PAP was both ideological and institutional. On the one hand, 'individualism' having been lauded and encouraged earlier as a motive to individual betterment and thus social progress, became subject to critique. It was equated with potentially destructive selfishness, and regarded as the source of alleged decay in the institutions and mores of advanced European and American societies. In its place, the regime explored various possibilities: first moral and religious education, then the official adoption of 'Confucianism', then the promulgation of 'shared values', and most recently the discourse of 'Asian values'. On the institutional front, co-optative, innovatory and feedback strategies were all employed to undermine criticism or absorb its perpetrators. Places in parliament were provided both for nominated MPs and also for those parliamentary candidates who were the closest runners-up at general elections, it being assumed that these would bring opposition or non-partisan voices to a chamber where there was very little real debate. The electoral system was further modified to ensure that some members of the minority races would always be present in parliament. And a 'Feedback Unit' was established in the Ministry of Community Development to hold regular consultative sessions with members of the public. There was also talk of the positive role that 'civic society' could play in the next stage of Singapore's development.[18]

Chua is convinced that the regime needs to go further if the trend towards democratisation is not to be stifled:

> A defining character of democracy is freedom of belief and freedom to speak freely about that belief. This remains difficult in Singapore at three levels; the level of conceptual practice, the level of building of non-government-sponsored social organisations in civil society, and finally, the generalised effect of legal constraints.[19]

His prescription for entrenching and consolidating democracy includes the relinquishment of controls on the media, the modification of such restrictions upon civil society as the Societies Act (which requires all voluntary associations to register and to restrict themselves to their particular sphere and not engage in 'politics) and the repeal of the Internal Security Act (which permits imprisonment without trial). But the democracy that would be thereby entrenched need not be liberal-democracy but could instead be 'communitarian'. Here Chua does not spell out the features of such a democracy—'the promoters of such a possibility ... have yet to work out just what a communitarian democracy looks like'[20]—except to say that it would be consistent with the PAPs anti-individualist policy stance, and might also match abiding ('Asian') features of the social system.

Which returns this critique to the neglect of the character and dynamics of the PAP, and indeed of the state. In reference to the abandonment in 1990 of the programme to promote Confucianism, Chua notes that 'while the PAP government has failed to Confucianise the population, it has indeed Confucianised itself.' However, he is adamant that:

> The Confucianisation of Singapore, with its emphasis on centralised leadership and unquestioning loyalty and obedience of the subjects, attempted to preempt, and even threatened [the] process towards greater democratisation.[21]

If the PAP has indeed become such a 'Confucianised' entity, it is surely important to determine whether there is any chance that the program of change recommended is likely to be supported. Chua's own work, and also that of Hill and Lian, shows that it is considerably at variance with the track record of the PAP thus far.

STATE AND ETHNICITY

If, indeed, the PAP has been so 'Confucianised', what has been the effect in Singapore on one of its major tasks, the management of ethnicity? Does this mean that ethnicity must be treated as an independent variable in analysis of the Singapore system? According to Lai Ah Eng, 'ethnicity' in this case is a particular and idiosyncratic construction of Chinese identity propagated by the Singapore political leadership. This has had powerful consequences not only for the majority community, but for all races in Singapore:

> The promotion of Mandarin and Confucianism in effect means a definition and perception of the Chinese as a homogeneous group. This view on the part of the government is guided by its ideology of CMIO (Chinese, Malays, Indians, and Others) multiracialism in which Chinese race = Mandarin language = Confucian culture. However ... the Chinese are extremely heterogeneous along the lines of class, language, culture, education, religion, and politics. The imposition of a particular conception of Chineseness confronts and contradicts this heterogeneity.[22]

'CMIO' insists upon moulding all groups according to a mainstream conception. While it facilitates the use of common space and facilities, with each group's practices and folkways having legitimacy, it also delimits and divides the population in a way that obstructs the development of commonalities. It is partly for this reason that cross-community marriages are still comparatively rare, and the use by one community of the language of another is unusual. The fate of the Chinese *Baba* community is particularly poignant, with their syncretic Sino-Malay culture and language being supplanted in the younger generation by a standard 'Chinese' identity. Ironically, given the PAP government's commitment to cooperation with its neighbours, the propagation of 'CMIO' has led to a loss of integration with the Southeast Asia region, as compared with 20 or 30 years ago, when *pasar* Malay was often the common language of the street and market.[23]

'CMIO' has not helped to eradicate the popular stereotypes of the various communities, indeed the PAP themselves have been responsible for maintaining them. Those who have watched successive National Day addresses by Lee Kuan Yew will be aware that questions of race have very much impinged upon his worldview. For Lee, the Malays were quite specifically under-achievers, who needed to make greater efforts to gain a place in the educational, economic, and governmental elite in proportion to their numbers. This sentiment has been internalised even by Malay community leaders themselves, who have often attributed their perceived backwardness to certain inherent cultural traits. The perception and self-perception of Malays in Singapore as 'marginal' has been comprehensively analysed by Lily Rahim.[24]

Tania Li has shown, however, that the Singapore Malays are a more heterogeneous group in terms of their origins than is often supposed, and there is more than one way to interpret their present status.[25] From the perspective of 1959 (the year of self-government), though the Chinese as an ethnic group were over-represented amongst the professional and economic elite, this fact obscures the division that then existed among them between the Chinese and English educated. Most ethnic Chinese members of the various elites were drawn from the latter, and the economic status of the vernacular educated Chinese and of the Malays was little different. While it is the case that certain social mores and practices presently disadvantage the minority Malay community by comparison with the Chinese (Chinese women, for example, place more of their income at the disposal of the household; they also exhibit lower fertility rates), it cannot be maintained that Chinese social patterns are uniquely conducive to modernisation.

For what purpose has ethnicity been thus managed? Raj Vasil contends that this construction of ethnicity is to be understood as part of a policy of 'Asianising' which has been introduced to help Singapore avoid the perils of Westernisation.[26] Lee Kuan Yew has spoken of the need to provide that 'cultural ballast' which would be lost if Singaporeans spoke only English (and were, presumably, all Christians). More pragmatic members of the elite have stressed the beneficent effects of fostering such 'Asian' values as loyalty to the family and respect for community. In addition, it should be observed that Singapore has suffered in the past from ethnic conflicts, and an ethnic policy was required which both allowed the expression of ethnic identity while requiring tolerance for the expression of the same by other ethnic groups.

However, alternative interpretations of this policy are possible. Ethnicity has always been a potential vehicle for opposition to the regime, and indeed did function as such in the early 1960s when the Barisan Socialis (the leftist leaders of which had split from the PAP, carrying many of the rank and file members with them) based their appeal on the local Chinese identity and its neglect by the English-educated elite. So constructing ethnicity as to redefine it according to the definition formulated by the state has ensured that the state has remained in charge of the ethnic agenda. This has had the added benefit, in the case of the majority Chinese community, that propagating the high culture has also allowed the state to embrace, in the interest of cultural ballast, its uncompromising message of the duty of loyalty to the ruler.

THEORISING THE STATE

This chapter has established that in much analytical writing on Singapore and the Singapore identity, 'the state' is central. 'Class' fails as a master narrative; the dynamics and characteristics of 'society' cannot be discussed without reference to 'the state'; and the very construction and meaning of ethnicity now conforms to a state agenda.

Now there is an extensive literature on 'relative state autonomy' in the Asian NICs/NIEs, in which can be found a range of explanations as to why this might be the case.[27] This ground has been well-covered, and will thus not be further considered. Rather, my purpose here will be to point to the fact that while 'the state' is centre stage, the meaning of the state remains often problematic in these works. It is variously an organisation (the PAP), a guiding group or clique (Lee Kuan Yew and his associates), a body of policies (CMIO, natal policies, and so forth), or an ideology (meritocracy and/or pragmatism)

Defining and delimiting the core of the Singapore state is evidently difficult. The PAP is clearly of some importance—hence the expression, 'the PAP-state'—but the most obvious function of the party is to be seen at the grass-roots, with the sponsorship of children's and youth groups, and the superintending of local government. The PAP is avowedly a mass party with a national mission, but the members neither aggregate policy nor orchestrate demands of the leadership, nor even choose the candidates who stand on the party ticket at election time. As Bilveer Singh observes:

> ... the PAP is a highly centralised organisation, ruled totally by the parliamentary-ministerial wing headed, in the past by the prime minister, and since November 1990, the senior minister, Mr Lee Kuan Yew.[28]

It would therefore seem that government and party and more or less interchangeable, and indeed this is the approach taken by local opposition leader, Chee Soon Juan, in his analysis of the city-state.[29] Further, the party is itself something of a shell. While it legitimises a particular team of parliamentary candidates at election time, and occupies an area in the political space that might otherwise be claimed by other contenders for power, it is neither a vehicle for grooming potential parliamentarians, nor an organisation in which policy is formulated, nor an aggregator of citizen demands. Under the party statutes, it is dominated by a small group of 'cadre members' (not always publicly identified). More informally, Lee Kuan Yew and his associates, co-existing with a potentially rival group led by Prime Minister Goh Chok Tong, are the source of all important policy and personnel initiatives.[30]

However, the conditions that make the dominance of this group possible are difficult to specify. It may be suggested that it is the specification, on the basis of empirical study, of these conditions which constitutes the agenda for studies of the Singapore state and thus of the Singapore identity. Here in at least four areas there have been some suggestions by contemporary analysts as to those conditions.

First, there is no independent entrepreneurial class in Singapore from which demands might arise that would undermine the PAP. There has been some argument that this absence has been a matter of design: there are undoubtedly some notable examples of business figures who have been undermined or ruined when they chose to contest the PAP's dominance.[31]

Second, Singapore's present political arrangements draw strength from the large state sector of the national economy. Partly in the space which might otherwise have been occupied by an entrepreneurial class, the state has created a number of government linked companies which, though dwarfed overall by the multi-national sector, dominate the domestic component of the economy. Holding companies linked to Temasek Holdings, Singapore Technology Holdings, and the Singapore Health Corporation, as well as to the Ministry of National Development are by far the biggest players in Singapore domestic business. It is Werner Vennewald's conclusion that the leading executives of these companies are the dominant elite:

> In Singapore highly motivated, economically trained professionals and not rent-seeking groups or an indigenous bourgeoisie conquered the heights of political power. Through their access to and command of political resources they changed the socio-economic structure of the country.[32]

Vennewald's study highlights two aspects of Singapore's state sector. The hundreds of business entities that make up the government linked sector are managed by a cadre of senior bureaucrats occupying multiple directorships in a range of companies. Around 40 such bureaucrats are at the very summit, being responsible for thousands of employees and billions of dollars of state assets. Though in formal terms these bureaucrats are answerable to ministers and departmental permanent secretaries, in practice much of their activity is autonomous. In many cases these companies have no obligation to publish their accounts and are free of many of the legal restraints that apply to private businesses; moreover their operations cannot be adequately scrutinised by parliament. These arrangements lead Vennewald to speculate that this personnel system is dependent ultimately upon patronage and especially upon loyalty to Lee Kuan Yew. As it becomes larger and diversifies further, these controls may be insufficient to ensure both the probity and the efficiency of this elite.

Third, it has been suggested that an important condition for the maintenance of PAP power has been the attentiveness of the state to the material demands and aspirations of the middle class. While explicitly delimiting 'no go areas' in respect of political opinion and action, the state has gone out of its way to provide an ever more prosperous material environment and ever greater material rewards, especially for the upwardly mobile. In this way a leadership, the older generation of which originally adhered to an austere Fabian socialism, have become the superintendents of a pleasure ground of shopping malls and restaurants. In the Singapore case, as yet, the banausic state appears to have both defined and satisfied the aspirations of that class who, in the other Asian NICs, seem to be the social force impelling democratisation.[33]

Finally, Singapore's geo-political predicament has acted as a powerful force in constraining and impelling the policies of the state. As Philippe Regnier remarks,

> It is ... imperative for the city-state never to forget that every break in relations with the regional environment whether brought about by its own action or by one of its neighbours, could spoil the geopolitical conditions which have governed its brilliant development.[34]

From the 1960s to the 1980s, to achieve the twin goals of independence and prosperity, it was necessary for Singapore to perform both a regional and an international role. This regional role, as much political as economic, built upon Singapore's existing connections and served to integrate the city-state with the region. Thus Singapore's pursuit of an entrepot role was paralleled by its embrace of ASEAN. However, Singapore had also to cultivate an international identity precisely because absolute reliance could not be placed on the policies and attitudes of those sovereign states in the neighbourhood, however much they became economic and diplomatic partners. This validity of this alternative strategy was demonstrated by the regional financial crisis of 1997 and its attendant economic and political fallout. Possessing only human resources, Singapore sought to provide a profitable haven for trans-national capital at the same time building the requisite physical and communications infrastructure and educating its population. These considerations still apply, and help locate the state's policies and political instruments.

CONCLUSIONS

The state is the key to analysing modern Singapore. It has shaped society, defied class, and redefined ethnicity. And this state would not exist without the linkages it has cultivated, for the city-state as much as for itself, with international sources of capital and information. But to defend this view, while it excludes some hypotheses is to raise a whole series of further questions. The Singapore state's character and dynamics remain obscure, and work is required to elucidate such areas as elite recruitment, patronage networks and citizen compliance. There are some issues, however, which will not be clarified until some of the occupants and former occupants of the upper reaches of the political system publish their own accounts. With the emergence of succession tensions such accounts may yet appear. Meanwhile, at a time when there is the wide presumption that the more extensive a political and economic system engages in globalisation the more transparent its processes become, Singapore provides a significant counter-example.

NOTES

1. This chapter draws in part on the following pieces: 'Singapore Scrutinised', *The Pacific Review* Vol. 4 (1991), 185- 87; 'Interpreting Singapore: class or power?', *The Pacific Review* Vol. 8 (1995), 558–63; 'State and Society in Singapore', *The Pacific Review* Vol. 9 (1996), 278–82.
2. Christopher Tremewan, The Political Economy of Social Control in Singapore (London: Macmillan, 1994).
3. c/f F C Deyo, *Dependent Development and Industrial Order: An Asian Case Study* (New York: Praeger, 1981); Garry Rodan, *The Political Economy of Singapore's Industrialisation* (London: Macmillan, 1989); J W Salaff, *State and Family in Singapore* (Ithaca: Cornell University Press, 1988); Walden Bello and S Rosenfeld, *Dragons in Distress: Asia's Miracle Economies in Crisis* (San Francisco: Food First, 1990).
4. Linda Y-C Lim, 'Social Welfare', in K S Sandhu and P Wheatley eds, *Management of Success: The Moulding of Modern Singapore* (Singapore: Institute of Southeast Asian Studies, 1989), 171–97.
5. Iaian Buchanan, *Singapore in Southeast Asia* (London: Bell, 1972); M Caldwell, *Lee Kuan Yew: The Man, His Mayoralty and His Mafia* (London: UK Malaysian and Singaporean Student Organisations, 1979).
6. Tremewan, *The Political Economy of Social Control in Singapore*, 29, 31, 34, 178.
7. Tremewan, *The Political Economy of Social Control in Singapore*, 231.

8 Francis T. Seow, *To Catch a Tartar. A Dissident in Lee Kuan Yew's Prison* (New Haven: Yale University Southeast Asia Studies, Monograph 42, 1994).

9 Chan Heng Chee, *The Dynamics of One Party Dominance. The PAP at the Grass-roots* (Singapore: Singapore University Press, 1976); James Minchin, *No Man is an Island. A study of Singapore's Lee Kuan Yew* (Sydney: Allen and Unwin, 1986); Philip Jeyaretnam, *Abraham's Promise* (Honolulu: University of Hawaii Press, 1995).

10 Seow, *To Catch a Tartar,* 265.

11 Michael Hill and Lian Kwen Fee, *The Politics of Nation Building and Citizenship in Singapore* (London: Routledge, 1995), Beng-Huat Chua, *Communitarian Ideology and Democracy in Singapore* (London: Routledge, 1995).

12 Hill and Lian, *The Politics of Nation Building and Citizenship,* 185.

13 Hill and Lian, *The Politics of Nation Building and Citizenship,* 244.

14 Hill and Lian, *The Politics of Nation Building and Citizenship,* 14, 13.

15 Hill and Lian, *The Politics of Nation Building and Citizenship,* 14.

16 Hill and Lian, *The Politics of Nation Building and Citizenship,* 245, 249.

17 Chua, *Communitarian Ideology and Democracy in Singapore,* ch 6.

18 This development is highlighted in chapter 9 of Hill and Lian, *The Politics of Nation Building and Citizenship.*

19 Chua, *Communitarian Ideology and Democracy in Singapore,* 179.

20 Chua, *Communitarian Ideology and Democracy in Singapore,* 200.

21 Chua, *Communitarian Ideology and Democracy in Singapore,* 36, 163.

22 Lai Ah Eng, *Meanings of Multiethnicity, A Case-Study of Ethnicity and Ethnic Relations in Singapore* (Singapore: Oxford University Press, 1995), 146.

23 On the politics of language in Singapore, see Nirmala Srirekam PuruShotam, *Negotiating Multiculturalism. Disciplining Difference in Singapore* (The Hague: Mouton de Gruyter, 2000).

24 Lily Zubaidah Rahim, *The Singapore Dilemma. The Political and Educational Marginality of the Malay Community* (Singapore: Oxford University Press, 1998).

25 Tania Li, *Malays in Singapore: Culture, Economy, and Ideology* (Singapore: Oxford University Press, 1989).

26 Raj Vasil, *Asianising Singapore. The PAP's Management of Ethnicity* (Singapore: Heinemann Asia, 1995).

27 For example, S Haggard, 'The East Asian NICs in Comparative Perspective', *Annals of the American Academy of Political and Social Science* No. 505 (1989), 129–141. For a review of the Korean case, see J Cotton, 'Understanding the State in South Korea: Bureaucratic-Authoritarian or State Autonomy Theory?', *Comparative Political Studies* Vol. 24 (1991–2), 512–31.

28 Bilveer Singh, *Wither PAPs Dominance? An Analysis of Singapore's 1991 General Elections* (Petaling Jaya: Pelanduk, 1992), 39.

29 Chee Soon Juan, *Dare to Change. An Alternative Vision for Singapore* (Singapore: Singapore Democratic Party, 1994), 27–30.

30 J Cotton, 'Political innovation in Singapore: the presidency, the leadership and the party', in Garry Rodan ed, *Singapore Changes Guard. Social, Political and Economic Directions in the 1990s* (Melbourne: Longman-Cheshire, 1993), 3–15.

31 On Singapore entrepreneurs, see Lee Tsao Yuan and Linda Low, *Local Entrepreneurship in Singapore: Private and State* (Singapore: Institute of Policy Studies/Times Academic Press, 1990); Chan Kwok Bun and Claire Chiang, *Stepping Out: The Making of Chinese Entrepreneurs* (New York: Prentice-Hall, 1994).

32 Werner Vennevald, *Technocrats in the State Enterprise System of Singapore* (Murdoch University Asia Research Centre, Working Paper No 32,1994), 16.

33 Garry Rodan, 'Class transformations and political tensions in Singapore's development', in D S G Goodman and R Robison eds, *The New Rich in Asia* (London: Routledge, 1996), 19–45; c/f D Brown and D M Jones, 'Democratization and the Myth of the Liberalizing Middle Classes', in Daniel A Bell et al, *Towards Illiberal Democracy in Pacific Asia* (London: Macmillan, 1995), 41–77.

34 Philippe Regnier, *Singapore: City-State in South-East Asia* (London: Hurst & Co, 1991), 98.

Chapter 5

MACAU'S TENUOUS IDENTITY

The format of the ceremonial conducted at midnight on 19 December 1999 at which China resumed administration of Macau from Portugal resembled the analogous events of 1997 in Hong Kong to an extraordinary degree. The presence of former Hong Kong Governor Chris Patten (in his capacity as European Union Commissioner for External Relations), and on the Chinese side the same honor guard for the raising of the flag, lent a particular air of *déjà vu* to the proceedings. Even the unseasonal cold weather that gripped the territory two days before the transfer seemed to parallel the unusually heavy rain of late June 1997. Appointed as Chief Executive of the new Special Administrative Region (SAR) was Edmund Ho Hau-wah, a member of China's National People's Congress, and a business figure indebted to the regime in Beijing in much the same way as his Hong Kong counterpart, Tung Chee-hwa. When his family's Tai Fung Bank was in trouble in 1984 the Bank of China acquired a large stake in the business rather than allow it to fail, and it is now the second largest financial house in Macau. This association with Hong Kong, which was perhaps the chief feature of the extensive international media coverage of the event, was also encouraged by the approach taken by Beijing. As President Jiang Zemin remarked in the speech delivered at the ceremony:

> It was [Deng Xiaoping] who initiated the principle of 'one country, two systems' with great political vision and extraordinary wisdom, pointing out the right road for the settlements of the issues of Hong Kong, Macau and Taiwan. The successful return of Macau is yet another historic monument built by the Chinese people on the road to national reunification following the return of Hong Kong.[1]

For their part, the line taken by Portuguese spokesmen was to observe that, as the territory now had an advanced infrastructure and the rights and freedoms of its inhabitants were protected by entrenched institutions, its future was bright.

The background to the transfer was also marked by many similarities with the Hong Kong experience. The April 1987 'Joint Declaration' of China and Portugal regarding Macau adopted the format and much of the phraseology of the 1984 'Joint Declaration' on Hong Kong. In particular, the Declaration which provided for the return of Macau to China from 20 December 1999 stated that from that date Macau would 'enjoy a high degree of autonomy', and that 'the current social and economic systems' and 'life-style' would 'remain unchanged for 50 years'. The most noteworthy difference regarded the fact that the United Kingdom agreed to 'restore' Hong Kong to Chinese sovereignty, a provision omitted from the later document undoubtedly on the grounds that Beijing considered Portugal to have been clearly a tenant (albeit one with an indefinite lease) on what was even under prevailing international rules Chinese territory.

The 9 chapters and 160 articles of the Hong Kong Special Administrative Region 'Basic Law' were closely followed in the 145 article 'Basic Law' for Macau, which was adopted by the National People's Congress of China in March 1993. Aside from some greater precision on the right of abode and on individual rights and freedoms, a significant difference between the two documents relates to the legislature. The goal specified for the Hong Kong legislature is the eventual election of all members by universal suffrage, whereas the relevant article for that of Macau states that 'the majority of its members shall be elected' (article 68). The actual provisions for Legislative Council elections provide that by the third term of the legislature, of the 29 members 12 shall be directly elected, and 10 indirectly elected. Nevertheless the institutional framework of the two Special Administrative Regions are very much alike. Thus in both a chief executive, in effect chosen from Beijing, dominates a weak and only partially representative legislature. In addition the geographical and administrative settings of Hong Kong and of Macau are analogous in that both are nested next to Special Economic Zones (SEZs), Shenzhen and Zhuhai respectively, both of which were established to turn to China's advantage cross-border trade, investment, and technology transfer.

DIVERGENCES FROM THE HONG KONG MODEL

But behind these parallels, the differences between the cases are extremely marked.[2] This extends even to the transfer processes that, though outwardly similar, have actually enhanced some of these differences.

Even after the very extensive reclamation of recent years, Macau's tiny size (21.45 squ kms) bears little comparison with that of Hong Kong (1095 squ kms). Macau's population stands officially at around 450,000 but even if unofficial estimates of as many as 700,000 are more accurate, this is only about one-tenth of that of Hong Kong. Macau's social structure exhibits many idiosyncratic features. Though the population has been swollen by a large number of recent immigrants from neighbouring Guangdong, so that around 96% of the population are Chinese, it still possesses a unique Sino-Portuguese element, the Macanese (*Macaense*) who, despite numbering only in the thousands (after recent emigration, now around 8,000) have long served as a bridge between the bulk of the inhabitants and the colonial government. Chinese in many habits but usually bi-lingual, they have been strongly represented in the administration, and have been vital to the functioning of the legal system, since even in the lead up to the transfer the language of law and legislation remained Portuguese. The Eurasian community in Hong Kong, by contrast, has never wielded such important social and economic power. Nor has the issue of citizenship and the right of abode been especially contentious in Macau. While Britain legislated to prevent Hong Kong inhabitants from using their 'British' status to facilitate emigration to Britain, more than a third of Macau's population were qualified for full Portuguese travel documents, and thus free to seek abode anywhere in the entire European Union.

Though Beijing's formula that Hong Kong and Macau are issues 'left over from the past' is accurate enough, the past in question is rather distinctive, as can be inferred from the fact that the conventional date for a Portuguese presence on the peninsula is 1557, long before the high tide of European expansion of which colonial Hong Kong was a product.[3]

For some time it was far from clear whether the Portuguese would become permanent occupants, and when they began erecting buildings and fortifications in the early seventeenth century their title to the territory was ill-defined. Without accepting the present account of either party,[4] it is reasonable to claim that for several centuries Chinese and Portuguese power coexisted. Resident Chinese officials collected customs and exercised some judicial powers, and if the Chinese considered that Portuguese officials were exceeding their authority they initiated boycotts of food supplies or required the Chinese population to decamp, thus usually asserting their will.

In the wake of the Sino-British confrontation that transmuted the island of Hong Kong into a British colony, the Portuguese attempted to acquire undisputed title to the peninsula and its neighbouring islands. The Chinese customs officials were expelled in 1849, and their superiors were informed that henceforth they would be considered as having no authority on the peninsula, an event which precipitated the assassination of the Governor, João Maria Ferreira do Amaral. In a later echo of this event the statue of this Governor which once graced the park at the front of the Lisboa Hotel was repatriated to Portugal as part of the transfer preparations. At the same time a road was driven through the park to form a link with new land reclamation which has rendered much of the water frontage of the former *Praia Grande* a stagnant pond. Taking advantage of British and French pressure on China in the later part of the century, Portugal negotiated a treaty with China in 1887, the Treaty of Peking, partly with the intention of asserting its undisputed ownership. But even this agreement, though it confirmed Portugal's sole and perpetual occupation, did not concede untrammeled Portuguese sovereignty since Lisbon agreed not to alienate the territory to any third power. Further, the precise limits of the territory of Macau were not defined, an ambiguity that was never resolved, despite further Portuguese efforts.

Portuguese neutrality in the Pacific war protected Macau from Japanese occupation, and at its conclusion the government of Chiang Kai-shek did nothing to achieve its stated objective of resuming control of Macau. Though the communist government in Beijing in 1955 stated the position that Macau was Chinese territory, nothing was done to advance this claim. But the Cultural Revolution precipitated riots and a confrontation between the administration and local leftist forces.[5] Unlike the outcome of the analogous events in Hong Kong, where Britain managed to reassert its authority, under overt Chinese pressure and with Chinese naval vessels patrolling the harbor, Portugal was forced to accept that its tenure over the territory could be continued only with Beijing's express consent. A key role was played in these events by Ho Yin, the leading pro-Beijing entrepreneur in Macau, then Chairman of the Tai Fung Bank as well as Chair of the Chinese Chamber of Commerce (and father of the man now Macau's Chief Executive).

In 1972 China successfully sought to withdraw the Hong Kong and Macau issues from consideration by the United Nations Special Committee for Decolonization on the grounds that these issues were entirely a matter for China, the sovereign power, to resolve. However it became clear that Beijing did not consider the time was 'ripe' to take any concrete steps. The 'carnation revolution' in Portugal in 1974 brought to power in Lisbon political forces committed to decolonisation and self-determination, and under the territory's 'Organic Statute' of 1976 Macau assumed a high degree of autonomy. Negotiation of diplomatic relations with Beijing in 1979 produced an agreement, not made public at the time, that Macau was 'Chinese territory under Portuguese administration' and committed Lisbon in due course to discuss a formal transfer of control. Thus the tortuous negotiation of the Sino-British 'Joint Declaration' through which London reluctantly conceded in 1984 eventual control of Hong Kong, a negotiation that proceeded amidst diplomatic confrontation and a run on the currency, was quite unnecessary in the Macau case.[6]

Macau's new autonomy launched it on a political trajectory which avoided many of the problems that be-devilled Hong Kong once China and Britain began to implement the 1984 document on the basis of their respective (and divergent) understandings. Macau's autonomous status having been defined in 1976, to assist the governance of the territory the Portuguese administration established a Legislative Assembly partly on elective principles. This replaced an entirely appointed body the members of which were generally Portuguese or Macanese. Initially, the six directly elected members (a further six were indirectly elected, with five appointed by the Governor) were only drawn from a narrow franchise and thus tended to be members of the relatively prosperous Macanese community. However, the extension of the franchise in 1984 (with some additional modifications in 1988) gave all residents irrespective of nationality the vote. This circumvented the problem caused by the presence of many immigrants of doubtful legality from China, and also ensured, after some confrontations between the Macanese élite and the colonial administration, that a majority of the elected representatives would be Chinese. The enlargement of the Assembly in 1991 entrenched these changes. At this time in Hong Kong political reform involving the extension of the elected element of the Legislative Council (where direct elections though mooted in 1984 were only introduced from 1991) became a matter of controversy. This issue ultimately derailed the 'through train' by which it was originally intended that the pre- and post-1997 political institutions would merge. The context for this reform was vocal criticism of Bejing's handling of the Tiananmen incident of 1989, which then reinforced the notion that Britain was duty bound to foster accountable institutions in Hong Kong in order to fashion an instrument available to the population after 1997 the better to defend their rights and liberties.[7] Lisbon's reaction to 1989, by contrast, was muted, and correspondingly no doubts were expressed as to the desirability of encouraging pro-Beijing forces to suffuse the political institutions. In this respect Macau's 'through train' permitted an easier merger of the identities of colonial and post-colonial authority, with no need to appoint an alternative body of legislators as in Hong Kong.

On the one hand, the appropriateness of elections as one of the legitimate means of determining the opinion of the inhabitants was never thereafter questioned. On the other, with the absence of a strong democratic movement in the territory, pro-Beijing political forces occupied the political space thus created. In Hong Kong the Democrats under Martin Lee Chu-ming became the dominant popular political force in the years between the Tiananmen incident and retrocession, and were outspoken in their criticism not only of Beijing's management of the political transition but also of the wider issues entailed in the continuing communist monopoly of the Beijing political system. In Macau, by contrast, in the elections for the 1992 legislature, pro-Beijing forces captured four of the eight directly contested seats with candidates supported by the Union for the Promotion of Progress (UNIPRO, a movement with its roots in the neighbourhood—*kaifong*—associations) and the Development Union (UPD, a political movement supported by the Federation of Labour Unions).[8] These movements commanded extensive mass support and were able to mobilize voters both to register as electors and subsequently to vote. Augmented by indirectly elected members from pro-Beijing business and professional groups, they formed the largest group in the legislature. Only two democratically aligned members were elected. There was some pluralisation of political forces in the 1996 elections, with the rise of distinctive 'pro-business' groups to rival the overtly pro-Beijing forces.[9] The latter managed to secure four of the elected seats, with UNIPRO and the UPD electing three between them. Of the avowed democrats, only one, Ng Kwok Cheong (having been elected in 1992) was re-elected. According to some observers the success of the pro-business forces derived from vote buying facilitated by the lax policing of uncertain electoral regulations.

But there is evidence to suggest that the inhabitants did not rate the performance of this government very highly, and thus the legitimacy of the administration was progressively eroded through the 1990s.[10] The declining state of law and order was undoubtedly a factor in this disenchantment, as was corruption in official ranks. In addition, the administration engaged in an orgy of museum building and historical conservation at the expense of the administration's budget that depleted the reserves available to the government of the new SAR. To its credit, however, the administration also pursued a vigorous program for the construction of infrastructure and public works, including a major international airport that was opened in 1995.

Overall the rise to prominence of candidates associated with business interests did not necessarily pose major challenges for the progress of the retrocession since, as in Hong Kong, the business sector is generally inclined to cooperate with Beijing. The political spectrum in Macau has thus been characterised by a good deal more conservatism and compliance than in Hong Kong, with very few voices raised to contest the main items in Beijing's agenda for the territory. This conservatism is reflected also in the media, though the ease of availability of Hong Kong media to an extent obviates the need for a separate critical voice. A measure of the distinctiveness of the political atmosphere in Macau can be gauged by the treatment of the Falun Gong religious cult, now outlawed in China, though still a legal organisation in the Hong Kong SAR. Cult members attempted to stage a protest on the morning of 19 December 1999 in public space outside the Lisboa Hotel. Police arrested about thirty of the group, and a number were later expelled from the territory. At the same time other members were prevented from entry after arriving from Hong Kong.

A further difference derives from the program of localization of the administration. When Tung Chee-hwa assumed the office of Chief Executive in Hong Kong, all of the secretaries of the government departments were local personnel, and he was able to maintain all but one in office. In Macau, the corresponding individuals were all expatriates, with the exception of one Macanese.[11] Of the five principal secretaries in the new administration of Edmund Ho, three (Florinda da Rosa Silva Chan, Secretary for Administration and Justice, Cheong Kuok-va, Secretary for Security, and Ao Man-long, Secretary for Transport and Public Works) were local members of the former colonial administration, though they were promoted in order to assume their new roles. Two further secretaries (Francis Tam Pak-un, Secretary for Economic and Financial Affairs and Fernando Chui Sai-on, Secretary for Social Affairs and Culture) were brought from industry and education to complete the localization of the top executive. The two Commissioners (Cheong U, Commissioner Against Corruption, and Fatima Choi Mei-lei, Commissioner of Audit) were also local personnel. With an average age in the middle 40s this group lacked experience, and in the case of the outside appointees little familiarity with the requirements of government. This was generally also true of the leading legal personnel, with the head of the Court of Final Appeal, Sam Hou-fai, being only 38 years old.

The context for this turnover of personnel is the arrangements for the localization of the civil service, which has been a matter of some controversy in Macau. Until the beginning of the 1990s, the civil service was dominated by expatriates, and with local members often Macanese. In 1992, of the 192 members of the three top levels of the civil service, 137 were expatriates. This issue was one considered by the Sino-Portuguese Joint Liaison Group managing the transition, and in response a plan was published to accelerate the promotion of local appointees so that by 1999, of the 147 occupants of these positions, 88 would be local.[12] The comparison with Hong Kong is revealing of the extent to which the SAR would continue to be reliant on Portuguese civil servants, many of them with little command of the Chinese language. In Hong Kong, the corresponding reforms resulted, as early as 1990, in a civil service that was already heavily localised. At the (senior) level of Director or above, 59.7% of the personnel were local appointees.[13] As to the administrative process in Macau, it was only from March 1998 that all the administrative acts approved by the government were published in both Portuguese and Chinese. The localization of the legal system has also proceeded slowly, with training of bi-lingual legal personnel only being introduced in 1995.

This raises the issue of language usage. The use of English is entrenched in Hong Kong because it has become the language of regional and international commerce. While standards may have declined, especially since there is more need post-1997 to learn and use *putonghua* (standard Chinese), Hong Kong will always have a stake in the knowledge and employment of English. The use of the Portuguese language in Macau was always limited, and is now diminishing through competition with English as well as *putonghua*. Macau's claim to belong to the Lusophone world is thus becoming more and more tenuous. The problems in the legal system are thus a microcosm of those in the larger society. As the existing body of law is in Portuguese, and official translation into Chinese will take some years to complete, the use of the Portuguese language will be essential for the legal system to function. But with sharply declining numbers of students studying Portuguese, an appropriately qualified body of specialists will be progressively harder to find.[14]

Regarding economic issues, the difference between the economy of Macau and that of Hong Kong is much more than a matter of size. Hong Kong is increasingly the service centre for a regional economy that embraces a good part of South China, having exported many of its light industrial production facilities to Shenzhen and beyond. Between 1980 and 1997 the contribution of industry to Hong Kong's GDP was halved, and that of services increased by around one-third. The Hong Kong currency circulates widely in this economy, and the tastes, fashions and language of the former colony are exerting a strong influence on the thinking and behaviour as well as the consumption patterns of the inhabitants of that region. Though the regional financial crisis struck Hong Kong immediately after the retrocession, its influence was reversed within two years. Growing at an annual rate of 5.4% in 1996, the Hong Kong economy returned to a strong positive performance in the second quarter of 1999 (registering a growth rate for that quarter of 3.2%).[15]

Macau gained its first advantage from surreptitious trade in gold, taking advantage of the fact that while Portugal had acceded to the Bretton Woods treaties pegging the price of the precious metal, it had not included Macau as one of the dependent territories in which this rule applied.[16] In the 1970s and 1980s, in common with other Asian newly industrializing economies, Macau began to develop light industry. However by contrast with Hong Kong, when its textile, apparel and toy production began to migrate to factories in the cheaper labour environment of South China, the Macau economy did not so readily find a new role. A relatively strong performer in the 1980s, Macau's economy slowed to register negative growth (–0.5%) in 1996, even before the advent of the regional financial crisis. The collapse of the housing market in 1994 was an early sign of deeper structural problems.[17] Thereafter the recession deepened, with the economy contracting by 4.0% in 1998. Unemployment exhibited an associated increase (from 4.3% in 1996 to 6.7% in 1999).[18] What remains of Macau's textile industry is threatened by the World Trade Organisation deadline of 2005 for the expiry of textile quotas, under which the territory has enjoyed ready access to the United States market.

THE GAMBLING MONOPOLY

The trend has been for Macau to become a one industry town, with that industry being gambling and associated tourism. This reliance is reflected in various measures. Employment in 'commerce and hotels' and 'transportation' combined stood at 34.7% of the workforce in 1996. By comparison manufacturing industry (largely textiles and apparel) accounted for 20.7% of the workforce, down from 49.9% in 1984. The income from taxes and charges on gambling is the mainstay of the government's income. Regarding the government budget in 1999 on the eve of the retrocession, of a total projected Current Revenue of P$9.3 billion, these charges were the source of P$5.4 billion or 58%[19]. Gambling depends upon tourist arrivals, but the trends have not been encouraging. Tourist arrivals peaked at 8.15 million in 1996, declining to 6.95 million by 1998. Of this diminishing total, arrivals from over the border in China are replacing dwindling numbers of visitors from Hong Kong. Given that the disposable funds of the former are a good deal less than the latter, the impact on the tourist and gambling sectors has been to further reduce their incomes. Meanwhile the spillover of corruption in coastal China, and the presence of vice and crime in association with gambling, have lowered the social tone of the territory and eroded public confidence in the probity of the administration.

Without the continuing support for government revenue and employment that derives from the gambling industry, therefore, Macau would be in serious economic straits. But here the position is complicated by the fact that in this sector the economy was for long reliant upon a monopoly provider.

In March 1962 the STDM (*Sociedade de Turismo e Diversões de Macau*) became responsible for the gambling monopoly and diversified its operations to include, most recently, participating in the construction of the international airport. Gambling had been a feature of the Macau scene from the nineteenth century, but the STDM, an investment syndicate organised by Stanley Ho in company with other Hong Kong investors including Henry Fok, grew to dominate the economy and society in a manner that had few precedents.[20] Ho (who is not a relation of the Chief Executive) first formed an association with the territory during the second world war, when he went into business trading with the Japanese to obtain rice for the inhabitants, their numbers more than doubled by an influx of wartime refugees, many from Hong Kong. Over the years Ho has become the most important local business figure, though he generally chooses to commute from his Hong Kong residence by helicopter. As well as a gambling magnate he is also a patron of a host of activities, from art galleries to Grand Prix racing, and through his role as a Trustee of the Macau Foundation he has been responsible for the support of a very diverse range of cultural and historical projects. In 1982 the Macau government extracted a fee of P$1 billion for a renewal of the gambling monopoly, and charges exacted on gambling grew from around 14% of government revenue in 1980 to over 33% (or P$5.4 billion) by 1995.[21] The STDM opened the tenth of its casinos in the territory in 1999. Stanley Ho's Shun Tak Holdings (based in Hong Kong) also controls a large number of associated businesses, including the jetfoils that are the most favoured form of transport from Hong Kong. Shun Tak and Ho's other businesses are also vehicles for investment abroad, including casinos in Vietnam, North Korea and a prospective venture in East Timor.

Gambling oriented tourism has become the staple of the Macau economy, but the trends in this respect have not always been positive. To an extent, tourism has expanded to fill the void left by the migration of manufacturing industry (mostly textiles and apparel) to neighbouring parts of China, especially Zhuhai, from the 1980s onwards. But the gaming monopoly is reliant upon facilitating conditions that may easily be disturbed. Thus, as has been indicated, the Macau economy experienced a significant decline from the middle 1990s, largely reflecting the regional financial crisis which restricted spending and limited tourist visits. At the same time, the industry was beset with problems ranging from the proliferation of prostitutes to the infiltration of criminals into aspects of its operations, including through the 'sub-letting' of the monopoly's gaming rooms to doubtful figures. The colonial authorities appeared powerless to deal with the rise in violent crime of which some of its own officials were victims. In 1998 a jail warder, a member of a prison guard team recently brought from Portugal, and a top official of the Gambling Inspectorate, Francisco Amaral, were all shot to death in the streets of Macau. A senior government prosecutor and a police director were also the targets of unsuccessful assassination attempts.

As a consequence of this direct challenge to the authorities, the colonial administration arrested a leading triad member, Wan Kuok-koi, also known as 'Broken Tooth'. He was sentenced in December 1999 to 15 years in prison for loan-sharking, money laundering and triad membership.[22] There is little doubt that an example was being made of Wan, who, in financing a fictionalized movie version of his life, *Casino*, with a Hong Kong pop star in the leading role, had perhaps courted retribution. At the same time, three of Wan's associates, including Ip Seng-kin from Hong Kong, were tried and executed over the border in the Zhuhai SEZ after being arrested in China. This case, though it demonstrated cooperation between Beijing and Lisbon on a grave issue, also raised problems of legality, in that Ip was a Hong Kong resident and his alleged crimes were committed in Macau. In the event, no protest was forthcoming from any jurisdiction. The need to preserve public order was also the ground for the unilateral announcement from Beijing that a PLA (People's Liberation Army) contingent would be based in the Macau SAR, and would be empowered to assist if necessary with law enforcement.

The gambling monopoly expired at the end of 2001, and the new Macau administration made it plain that a more diversified structure for the industry was expected by granting licenses to two international operators in addition to the STDM.[23] But the prospects for even a reformed gambling sector are being threatened by the consideration being given in Hong Kong to the introduction there of some gambling establishments, which would drastically curtail traffic from across the Pearl River and thus undermine government revenues. From being reliant on one industry, Macau may graduate to having no industry.

MACAU'S FUTURE

Macau's international connections are many, with the territory being party to over 100 international conventions and bilateral agreements (including a Trade and Cooperation Agreement signed with the European Union in 1992), and with membership of more than 30 international economic institutions. Strenuous efforts to enmesh Macau into a number of international regimes was a feature of Portuguese policy in the 1990s.[24] However, Macau, unlike Hong Kong, is not part of the Anglophone world, and though the wider Portuguese community includes the most important state of Latin America and a member of the European Union, it is not sufficiently influential to focus world attention on Macau's fate for long. The declining usage of the Portuguese language and the limited scale of investments in Macau from the metropolitan country have left the territory with slim resources to facilitate the pursuit of an identity distinct from its immediate neighbourhood. There may be indications of the emergence of a more participatory political culture on the part of the younger inhabitants of Macau[25], but the political and civic space no longer exists for this culture to be adequately expressed.

The physical obliteration of much of old Macau (that has proceeded apace through the 1990s) on the one hand and the construction of extensive transport and infrastructure links on the other have erased much of the sense of place that formerly existed. As the Inner Harbor continues to narrow, a victim of the combined effects of siltation and landfill, Macau has become harder to distinguish even physically from more populous Zhuhai. The major infrastructure projects for which the Portuguese were responsible—the container-port and the airport—are now easily accessible (the former by way of the new *Ponte Flor de Lótus* bridge from Taipa) directly from the neighbouring Zhuhai SEZ so the benefit to the territory may over time prove limited. At the same time the operators of the Zhuhai airport, the largest in China when it was constructed, are seeking approval for its use by international traffic, thus threatening Macau's overseas gateway role. In any case between 60% and 70% of the passenger traffic passing through Macau consists of passengers from Taiwan, whose presence on the routes in question derives from decidedly temporary political arrangements. Direct flights between Taipei and Shanghai or Xiamen, not an unlikely development by any means, would divert much of this traffic. The merger of Macau with its surroundings is also proceeding in other dimensions, demographic as well as economic, and political merger in the future may be impossible to avoid. Presuming a formula is eventually found to mitigate or legitimise the differences between China and Taiwan, the rationale for a separate SAR for less than a million inhabitants (and many of those recent immigrants) may well disappear.

Macau's one hope, however tenuous, is to remain the Monaco of the Far East. Given that Hong Kong and Macau are now both SARs, the Chinese government might be expected to take measures to protect the gambling industry from competition in Hong Kong, preserving at least for the present the one source of ready revenue for the territory. They may be uncomfortable, however, with the irony of an avowedly socialist government intervening to maintain conditions that require its citizens to travel between one part of their territory and another in order to enrich a gambling monopoly the profits of which are not necessarily locally invested.

NOTES

1 *China Daily*, 21 December 1999, 6.

2 Arnaldo Gonçalves, 'A Paradigm of Autonomy: The Hong Kong and Macau SARs', *Contemporary Southeast Asia* Vol. 18 (1996), no. 1, 36–60; Jonathan Porter, 'Macau 1999', *Current History* No. 96 (1997), 282–6.

3 Austin Coates, *A Macao Narrative* (Hong Kong: Oxford University Press, 1987); Geoffrey C. Gunn, *Encountering Macau. A Portuguese City-State on the Periphery of China, 1557–1999* (Boulder: Westview Press, 1996); Jonathan Porter, *Macau The Imaginary City. Culture and Society, 1557 to the Present* (Boulder: Westview Press, 1996).

4 Wang Qiaolong, *The Homecoming of Macao* (Beijing: China Intercontinental Press, 1999); c/f Fernando Lima, *Macau. A Portuguese Adventure* (Macau: Fundação Macau, 1999).

5 Geoffrey C. Gunn, *Encountering Macau. A Portuguese City-State on the Periphery of China, 1557–1999*, 155–58.

6 Stephen Vines, *Hong Kong: China's New Colony* (London: Aurum Press, 1999), 32–47.

7 Michael Yahuda, *Hong Kong. China's Challenge* (London: Routledge, 1996), 69–75.

8 Lo Shiu Hing, *Political Development in Macau* (Hong Kong: The Chinese University Press, 1995), 81–98.

9 Herbert Yee , 'Money Politics and Political Mobilization in Macau. The 1996 Legislative Assembly Elections', *Asian Survey* Vol. 37 (1997), no. 10, 944–60.

10 Herbert Yee, Liu Bolong and Ngo Tak-wing, 'Macau's Mass Political Culture', *Asian Journal of Public Administration* Vol. 15 (1993), no. 2, 177–200; Richard Louis Edmonds and Herbert S. Yee, 'Macau: From Portuguese Autonomous Territory to Chinese Special Administrative Region', *The China Quarterly* No. 160 (December 1999), 801–817.

11 *Hong Kong Standard*, 20 December 1999, 4.

12 Lo Shiu Hing, *Political Development in Macau*, 157–60.

13 Norman Miners, *the Government and Politics of Hong Kong*, 5th edition updated (Hong Kong: Oxford University Press, 1998), 94–5.

14 J. A. Berlie, 'Macao's Education: A Question of Language—Chinese, Portuguese, and English', in J. A. Berlie (ed.), *Macao 2000* (Hong Kong: Oxford University Press, 1999), 71–104.

15 Hong Kong Government, <http://www.info.gov.hk/cestatd/eng/hkstat.htm>, accessed 2.16.00; Hong Kong Government, *Hong Kong 1997* (Hong Kong: Government Information Services Department, 1997), 36–62.

16 *Far Eastern Economic Review*, 30 December 1999, 15.

17 Raymond Y. C. Tse, 'Real Estate and the Housing Market', in J. A. Berlie (ed.), *Macao 2000*, 145–161.

18 Macau Government, <http://www.economia.gov.mo/english/dei/engind.htm>, accessed 2.16.00.

19 Macau Government, <http://www.economia.gov.mo/english/dei/engind15.htm>, accessed 2.16.00. See also, Government Information Services, *Macau 99 Report* (Macau: Government Information Services, 1999), 68–95. The Macau *pataca*—P$—is pegged at 1.03 to the HK$. Both currencies circulate in the territory.

20 *Far Eastern Economic Review*, 9 December 1999, 8–12.

21 Torojiro Maruya, 'Macroeconomy: Past, Present, and Prospects', in J. A. Berlie (ed.), *Macao 2000,* 123–144; Macau Government, <http://www.economia.gov.mo/english/dei/engind15.htm>, accessed 2.16.00.

22 *Hong Kong Standard*, 23 November 1999, 1–3.

23 *Far Eastern Economic Review*, 30 December 1999, 14–15.

24 Susan J. Henders, 'So What if It's Not a Gamble? Post-Westphalian Politics in Macau', *Pacific Affairs* Vol. 74 (2001), no. 3, 342-360.

25 Herbert S Yee, 'Mass Political Culture in Macau: Continuity and Change', *Issues and Studies* Vol. 35 (1999), no. 2, 174–197.

Chapter 6

EAST ASIAN DEMOCRACY: CONSOLIDATION OR CONTAINMENT?

Democratization is undoubtedly the most significant example of 'cross-border' politics in the contemporary Asia Pacific. A type of political system with origins in Western classical and early modern thought and also in the practice of seventeenth and eighteenth century European states is being progressively adapted in nations with distinctive and utterly different local political cultures and political and intellectual traditions. This process is an example of cross-border politics in many other respects, with international pressure groups, for example, censuring Asian political systems for failures to observe human rights or labour standards, and US and Western foreign and trade policy oriented towards those polities that affirm democratic principles.

How successful has this process of adaptation (or 'importation'[1]) been? This chapter considers the prospects for the consolidation of democracy in the Asia Pacific, focusing on the Philippines, South Korea, Taiwan, and Thailand, with some attention paid as well to Malaysia and Singapore. In all of these cases, democratic forms are embedded, with more or less regular electoral mechanisms for managing political change. This geographical approach is taken in an attempt to identify as wide a basis as possible for the comparative analysis of the Asian examples of democracy's third wave.

Using Samuel Huntington's framework for understanding the recent global trend toward democratization, a trend for which he coined the term 'third wave,'[2] democratization in Taiwan is considered an example of 'transformation' (with the government in charge of the democratization process), while in South Korea it is an example of 'transplacement' (with government and opposition both affecting the outcome), and in the Philippines an example of 'replacement' (with the opposition supplanting the government). Thailand was a 'semi-democracy' when Huntington's book *The Third Wave* was written in 1991; just one year later, however, in 1992, the military brought extra-constitutional pressures to bear on the political system. Mass demonstrations ensued, ultimately forcing a constitutional amendment and new elections that returned a democratic coalition to power. At first, this seemed to indicate that a process of leadership 'replacement' had been launched. Subsequent developments, however, notably the constitutional reforms of 1997 and the elections of 2001, throw a different light on the Thai case. The former would appear to support the 'transplacement' analysis, the latter seems to mark something of a regression. In the Philippines the situation is as unclear, with elements of 'People's Power' combining with old elites in 2001 to remove the president, Joseph Estrada, elected in a landslide in 1998. Finally, those regional systems in which political contestation also occurs—Malaysia and Singapore—are not considered as part of Huntington's group for the purposes of this kind of comparison.

Without rejecting the utility of Huntington's approach, or positing the existence of an 'Asian style' of democracy, I propose that a wider regional approach to understanding the character and limits of democratization is of value, for several reasons. First, despite differences in the original democratization experiences of the cases discussed here, these differences have become less important than certain key similarities during the course of democratic consolidation. To take the Taiwanese and South Korean cases as examples, the initial democratization processes were clearly distinct, though both occurred during the third wave. In Taiwan the established elite remained in charge during the transition, while in Korea popular pressures contributed to defining the pace and character of change. By 1996, however, one key similarity had emerged. In both cases, opposition candidates had emerged triumphant in the most important local elections in Taiwan and South Korea, specifically in the mayoral contest in Taipei in 1994 and in a similar contest in Seoul in 1995. The election of oppositionists proceeded a stage further with the assumption to the presidency, respectively, of Chen Shui-bian (in 2000) and Kim Dae-jung (in 1998). Another similarity was that generalized political factionalism largely accounted for the character of the opposition in both cases. In both political systems, two major groups with little in common besides hostility to the government by that time had come to dominate the opposition. Kim depended on unlikely allies to win a narrow victory, and Chen's plurality of this presidential vote was directly a product of factional rivalry within the former ruling party.

A second striking characteristic of the Asian experience with democracy is that even after the transition to democracy it took several electoral cycles before an opposition group or candidate assumed control of the national government, though this may be due in part to definitional problems with the term 'opposition.' Liberal democratic theory assumes that a genuine opposition is an alternative government, while in less than full democracies the term is often used in a more diffused sense. As Huntington observed in 1993, 'In none of these countries . . . in East Asia, except for the ... Philippines, has a turnover of power occurred from an elected government of one party to an elected government of another party.'[3] This suggests that there may be some important comparisons to be made across the region. It also alerts us to the possibility that while democracy may be further extended and consolidated in some cases, in other cases constitutional systems may evolve to a point of equilibrium where the degree of political contestation and inclusiveness consistently falls short of that required for full democracy to exist. In such cases, democracy may be contained rather than consolidated, with neither elites nor major social interests committed to its further or full realisation. I propose, therefore, to add Malaysia and Singapore to the category of 'East Asian constitutional systems,' all of which will be shown to have significant similarities for these comparative purposes. On Huntington's view, such democratic features as Malaysia and Singapore possess are the result of the 'second wave' that he associates with post-war decolonisation.

This chapter will first identify some of the major characteristics of the constitutional systems in the cases analyzed here. It then considers how far and in what respects the democratic features of these systems might be consolidated, and to what extent democratization might be contained, especially in view of the likely international environment in the post-Cold War era.

THE RULES OF THE GAME

In Taiwan from 1986 to the watershed year of 1991, in South Korea from 1985 to 1993, in the Philippines since the 1986 ouster of Ferdinand Marcos, and progressively in Thailand since 1975, competitive political systems have replaced authoritarian rule. In recent years, each of these political systems has adopted a constitution embodying many if not all of the major formal requirements of democracy. South Korea adopted its new constitution in 1987. Likewise, Taiwan amended its constitution in May 1992 (and again to enable the direct election of the president in 1996), as did the Philippines in 1987, while Thailand adopted a reformed constitution in 1991, amended it a year later with a provision requiring that the prime minister be an elected member of parliament, and then (largely as a response to the regional financial crisis) completely recast the document in 1997. Significantly, the Philippines functioned at least in a formal sense as a democracy prior to the declaration of martial law in 1972, as did South Korea from 1960 to 1961, and Thailand from 1973 to 1976. Only Taiwan never functioned prior to the 'third wave' as a democracy—setting aside, that is, the elections held under civil war conditions in November 1947. Nevertheless, the brevity and interrupted nature of constitutional order in all of these systems suggests that it is premature to regard consolidation as having been achieved.

The Singapore and Malaysia cases are both more settled in their usage, and more suggestive as to the limits that may be placed on democratic contestation. In Malaysia and Singapore, the rules permitting democratic political competition were established during British decolonisation in the 1950s. Though these rules have been suspended on some occasions, they have nevertheless endured. However, although the constitutions of Malaysia and Singapore have remained in force, the procedures by which they may be amended have been made progressively easier. In Malaysia, where apart from a limited number of entrenched provisions relating primarily to the rights of ethnic Malays the constitution may be amended by two-thirds of the members of the parliament, the ruling coalition has commanded a majority nearly continuously since 1969. The constitution was amended at the formation of Malaysia in 1963 and has been amended frequently since then, with this frequency increasing over time, often at short notice and with little if any public debate.[4] The malleability of the Singaporean constitution, as amended in 1965, is also generally acknowledged, and has been facilitated by the virtual monopoly of parliament by the People's Action Party (PAP). Another British legacy in Malaysia and Singapore is the continuing existence of an Internal Security Act, originally introduced by the British colonial authorities in an attempt to control the activities in both of the Malayan Communist Party, under the 'Emergency' declared in 1948. Since decolonisation, internal security acts in Malaysia and Singapore have been used to detain opposition figures without trial and have generally been employed against both dissidents and opposition members, most notably in a series of arrests and detentions involving political activists in 1986 and 1987, and alleged terrorists in 2001–2.

Political actors in each of the cases examined here have not always adhered to the formal rules. Although laws have been established to restrain corrupt electoral practices, these laws have not always been enforced. In both South Korea and Taiwan, influence-peddling and vote-buying have been particularly problematic. In Taiwan, for example, the long association of party and state gave the Kuomintang access to resources unavailable to its rivals. Likewise, in South Korea, the munificent funding of the regime and its political machine by the *chaebol*, or industrial conglomerates, was fully exposed in the trial of former president Roh Tae-woo, who was found guilty of accepting campaign funds of over $600 million in exchange for special favours. Even though Kim Young-sam began his presidency with reforms that were designed to prevent such corruption, he left office with his own son in gaol for accepting illicit funds from an industrial conglomerate. To help redress the political imbalance in Taiwan and South Korea, party reforms (including primaries to chose parliamentary candidates) have been established in the former while stringent laws against improper campaign funding have been introduced in the latter. Nevertheless, in South Korea organizations such as trade unions are still not permitted by law to contribute funds to political parties, obstructing the development of linkages between parties and civil society.

Moreover, political contestation for office may be deflected or contained through veto powers accorded to institutions that are formally subordinate to those offices. For example, the independent power of the Thai bureaucracy, though it has diminished somewhat since the heyday in the 1960s of the 'bureaucratic polity', is still a feature of government in Bangkok. Similarly, in South Korea until the mid-1980s, the military and security establishments wielded a measure of independent power.

Constitutional rules also coexist with laws that can be used by ruling parties to undermine the formation of opposition parties and political competition in general. In Singapore, for example, several opposition figures have fallen afoul of libel laws. The award of punitive damages to the ruling PAP has crippled such oppositionists as J.B. Jeyaretnam and Dr. Chee Soon Juan. Overall, the judgments in these and other cases have allowed the ruling party to use the courts as yet another weapon for restricting the opposition.[5] In Singapore and Malaysia, very short campaign periods constrain the opposition, while constitutional changes have put opposition parties at a decided disadvantage. For example, Singapore has switched from a parliamentary to a presidential system, with the rules for candidacy so hedged with qualifications that few individuals other than former cabinet members are eligible to run. Likewise, national security laws in South Korea, still in force pending a final reconciliation with North Korea, constrain internal political organization and expression.

Media Controls

Another essential element of a genuinely competitive political system is access to nonpartisan, independent information and commentary. Here, the terrain of constitutional East Asia is quite distinctive, with the principal of a completely independent, non-monopolistic media far from universally entrenched.

Progress toward a free press has been greatest in South Korea. In the Chun Doo-hwan era, dissident journalists were driven out of the media by the government but later played a role in popularizing the critique of authoritarianism.[6] Though the press now publicizes the deeds and misdeeds of the government, and South Koreans may, under particular circumstances, gain access to North Korean media, national security laws still provide some constraints. For example, in 1994, a writ was issued against a group of university professors who allegedly produced a textbook showing North Korea in a favorable light. Similarly, insinuations of treason resulted from the mere suggestion in the National Assembly that Seoul send a delegation to Pyongyang for former president Kim Il-sung's funeral. During Kim Dae-jung's tenure of the presidency, relations between the press and the government were not harmonious. Though no new legal restraints were placed on the newspapers, publishing groups were subject to strict taxation audits and the proprietor of a major newspaper was sentenced to a gaol term. Such actions serve as stark reminders that neither information nor commentary can be disseminated in South Korea entirely without fear of the consequences. It is also noteworthy that Seoul has yet to legalize and regulate the possession of satellite dishes, though the government has justified its inaction on 'cultural' grounds. The government of Korea is still wary of allowing free access to international, and especially Japanese, media.

While South Korea has taken some strides toward greater press freedom, controls on the media in Singapore are without parallel.[7] Agencies answerable to the government control the press and television, which devote considerable, generally uncritical coverage to government initiatives. Legislation introduced in 1987 also gives the government the power to ban or limit the circulation of foreign media. In the late 1990s, the government also constrained the use of the internet to obstruct political commentary using that medium, with the result that a number of popular political websites suspended their operations. Controls on the media in Malaysia were for a long period less stringent than in Singapore, though the Malaysian authorities often block opposition access to the media. For instance, in the April 1995 national parliamentary election campaign, the opposition was hamstrung by its inability to gain significant television or press coverage, due to the fact that most important media organs are government controlled, and all are government licensed. Since the arrest and trial of former Deputy-Prime Minister, Anwar Ibrahim, in 1998, controls on the press and media have become highly restrictive, with the major opposition party effectively prevented from publishing what had become a very popular party newspaper, and the Malaysian Chinese Association (a subordinate party in the ruling coalition) acquiring financial control of the only independent Chinese medium newspaper.

In Taiwan, magazines once provided a focus for opposition activity, since most newspapers and all television stations were controlled by the Kuomintang or influential members of the ruling party. This kept the opposition at a disadvantage, limiting its ability to convey its message to the electorate. Until the mid-1990s, the predominance of Mandarin in the media was also a contentious issue, as the language of the bulk of the population, Taiwanese, was downgraded to the status of a 'dialect'. At that time, laws were enforced to close unlicensed radio stations. Though this had a Taiwanese cultural dimension, it became a partisan political question as well. For example, in 1994 local elections for the governorship of Taiwan and for the positions of mayor of Taipei and Kaohsiung, critics maintained that opposition candidates did not receive entirely independent or impartial coverage in the official media. Further, without the unlicensed radio stations as a popular source of unofficial, often irreverent political commentary, access to such coverage became a political issue. The 1995 elections to the Legislative Yuan were the first in which the opposition enjoyed relatively equal access to and coverage in the media, with the acceptance by the ruling party of the need for a better-informed public. Meanwhile, in Thailand, the military still owns most major radio stations, as it has since the popularisation of the medium in the 1960s, and there are few pressures to change this arrangement.[8] With the rise to power of media billionaire Thaksin Shinawatra, family linked companies acquired the only completely independent television company, and foreign publications that criticized his policies were banned. In the Philippines, by contrast, there is no monopolistic control of the media, though journalists have been known to avoid open criticism of major political figures.

PARTIES AND PARTY SUPPORT

There are many examples of weak party institutionalization in Asian democracies, especially where formal or informal political rules have impeded the formation or activities of political parties. Opposition movements have sometimes found ways to circumvent such rules, however. The Taiwanese case is instructive. Although elections for local government were instituted in 1950 and elections for a limited number of positions in the National Assembly and Legislative Yuan were introduced in 1969, the formation of new political parties was proscribed in Taiwan until 1986. Non-Kuomintang candidates did run for office and over time cooperated through the *tangwai* ('outside party') movement to circumvent the existing prohibitions.

There are some parallels in the case of South Korea. From the installation of President Park Chung-hee's *Yushin* ('Revitalizing') constitution in 1972 until 1985, when party formation and competition were liberalized under Chun Doo-hwan, party activity was sidelined. Though it had taken Park almost two decades to build his political machine from his original seizure of power in 1961, it did not survive him. Chun was more successful, though only a fragment of the party he created, the Democratic Justice Party, survived (as part of the Democratic Liberal Party) through a merger of forces with those of Kim Young-sam. The opposition also suffered fragmentation, as personality conflicts among leaders led to a series of party splits and realignments, underlining the weakness of party structures and their shallow popular roots. While the opposition's New Korea Democratic Party did well in 1985 elections to the Assembly, the party was subsequently shown to be a marriage of convenience, with its two leading personalities founding their own parties, thereby dividing the forces opposed to authoritarianism. Election of former general and coup maker, Roh Tae-woo, was the result.

The history of political parties in South Korea reflects, in part, the deleterious effects of authoritarianism. From the time of the First Republic (1948-60), there have been more than a hundred South Korean political parties, and a relatively small number of leading political figures have been associated with several different parties during their careers. Even in the era of Kim Young-sam (1993-97), the first civilian to head the government since the military coup of 1961, parties functioned more as the creations of powerful leaders than as vehicles for policy or the advocacy of interests. The party realignments that occurred in 1995–96 attest to this. The Korean political landscape was remade, yet while all the major parties adopted new names and were constituted on the basis of new power alliances, the same leading personalities remained in charge.[9] While in opposition, Kim Dae-jung headed one party, came to the presidency while leader of another, and then created a third political party while in office.[10]

In Thailand, party proliferation has been a constant of the political environment. Party factionalism has also been common, with few parties espousing distinctive policies. Under the current constitution, attempts have been made to enhance party institutionalization by permitting only those parties with the minimum required number of members to register officially. Similarly, only those parties that agree to mount candidates in all constituencies for the national legislature are now eligible to run in the general elections. Following the political crisis of 1992, there was an attempt to characterize some political parties as 'devilish' (or pro-military) and others as 'angelic' (or anti-military), but this lasted only until the subsequent parliamentary elections in 1995. Indeed, the reason for the fall of the coalition government of Chuan Leekpai (leader of the Democrat

Party) and the subsequent scheduling of the elections was the defection of Palang Dharma from the 'angelic' coalition led by the Democrat Party.[11] The elections of 2001 resulted in a victory for an entirely new party, Thai Rak Thai, largely a personal vehicle for Thaksin Shinawatra. Thaksin's initial strategy was to incorporate as many existing members of parliament into his movement as possible, and once in power continued to pursue that strategy. Soon very little was left of the Thai political landscape, with the exception of the Democrat Party.[12]

In the Philippines, competition between the *Nacionalista* and Liberal parties after independence in 1946 until martial law in 1972 appeared to herald the emergence of regular political contestation.[13] Despite the appearance of a competitive two-party system, however, factionalism was common, as was movement between the two parties by leaders and other key individuals. Since the ouster of Ferdinand Marcos in 1986, political contestation has revived, but there has been little progress toward party institutionalization, with loose party coalitions forming and dissolving with each electoral cycle. Following the 1992 presidential election, major realignments occurred in the House of Representatives, with 71 members defecting from their parties in order to join the *Lakas*-National Union of Christian Democrats party of newly elected president Fidel Ramos. In subsequent midterm elections, Ramos managed to negotiate an electoral pact with the *Laban ng Demokratikong Pilipino* (LDP), which had been his toughest competitor in the earlier presidential contest. The *Lakas-Laban* coalition then won an overwhelming majority in the House and consolidated its majority in the Senate, only to have the coalition dissolve a year later in acrimonious circumstances. Joseph Estrada was supported in the presidential elections of 1998 by a coalition including *Laban* and his own party, *Partido ng Masang Pilipino*.

In Singapore, there are many officially registered parties, most of which are small and unconsolidated. The present Workers' Party, despite using a name that has been in currency since 1957, was in fact a creation of the 1970s. Its membership is small and its finances uncertain, though its performance at the polls suggests that it would be a more credible entity in a benign environment. The Singapore Democratic Party is of similar vintage. It was created in 1980 largely as a vehicle for Chiam See Tong, the sole opposition member of the legislature from 1988 to 1991. In 1995, Chiam disagreed with other leading members of the party, and eventually left to found another party even more a vehicle for his personal political role.

Despite such weaknesses in party structure, some Asian political parties have enjoyed remarkable continuity. In particular, the United Malays National Organization (UMNO) in Malaysia and the PAP in Singapore both date from the era of anti-colonial struggle in the 1950s. Likewise, the Kuomintang grew out of the movement that fought to displace the Manchu rulers of imperial China.

Each of these three parties, however, has sought to exercise a hegemonic role in its political system, and it is possible that none would be readily recognized by its founders. Though Singapore's Lee Kuan Yew (since 1990 Senior Minister in the cabinet) remains the intellectual leader of the PAP, its program, structure, and rationale are profoundly different from what they were in 1954. Indeed, many party elders, including former party chairman Dr. Toh Chin Chye and former Singapore President Devan Nair, have expressed uneasiness with the party's evolution. Similarly, Malaysia's UMNO endured a major split in 1987, and is now officially UMNO Baharu (new UMNO). Party factionalism within the Kuomintang, as well as defections to the New Party (essentially a mainlander group unhappy with concessions made to the Taiwanese and Taiwanese issues), transformed the ruling party on Taiwan. In fact, the New Party, by competing with the Kuomintang for the votes of those with mainlander affiliations, was a major factor in the opposition's success in 1994 with the election of the Democratic Progressive Party (DPP) candidate as mayor of Taipei. The leadership of the Kuomintang at that time was criticized by figures associated with the old regime (such as Chiang Wei-kuo and Sun An-ti) who implied that the original guiding ideology of Sun Yat-sen was being ignored through a focus only on Taiwan rather than all of China.[14] The formation of the New Party, which attracted 13 percent of the popular vote in the 1995 Legislative Yuan elections, was in part a response to such criticisms. Kuomintang disunity persisted, allowing the DPP's Chen Shui-bian to win the presidency in 2000. With the Kuomintang remaining the most important party in the Legislative Yuan until December 2001, Chen was forced to accept the principle of political cohabitation in the context of an unruly and divided political atmosphere.

The pattern of electoral support for the parties in these systems is difficult to characterize. It can be asserted, however, that the cross-cutting and overlapping affiliations which in Western liberal democracies facilitate democratic contestation are often absent in these cases.[15] Pluralist structures are weak, and multiple allegiances to interest groups that have contending political identities are unusual. At the same time, attitudes and social structure alike are in rapid change, with continued economic growth and associated social transformation, making it uncertain how this picture will look a decade from now.

For Malaysia, it is impossible to account for the political dynamics of electoral politics without reference to communalism. Indeed, the ethnic character of political competition is openly affirmed, with the dominant party in the ruling coalition being UMNO, the party of the majority (53%) Malay community.[16] The most important of Malaysia's opposition parties is the Democratic Action Party, most of whose supporters are ethnic Chinese (who constitute around 30% of the population) and whose most significant opponent is the Malaysian Chinese Association, an UMNO ally.

Communal identification can also be discerned in Taiwan, the most modernized and affluent of Asian states after Singapore and Japan. There is some evidence that an individual voter's perception of his or her ethnic identity as 'Taiwanese' (as opposed to Chinese mainlander) is the best indicator of a propensity to vote for the DPP.[17] Recent elections in Taiwan, however, indicate that this is changing, as voters focus on new issues such as corruption and environmental pollution that transcend longstanding debates about whether the political system on Taiwan should or should not be considered part of 'China'.[18] There is no reliable data on opposition support in Singapore, but it is often alleged that the Chinese-educated are less likely to vote for the ruling party than are the English-educated. The ruling PAP may therefore be an uncertain coalition of an English educated elite, and a Chinese educated following.

In South Korea, despite rapid modernization and the retirement of the military from government, factors other than those anticipated by conventional analysis have greatly affected support for political opposition. In short, Koreans still tend to view politics from the point of their regional affiliation, rather than being influenced by education or income level. In both 1987 and 1992, Kim Dae-jung was a candidate in presidential elections. In this period, the Kim Dae-jung vote was remarkably consistent. Over 80 percent of the voters who supported him in 1987 voted for him again in 1992. This support did not, however, bring him office in those contests.

In 1992, Kim Dae-jung and Kim Young-sam, both longstanding opposition figures, competed in the presidential elections. The two Kims had also contested, unsuccessfully, the 1987 elections. In the meantime, Kim Young-sam had shifted his position in the party realignment of 1990 in which he brought his erstwhile opposition grouping into the government. Industrial magnate Chung Ju-yung of the Unification National Party was the third candidate. As Kim Young-sam was perceived by many to have changed sides, it was expected that he would lose at least some votes to the other candidates. With Chung not likely to amass enough of a following to win office, Kim Dae-jung had to pick up most of these defectors to win. In the event, the defectors favored Chung, however, thereby denying Kim Dae-jung victory. Kim Dae-jung kept his loyal followers, but was unable to broaden his support base.

The most likely explanation for Kim Dae-jung's failure to gain office at that time was the regional nature of political support in South Korea. In the

Honam/Kwangju region (in Korea's Southwest), Kim Dae-jung consistently captured between 80 and 90 percent of the vote; in Seoul, which accounts for about 25 percent of the electorate, he managed to capture only about 30 percent of the vote. Interestingly, many in Seoul regard themselves as affiliated with the Honam region despite different voting patterns. In other regions, he performed poorly.[19] Moreover, those deserting Kim Young-sam in 1992 were primarily from areas beyond his regional base in Yongnam (in the Southeast). South Korean electoral behavior is further complicated by education, but regional affiliation appeared to be the strongest factor in the 1987 and 1992 results, and also in the 1995 local elections.[20] In the 1997 presidential contest regionalism was once again a major factor. Kim Dae-jung did well in his home area, but not elsewhere. He was however assisted by the fact that Kim Young-sam's political movement was in effect divided between two rival candidates, neither of whom were native sons of Kim's home region. Kim Young-sam's key ally, Kim Jong-pil, had also joined him in a cooperative alliance. Even in these circumstances, Kim Dae-jung's margin of victory was very small (winning 39.7% of the vote against 38.2% for his nearest rival).[21]

A consideration of elections in Thailand and the Philippines demonstrate that similar dynamics are at work in these Asian democracies. In Thailand, the 1995 elections brought to power a new coalition led by Chart Thai. This led, in turn, to a major realignment of the parties. The pattern of representation was striking testimony to the bases of party support in the country. For example, although Chart Thai had the largest representation nationwide, in the capital it did not win a single seat. Instead, Palang Dharma, Prachakorn Thai and the Democrat Party, parties much more attuned to policy issues and thus of greater appeal to the more educated voters in Bangkok, captured the great majority of the seats.

The bulk of Chart Thai's support came from the rural areas outside the capital, though not from the South, and much of the party's success could be attributed to the mobilization of voters or rural leaders. This mobilization was achieved either through vote-buying or by simply addressing the particular needs of voters from these areas. In the capital, the buying of votes was much less extensive, and issues and policies were correspondingly more important. One explanation for this difference was that, in the capital, the middle class accounted for about 30 percent of the population.[22] With leadership and other changes, the place of Palang Dharma as the party of urbanized Thais was subsequently taken by the Democrat Party, which led the government that came to power in November 1997.

In the Philippine presidential contest of 1992, neither candidate of the large party machines won, though the power of these parties persisted. Specifically, both Ramon Mitra of the LDP and Eduardo Cojuangco, the chief inheritor of the patronage network of Ferdinand Marcos, lost to Fidel Ramos. The factor that was probably crucial to his victory was outgoing president Corazon Aquino's endorsement. Nevertheless, with only 23.4 percent of the popular vote, his victory was a narrow one and so did not provide overwhelming evidence of a new style of politics. Following the election, Ramos assembled a coalition with the main competing party, as described above, in order to command a majority in the House and Senate. Although 1995 legislative elections increased the coalition's majority in both the House and the Senate, the Ramos administration continued to depend upon the cooperation of the LDP to command a floor majority.[23] The presidential contest of 1998 produced a landslide for the coalition supporting Joseph Estrada, LAMP (*Lapian ng Masang Pilipino*), which included Laban as well as Estrada's own movement, the PMP (*Partido ng Masang Pilipino*). Later Lakas joined forces with former 'People's Power' NGOs to force Estrada from office as a result of corruption scandals. Even in Taiwan, the relative success of the Kuomintang in local politics can be explained by the party's ability to mobilize voters using patronage and faction ties, as a number of studies have demonstrated.[24]

Civil Society and Political Culture

It should not be presumed that such patterns of political support are static. Though civil society is relatively weak in East Asia, there are indications that the new politics of citizen mobilization is winning an increasing number of converts. This has influenced parliamentary opposition in Taiwan, and was one reason the DPP took an interest in problems of pollution and environmental degradation, since alliances with groups formed to address these problems brought the party voting support.[25] The more general pattern for organizations of this type, such as the Citizens' Coalition for Economic Justice in South Korea and the Taiwan Environmental Protection Union, has been to advance their specific issues through selective contact with a variety of political and governmental figures as well as with the media.[26] This pattern of selective contact was not followed in Malaysia, where the Malaysian Trade Union Congress in the early 1990s openly backed the opposition party Semangat '46. In that and other such cases where special-interest groups have not followed a pattern of selective contact, civil society has suffered divisions.[27]

As Philippe Schmitter has pointed out, state policy has a specific impact (via regulation, encouragement, prohibition, and the like) on the capacity and scope of the elements of civil society to influence policy outcomes.[28] Evidence from at least one East Asian case suggests that in principle the state may permit these elements to proliferate while in practice still containing their influence on politics. For example, under the provisions of the Singapore Societies Act, any association of ten or more individuals must be registered and must restrict its activities to those for which the association has been formed. The Registrar of Societies may refuse to register or may expel any association on a variety of grounds, including affiliation with an overseas organization deemed contrary to the national interest. Most significantly, any association seeking to influence public policy must register as a political party or movement, effectively rendering illegal any activities defined as 'political' by other associations such as lobbying or the dissemination of political information.[29] Although some social organizations in Singapore such as the Association of Women for Action and Research (AWARE) have managed to remain active, considerable obstacles to the emergence of an autonomous civil society persist. At the same time, the government has created official channels for managing public demands. One such channel is the Feedback Unit in the Ministry of Community Development, the operations of which encourage especially the better educated to voice in hearings which are off the record their views on government policies. A similar, though in practice somewhat less restrictive, Societies Act also exists in Malaysia. Since 1998 in Malaysia the powers of the Police Act have been used to require all meetings larger than four members to be licensed, an arrangement that has permitted the government to criminalise dissident activities almost at will.

Selective political action by special interest groups is a marginal trend at present, but it is likely that this form of politics will have a greater impact on electoral outcomes in the future. Given that East Asian democracies exhibit considerable variations in their treatment of organised social interests, from Singapore's restrictive approach, as discussed above, to the increasingly demanding, even unruly civil society that emerged in Taiwan through the 1990s, there is clear potential for change in this aspect of Asian constitutional systems.[30]

Although social dynamics are changing constitutional Asia's patterns of political orientation, the distinctiveness and durability of the received political culture should nevertheless be acknowledged. Lucian Pye and others have maintained that Confucianism has had a powerful impact on East Asian approaches to authority, which in turn have conditioned notions of political opposition and contestation.[31] If the term 'political culture' includes not merely popular beliefs about authority but also the essentials of the high culture, then this will serve as another important obstacle to the development of a democratic opposition in those cases where Confucianism continues to have some influence, for several reasons. First, central to Confucianism is an ethical view of government that renders compromise morally repugnant. Second, a belief in the superiority and duty to lead of the educated man undercuts the functionality and legitimacy of contending interests. Finally, a generally collectivist and organic conception of the state creates conditions unfavorable to adversarial rules of political competition.

Although some East Asian statesmen have argued that there is not necessarily an inconsistency between Confucianism and democracy, such arguments are difficult to support.[32] According to Confucian theory, the superior men, or *junzi*, have a duty to rule irrespective of the wishes of the masses, while the masses are seen as concerned primarily with their own interests and personal profit and therefore without the moral perception to comprehend the basis of the *junzi's* duty. Giving the masses the vote and thus the power to dismiss the *junzi* contravenes the central element of Confucian political thought.

This is not a matter of interest only to historians of ideas. Confucianism still influences school curricula in Taiwan, while South Korea's Confucian lobby is vocal in its criticism of some measures of social reform. Singapore has even tried, with the help of Harvard professors, to reinvent Confucianism for consumption by a population never especially familiar with it (given the historical lack of a Confucian ruling elite in what had its origins as an emigrant community).

While Thailand and the Philippines have not been directly influenced by the texts and history of Confucianism, in both cases patron-client relations are pervasive and important enough to be considered crucial elements of the political culture. Thailand also has a deeply entrenched monarchical tradition, which further strengthens a deferential attitude on the part of the masses towards the elites.[33] In both systems, party solidity and strategy are as likely to result from networks of personal ties to political leaders as from competition for office. This is not to say, however, that conditions in either political system are static.

CONSOLIDATING DEMOCRACY?

Other features could be added to those considered above, but none would alter the basic character of the political syndrome that has here been identified. Two central judgments emerge from this analysis. The first concerns the extent to which the cases examined have certain important political features in common. Although a broadly inductive approach to operating constitutions—an approach exemplified by Books IV through VI of Aristotle's *Politics*—is beyond the scope of this essay, the systems analyzed here as a class resemble neither the democracies of Western Europe and North America nor the other political systems of the East Asian region. The second conclusion we can draw relates to the extent to which the cases analyzed here can be described as 'democratic.' Though none conforms in every respect to the more stringent definitions of democracy, all satisfy to a degree the view of democracy held by Joseph Schumpeter. That is, each allows for a competitive struggle between potential governing elites for the people's vote. Moreover, all are in the process of social as well as political change.

Summarising the features of the cases that have been considered, the rules of the game in the East Asian constitutional systems described here facilitate political competition, the outcome of which determines the composition of the government, though within established parameters. The rules do, however, favor incumbents. Further, party institutionalization is generally weak (even in the case of hegemonic political movements such as Singapore's PAP). Finally, the political sociology and culture of electoral support is not generally conducive to a two-party system. Even in those systems where democracy is furthest advanced, South Korea and Taiwan, office is as much decided by factional realignments within political movements as by an institutionalized alternation of power between contending political parties. And evidence of popular orientations towards politics exhibits a consistent pattern of skepticism regarding the extent to which these two political systems are held to be democracies by their citizens.[34]

Further consideration of this group of political systems requires a review of their dynamics. While South Korea and Taiwan appear to be moving toward institutionalizing and extending democratic forms, Malaysia and Singapore seem to have succeeded in institutionalizing a form of 'semi-democracy,'[35] 'electoralism,'[36] or 'democracy by default.'[37] With regard to Thailand and the Philippines, it is too soon for a definitive judgment, though if the whole group of cases analyzed here were to be placed along a continuum from most to least democratic, these two cases would fall somewhere in the middle. It is not clear how long these semi-democracies will persist in their present forms, but their stability at this level of democratization is a reminder that, even after important democratic forms have become entrenched, continued democratization is not inevitable.

If democracy is to be consolidated rather than contained, several immediate steps must be taken.[38] First, constitutionalism itself must be further embedded. This requires, at the very least, a settled period during which the existing constitutional order is recognized and respected. Following this period, changes must be made only after extensive consultation and debate, and with the clear understanding that such changes are being made for the sole purpose of enhancing the operations of the constitutional order. In performing this task, it is important to avoid the predicament Thailand found itself in during the 1980s:

> What Thailand experienced was neither constitutionalism nor constitutional government, but rather different types of regimes that adjusted and readjusted institutional relationships between the executive and the legislative branches in order to strengthen their own positions vis-à-vis their opponents.[39]

Here, there is no easy remedy for the present lack of solidity in constitutional arrangements. The Thai case is instructive. The 1997 constitution is profoundly democratic, amongst its features being an independent Electoral Commission and a National Counter-Corruption Commission. Yet despite Thaksin's Thai Rak Thai Party receiving the most numerous counts of censure for corruption in the 2001 elections, and the prime minister-elect himself being required to face the Constitutional Court for concealing his assets (and facing disqualification if found guilty) in the event his movement has come closer to dominating Thai politics than since the (decidedly semi-democratic) era of reforming military prime ministers of the 1980s. Nevertheless, in East Asia the oldest constitutions have generally been among those most easily altered, while some of the newest constitutions have proved most conducive to political contestation. Here the comparison between Singapore and South Korea is revealing.

Establishing a robust framework for laws relating to electoral procedures and the conduct of political parties is vital if democracy is to be consolidated. In South Korea, for example, the reforms of 1994 introduced stringent penalties for improper campaigning and corrupt political practices. Under the new rules, candidates must channel all campaign funds through registered bank accounts, with total funds committed not exceeding a specified limit. Further, government funding of political parties was made proportional to the level of national support the parties receive. This approach followed the German model, and was instituted in South Korea in an attempt to reduce the reliance of parties on funding from business groups.[40] Yet both the Kim Young-sam and Kim Dae-jung administrations were disfigured by repeated exposures of malfeasance by officials and politicians. Though Singapore's Westminster type institutions have functioned since 1959, arbitrary and partisan changes to electoral arrangements and the duration of the campaigning period have undermined their original democratic impulse.

To a great degree, the ability of a political system to entrench constitutionalism rests on durable guarantees for the rule of law.[41] In the past few years, considerable efforts have been made in Taiwan and South Korea to strengthen the rule of law and provide for the independence of the judiciary. In South Korea in particular, many legal officers tainted by their experience with the authoritarian era have resigned or retired, and the legal profession has reorganized itself in order to uphold proper professional standards. In Malaysia and Singapore, however, legal developments have followed a different course. In Malaysia, Lord President Tun Salleh Abas (the most senior of the judges in Malaysia's highest court) was removed in 1988 as a result of a direct confrontation with the prime minister. Likewise, in Singapore, the Law Society (the official association of the legal profession) was dissolved after the government criticized its leadership. Both cases indicate the ease with which this aspect of democratization may be contained.[42]

Across the region, hegemonic parties are either a structural feature or an aspiration. A means needs to be found to ensure that if they do claim to speak for an all-inclusive national consensus, or shared fundamental values, or embody some deep cultural inheritance, they also recognise that these claims require substantiation and fair electoral tests. Similarly, claims of 'performance legitimacy' are much easier to state than to prove.

Another difficult problem to consider is the role of regional or communal sentiment in determining political affiliation. As long as politics is conceived in these terms, parties will be able to appeal to such sentiments in order to assemble a majoritarian base of support while excluding minority regions or communities. Some evidence suggests that this strategy is a matter of political generations, but in some East Asian constitutional systems the older generations have been slow in passing. Taken together, the communal or regional approach to party affiliation and the generational approach to leadership support the argument that democracy in the region may not follow the pattern prescribed in Western theory. In order for this to change, a more inclusive type of political leadership as well as popular demand for such leadership will be required.

Democratic consolidation will not proceed without an increase in the power and status of the opposition. The tasks to be performed by opposition groups in these systems are challenging, yet without any real prospects for a change of government, such systems lack public contestation and inclusiveness, the two essential components of democracy as defined by Robert Dahl.[43] In parliamentary systems, where opposition groups are allowed an official presence even if they do not hold office, the opposition must walk a particularly fine line, subjecting members of the governing party to a sustained critique while respecting as legitimate the existing political structures.[44] In constitutional East Asia, the exact position of this line is often unclear.

Politics in constitutional East Asia has been as much about the persistence, moderation, or eradication of authoritarianism as about more conventional issues such as wealth redistribution, welfare, employment, and education. While the mobilization of opinion against authoritarian systems has been an important factor in the demise or modification of authoritarian regimes, anti-regime movements have not necessarily been able to manage the transition to the role of opposition parties. Indeed, as Alfred Stepan has noted, the (on occasion, conspiratorial and always single-minded) strategies and predilections appropriate to the struggle against authoritarianism may obstruct the capacity to aggregate opinions or pursue policy consensus.[45]

In some of the cases analyzed here, it is not yet clear whether the term 'opposition' is entirely appropriate for many of the parties engaged in political contestation. In order for an opposition to be credible, it must be viable as an alternative to the ruling party in government. In Taiwan and South Korea, opposition groups may have reached the point at least in electoral terms where they can claim that status. In Thailand, it is difficult to speak of a genuine opposition given that the established practice of the ruling coalition moving parties in and out of government with regularity. Similarly, in the Philippines, electoral contestation is as much about securing a leader's local power base (often held as a traditional family fief) as it is about changing the shape of national politics.

In Malaysia and Singapore, opposition parties are even less viable politically. Cooperation between Semangat '46, PAS (Partai Islam Se Malaysia) and the Democratic Action Party (DAP) of the type attempted during the 1995 general election conformed to the tactic of opposing Dr Mahathir by all available means, but did not make for a coherent program for an alternative government. While Semangat '46 was part of the political mainstream, the other parties had a reputation for (Malay and Chinese respectively) communalism and exclusivity. The same incoherence was manifest in the *Barisan Alternatif* (composed of PAS, KeADILan, a new political movement convened by Anwar Ibrahim's supporters, the DAP and a further minor party) that competed against UMNO and its allies in 1999.[46] Meanwhile, in Singapore, the major opposition parties have even cooperated in fielding at election time such a distribution of candidates that it would only be possible for them to win in a minority of seats, precisely to prevent the ruling party from losing office.

Finally, in order for democratic consolidation to progress, the various elements of civil society, will need to have more freedom as well as more responsibility. For example, in some of the cases described here, civil society has been unable to expand much beyond the restrictive parameters established by the state. Elsewhere, especially in states where civil society is a relatively new phenomenon given the recent transition from authoritarianism, its manifestations are still not sufficiently linked to the political process which is often regarded as a limited space dominated by democratizers and authoritarians. In South Korea, for example, elements of civil society were very active in the original democratization movement in the late 1980s, but civil society has not adapted as well as might then have been expected to the open political environment of the 1990s.[47]

All of the five conditions regarded by Juan Linz and Alfred Stepan as prerequisites for the consolidation of democracy are to be found in this region; yet none is sufficiently entrenched as to be completely unproblematic.[48] While the necessary economic prerequisites of democratic consolidation are less of a problem in this region than in other regions, such critical political requirements for democracy as the rule of law, the presence of an autonomous political sphere, and a free and lively civil society cannot yet be taken for granted in the cases examined here. In addition, strenuous efforts have been made to build national identities in multi-ethnic states. Though these efforts have been successful, they must be continued if democratic consolidation is to continue. Democratic consolidation in the cases covered here is decidedly a process, not a result.

The Question of Timing

The timing of democratization in the cases reviewed here has had and will continue to have a powerful bearing on prospects for consolidation. Malaysia and Singapore have been seen as examples of democracy's 'second wave'; South Korea, Taiwan, and perhaps Thailand as examples of the third wave; and the Philippines as at least a partial example of both. For all of these systems, the timing of democratization was crucial. The second wave was part of the process of decolonisation, the third wave arose during the era of American hegemony.

In Malaysia and Singapore, British decolonisation proceeded on the assumption that the political institutions to be left as a legacy should be modeled on the British system. The only concessions made were those deemed expedient and necessary for a constitution to be adopted. For example, in Malaysia, a role for the Malay sultans was preserved while many Chinese were denied the rights of citizenship. In fact, UMNO was dominated for decades by aristocrats with a specifically Malay mission, though they also were strongly influenced by British education and ideas. Similarly, in Singapore, political rights were abridged, with citizenship not initially extended to all inhabitants, and detention without trial permitted for reasons of national security. The general perception was that the only alternative to a decolonized political order of this kind was communism, though communism was rejected after intense domestic conflict. During the process of decolonization, British-educated elites inspired largely by Fabian socialism captured the political high ground.

While the second wave of democratization in Asia was dominated by British political ideas, the third wave was given impetus by the general perception that American political ideas and institutions were superior to those of Britain. The sources of this perception were various, but included the fact that American originals were already an important inspiration for the ROC (Republic of China) on Taiwan and (from 1948) successive Korean constitutions, and were also largely replicated in the Philippines constitution of 1935, and democratic movements and critics took succour from and were often based in that country. Moreover, by the time the third wave was under way, the alternative economic and social systems of America's Cold War antagonists were in visible decline. American approaches to political science dominated the academic discourse in all of the countries studied here, generally overlooking any arguments to the contrary aside from an increasingly discredited Marxism.

Democratization in the 1980s, insofar as it was affected by external influences and trends, thus proceeded according to an American formula. Democratic consolidation in the 1990s occurred in a radically different context. In particular, the disappearance of the Cold War as a reference point stimulated a search for new foundations. The perception became widespread, in the years immediately prior to the regional financial crisis of 1997, that the apogee of American power was over, and that serious fissures in the American social order were a warning to any who would emulate the American system too closely. On the one hand, there was a rise in the number of indigenous or cultural theories of the polity, including Islamic and Buddhist approaches in Malaysia and Thailand, and Confucianism in Singapore. Similarly, suitable local models were actively sought in Taiwan and South Korea.[49] The Japanese model was also influential, owing in part to the resurgence in Japan of cultural nationalism and also to the development of the 'contempt for America' school of thought. Even in South Korea, though there was a great deal of residual hostility toward and cultural fear of Japan due to historical experiences, notably World War II, Japan's political dynamics were nevertheless much studied following the democratic transition of 1987.

The extent to which there exist alternatives to the Western model of democracy continues to be disputed. Even so sanguine a critic as Francis Fukuyama presents a 'new Asian authoritarianism' as his alternative vision for the end of history, if liberal democracy is not universally triumphant. In this case, such a 'systematic, illiberal and non-democratic alternative will combine technocratic economic rationalism with paternalistic authoritarianism.'[50] Without adopting this extreme view, the kind of democracy that is still being consolidated in East Asia may nevertheless be less like American democracy than might have been the case in the 1980s. This may affect, in turn, a whole range of political characteristics, possibly including mobilization strategies employed by parties, the prerogatives of government, and conceptions of legitimate rights.

A further point related to timing may have even greater consequences for democracy in East Asia than the ones described above. Although any prognosis in this area remains uncertain, democratic consolidation is proceeding in an era of increasing regionalization and globalization.[51] This trend was, in fact, one factor contributing to the third wave itself ('People's Power' in the Philippines and American support for Corazon Aquino were powerful influences on Korean popular opinion in 1986) but its influence is now increasing to the point where the national polity is both too large and too small a unit of analysis in much political science. The polity is too small, since its borders are so porous and flexible; it is too large because its constituent elements are influenced as much by what goes on outside those borders as what transpires within, and so must be analysed in their own terms. As Kenichi Ohmae has remarked, 'the nation state has become an unnatural, even dysfunctional unit for organizing human activity and managing economic endeavor.'[52] Individuals may draw their tastes and wants from cosmopolitan models, while organized interests may either focus locally or look beyond their own polities for support, alliances, or resources. These trends have been further magnified by the spread of the internet in the Asia Pacific region. Likewise, transnational economic and political actors, including business conglomerates, regional economic groupings, and world organizations, will continue to erode the state both as a source of sovereign prerogatives and as a unit of analysis. All of these trends will therefore influence the scope and character of democratic consolidation, though some will likely operate in ways as yet unforeseen. While the limited reach and increasing permeability of the state has been an enduring theme of political science in its approach to 'developing nations' since the 1960s, this approach will have to be more broadly applied in the current era.

International and regional linkages will have an impact upon the progress of democracy in the cases analyzed here. For example, the emerging international human rights regime—embodied in United Nations instruments and obligations and now a major issue in diplomacy—elicited a skeptical response from Asia in the form of the Bangkok Declaration of 1993, which contained the region's contribution to the UN convened World Conference on Human Rights. Though this response sought to limit the scope of the international instruments protecting such rights,[53] democratic consolidation has seen the incorporation of structures for protecting and promoting human rights. On the other hand, regional linkages in East Asia, spanning economic, cultural, and security concerns, will be of great importance. Japan and China will loom large as markets, as sources of capital and technology, and as powerful cultural influences. Already security dialogue in the ASEAN Regional Forum has become preoccupied with conflicting territorial claims in the South China Sea. Perhaps the biggest uncertainty is the future shape of China and its role in the international system.[54]

Globalization can have both beneficial and deleterious implications for democratization and democratic consolidation. On the beneficial side, new and less easily censored global telecommunications networks, especially the internet, can expose authoritarian governments to external criticisms while informing the subjects of such regimes of alternative forms of organizing political life. Globalization may, however, have less than benign effects as well. For example, the development of the world market to incorporate major trans-national actors and methods of production has increased worldwide demand for the products of the advanced economies, generating also a popular belief in the right to a comparable standard of subsistence and consumption. Many may also find, however, that globalization undermines their freedom to consume by weakening the capacities of their communities to deliver the requisite political and social goods. Evidence of this is abundant. One only has to consider the almost complete destruction in many areas of China in the post-1979 era of market oriented reforms of the system of social welfare, which provided (albeit at a low level in some localities) housing, health and education. If this can occur in what is held to be one of the region's 'strongest' states, weaker states in pursuit of globalisation may pay an even higher price.

Extending this point directly to the political systems in the cases analyzed here, both Malaysia and Thailand have modernized rapidly in the past three decades and exemplify a form of development that employs very little indigenous technology.[55] The people in these societies who have prospered have been the elites, and especially those with foreign linkages. Moreover, the benefits of development have been spread very unevenly.[56]

If international conditions change radically, as the result of major economic disputes disrupting the international trading order, or as the consequence of the machinations of the global financial regime, this technology may be withdrawn or redirected, with possibly drastic consequences for employment and welfare in the region. For example, Singapore has now reached income levels comparable to those of Western Europe, but is heavily dependent on trans-national capital, with about three-quarters of the city-state's manufactured exports deriving from the operations of foreign investors. Even South Korea and Taiwan, the most successful at fostering local technology of the cases considered here, are still located in hierarchies of production. They are host to the basic processing entailed in the production of trans-national commodities while design and other value-added activities are often based in Japan.[57]

In such an environment, the consolidation of democracy may become devalued. Democracy may be seen as a political system that is incapable of delivering important social and political goods, thereby weakening state capacity at a time when globalizing forces have already eroded the resources and reach of the state. Further, the state's ability to successfully engage with the trans-national economy or the world market may be regarded as a much more important task than the extension and entrenchment of democracy. This argument is frequently made in Singapore and Malaysia, where the leaders of the PAP and UMNO assert that fully fledged liberal democracy is undesirable because it would shift the focus of state policy to redistributive and welfare issues or ethnic differences and away from the maintenance of those linkages and conditions which make those polities attractive and profitable for trans-national business.

CONCLUSION

Considered as a group, the political systems of the Philippines, South Korea, Taiwan and Thailand, and to some extent Malaysia and Singapore as well, are ranged across a continuum in terms of democratic practice and prospects. While progress is being made toward the consolidation of democracy in some respects, various democratic institutions and practices have also been constrained in each of the cases, indicating that democratization may stop short of full political contestation. Moreover, some of the democratic forms that have been successfully adopted suggest that even consolidated East Asian democracies may be distinct from their counterparts elsewhere.[58] In particular, hegemonic parties have been slow to relinquish their control, and party support has not followed the typical prescription of pluralist theory.

In short, where consolidation has been proceeding, it has not always established some of the conditions that are fundamental for the reproduction of a Western-style democracy. Finally, the present era may not be as favorable to democratization as was the latter part of the 1980s. In particular, the imperatives of globalization may reduce the attractiveness of democracy, either because the state may lose its capacity to deliver traditional public goods or because the state's linkages to regional and global economic orders may take on more importance for policy makers.

NOTES

1 Bertrand Badie, *The Imported State. The Westernization of the Political Order* (Stanford: Stanford University Press, 2000).

2 Samuel P. Huntington, *The Third Wave: Democratization in the Late Twentieth Century* (Norman: University of Oklahoma Press, 1991).

3 Samuel P. Huntington, 'American Democracy in Relation to Asia,' in Robert Bartley, Chan Heng Chee, Samuel P. Huntington, Shijuro Ogata, *Democracy and Capitalism: Asian and American Perspectives* (Singapore: Institute of Southeast Asian Studies, 1993), 39–40.

4 Michael Ong, 'Government and Opposition in Parliament: The Rules of the Game,' in Zakaria Haji Ahmad, ed., *Government and Politics of Malaysia* (Singapore: Oxford University Press, 1987), 40–55.

5 Christopher Tremewan, *The Political Economy of Social Control in Singapore* (London: Routledge, 1994), 187–227; Francis T. Seow, *To Catch a Tartar: A Dissident in Lee Kuan Yew's Prison* (New Haven: Yale Center for International and Area Studies, 1994).

6 Chin Sok Chong, 'The South Korean Press,' in Donald N. Clark, ed., *Korea Briefing, 1992* (Boulder, Colo.: Westview/Asia Society, 1992), 117–39.

7 Tan Teng Lang, *The Singapore Press: Freedom, Responsibility and Credibility* (Singapore: Institute of Policy Studies, 1990).

8 Chai-Anan Samudavanija, 'Thailand: A Stable Semi-Democracy,' in Larry Diamond, Juan J. Linz, and Seymour Martin Lipset, eds., *Democracy in Developing Countries*, vol. 3, *Asia* (Boulder, Colo.: Lynne Rienner, 1989), 324; Chai-Anan Samudavanija and Parichart Chotiya, 'Beyond Transition in Thailand', in Larry Diamond and Marc F. Plattner eds., *Democracy in East Asia* (Baltimore: Johns Hopkins University Press, 1998), 147-167.

9 Ahn Chung-Si, 'Democratization and Political Reform in Korea: Development, Culture, Leadership and Institutional Change,' in Doh Chull Shin, Myeong-han Zoh, Myung Chey, eds., *Korea in the Global Wave of Democratization* (Seoul: Seoul National University Press, 1994), 161–78.

10 Sunhyuk Kim, 'Patronage Politics as an Obstacle to Democracy in South Korea: Regional Networks and Democratic Consolidation', in Howard Handelman and Mark Tessler eds, *Democracy and Its Limits. Lessons from Asia, Latin America and the Middle East* (Notre Dame: University of Notre Dame Press, 1999), 115-129.

11 Daniel E. King, 'The Thai Parliamentary Elections of 1992: Return to Democracy in an Atypical Year,' *Asian Survey* Vol. 32 (1992), 1109–23.

[12] John Funston, 'Thailand: Reform Politics', in John Funston ed., *Government and Politics in Southeast Asia* (Singapore: ISEAS, 2001), 328-71.

[13] David Wurfel, *Filipino Politics: Development and Decay* (Ithaca, N.Y.: Cornell University Press, 1988), 93–103.

[14] *Far Eastern Economic Review*, 27 April 1995, 29.

[15] Fu Hu and Yun-han Chu, 'Neo-Authoritarianism, Polarized Conflict and Populism in a Newly Democratizing Regime: Taiwan's Emerging Mass Politics,' working paper no. 9, Conference Group on Taiwan Studies of the American Political Science Association, (Durham NC: Duke University Political Science Department, 1995).

[16] Gordon P. Means, *Malaysian Politics: The Second Generation* (Singapore: Oxford University Press, 1991), ch. 5; A.B. Shamsul, 'Religion and Ethnic Politics in Malaysia,' in Charles F. Keyes, Laurel Kendall, Helen Hardacre, eds., *Asian Visions of Authority: Religion and the Modern States of East and Southeast Asia* (Honolulu: University of Hawaii Press, 1994), 99–116.

[17] Fu Hu and Yun-han Chu, 'Electoral Competition and Political Democratization,' in Tun-jen Cheng and Stephan Haggard, eds., *Political Change in Taiwan* (Boulder, Colo.: Lynne Rienner, 1992), 186–97.

[18] Yun-han Chu and Tse-min Lin, 'The Process of Democratic Consolidation in Taiwan: Social Cleavage, Electoral Competition, and the Emerging Party System,' in Hung-mao Tien, ed., *Taiwan's Electoral Politics and Democratic Transition: Riding the Third Wave* (Armonk, N.Y.: M.E. Sharpe, 1996), 79–104.

[19] Bae Sun-kwang, 'Continuity or Change: The Voter's Choice in the 1992 Presidential Election,' in James Cotton, ed., *Politics and Policy in the New Korean State: From Roh Tae-woo to Kim Young-sam* (New York: St. Martin's, 1995), 66–82; Bae Sun-kwang and James Cotton, 'Regionalism in Electoral Politics,' in James Cotton, ed., *Korea Under Roh Tae-woo: Democratisation, Northern Policy and Inter-Korean Relations* (Sydney, Australia: Allen and Unwin, 1993), 170–84.

[20] *Korea Newsreview*, 1 July 1995, 4–7; *Far Eastern Economic Review*, 13 July 1995, 28.

[21] Kim, Byung-Kook, 'Party Politics in South Korea's Democracy: The Crisis of Success', in Larry Diamond and Byung-Kook Kim eds 2000, *Consolidating Democracy in South Korea* (Boulder & London: Rienner, 2000), 53-86.

[22] *Far Eastern Economic Review*, 29 June 1995, 14–20; Sukhumbhand Paribatra, 'State and Society in Thailand: How Fragile the Democracy?' *Asian Survey* Vol. 33 (1993), 879–93.

[23] *Far Eastern Economic Review*, 18 May 1995, 16; and 18 June 1995, 16–22.

[24] Joseph Bosco, 'Taiwan Factions: *Guanxi*, Patronage and the State in Local Politics,' *Ethnology* Vol. 31 (1992), 157–83.

[25] David W. Chen, 'The Emergence of Environmental Consciousness in Taiwan,' in Murray A. Rubinstein, ed., *The Other Taiwan: 1945 to the Present* (Armonk, N.Y.: M.E. Sharpe, 1994), 257–86.

26 Lee Su-Hoon, 'Transitional Politics of Korea, 1987-1992: Activation of Civil Society,' *Pacific Affairs* Vol. 66 (1993), 351–67.

27 James V. Jesudason, 'Statist Democracy and the Limits to Civil Society in Malaysia,' *Journal of Commonwealth and Comparative Politics* Vol. 33 (1995), 335–56.

28 See Philippe C. Schmitter, 'Civil Society East and West', in Larry Diamond, Marc E. Plattner, Yun-han Chu and Hung-mao Tien eds., *Consolidating the Third Wave Democracies. Themes and Perspectives* (Baltimore: Johns Hopkins University Press, 1997), 239-62.

29 Beng-huat Chua, *Communitarian Ideology and Democracy in Singapore* (London: Routledge, 1995), 204–5; Tremewan, *The Political Economy of Social Control in Singapore,* 195–96.

30 Thomas B. Gold, 'Civil Society and Taiwan's Quest for Identity,' in Stevan Harrell and Huang Chun-chieh, eds., *Cultural Change in Postwar Taiwan* (Boulder, Colo.: Westview, 1994), 47–68.

31 Lucian W. Pye, *Asian Power and Politics: The Cultural Dimensions of Authority* (Cambridge: Harvard University Press, 1987); Peter R. Moody, *Political Opposition in Post-Confucian Societies* (New York: Praeger, 1988).

32 For an energetic exposition of this position, see Lee Teng-hui, 'Chinese Culture and Political Renewal', in Larry Diamond, Marc F. Plattner, Yun-han Chu and Hung-mao Tien eds., *Consolidating the Third Wave Democracies. Regional Challenges* (Baltimore: Johns Hopkins University Press, 1997), 192-97.

33 Alfred W. McCoy, ed., *An Anarchy of Families: State and Family in the Philippines* (Quezon City, the Philippines: Ateneo de Manila University Press, 1994); *Far Eastern Economic Review,* 27 April 1995, 21.

34 Chu, Yun-han, Larry Diamond and Doh Chull Shin, 'Halting Progress in Korea and Taiwan', *Journal of Democracy* Vol. 12 (2001), no 1, 122-136

35 William Case, 'Semi-Democracy in Malaysia: Withstanding the Pressures for Regime Change,' *Pacific Affairs* Vol. 66 (1993), 183–205; Harold Crouch, 'Malaysia: Neither Authoritarian nor Democratic,' in Kevin Hewison, Richard Robison, Garry Rodan eds., *Southeast Asia in the 1990s: Authoritarianism, Democracy and Capitalism* (Sydney, Australia: Allen and Unwin, 1993), 133–58; Garry Rodan, ed., *Singapore Changes Guard: Social, Political and Economic Directions in the 1990s* (New York: St. Martin's, 1993); Huntington, *The Third Wave,* 295.

36 Terry Lynn Karl, 'Dilemmas of Democratization in Latin America,' *Comparative Politics* Vol. 23 (1990–91), 14.

37 Laurence Whitehead, 'The Alternatives to `Liberal Democracy': A Latin American Perspective,' in David Held, ed., *Prospects for Democracy: North, South, East, West* (Cambridge: Polity Press, 1993), 325.

38 On consolidation, see: Larry Diamond, *Developing Democracy. Toward Consolidation* (Baltimore: John Hopkins University Press, 1999).

[39] Samudavanija, 'Thailand: A Stable Semi-Democracy,' 320.

[40] Huh Young, 'Laws Alone Cannot Bring Political Reform,' *Korea Focus* Vol. 2 (1994), 22–31.

[41] Dae-Kyu Yoon, *Law and Political Authority in South Korea* (Seoul: Kyungnam University Press, 1990), 214–15.

[42] Tun Salleh Abas, *The Role of the Independent Judiciary* (Kuala Lumpur, Malaysia: Promarketing, 1989); H.P. Lee, *Constitutional Conflicts in Contemporary Malaysia* (Kuala Lumpur, Malaysia: Oxford University Press, 1995); Seow, *To Catch a Tartar.*

[43] Robert A. Dahl, *Polyarchy: Participation and Opposition* (New Haven: Yale University Press, 1971), 6–7

[44] Adam Przeworski, *Democracy and the Market* (Cambridge: Cambridge University Press, 1991), 89.

[45] Alfred Stepan, 'On the Tasks of a Democratic Opposition,' in Larry Diamond and Marc F. Plattner, eds., *The Global Resurgence of Democracy* (Baltimore: Johns Hopkins University Press, 1993), 67.

[46] John Funston, 'Malaysia's Tenth Elections: Status Quo, *Reformasi,* or Islamization', *Contemporary Southeast Asia* Vol. 22 (2000), no 1, 22-59.

[47] Sunhyuk Kim, *The Politics of Democratization in Korea. The Role of Civil Society* (Pittsburgh: University of Pittsburgh Press, 2000)

[48] See Juan J. Linz and Alfred Stepan 'Toward Consolidated Democracies', in Larry Diamond, Marc F. Plattner, Yun-han Chu and Hung-mao Tien eds., *Consolidating the Third Wave Democracies. Themes and Perspectives* (Baltimore: Johns Hopkins University Press, 1997), 14-33.

[49] Clark D. Neher, "Asian Style Democracy," *Asian Survey* Vol. 34 (1994), 949–61; Kishore Mahbubani, 'The Dangers of Decadence,' *Foreign Affairs* Vol. 72 (1993), 10–14.

[50] Francis Fukuyama, *The End of History and the Last Man* (London: Penguin, 1992), 243, and 'The Primacy of Culture,' *Journal of Democracy* 6 (1995): 3–10.

[51] David Held and Anthony McGrew, 'Globalization and the Liberal Democratic State,' *Government and Opposition* Vol. 28 (1993), 261–88.

[52] Kenichi Ohmae, 'The Rise of the Region State,' *Foreign Affairs* Vol. 72 (1993), 78.

[53] James T.H. Tang, ed., *Human Rights and International Relations in the Asia Pacific* (London: Pinter, 1995); Bilahari Kausikan, 'Asia's Different Standard,' *Foreign Policy* Vol. 92 (Fall 1993), 24–41.

[54] David S.G. Goodman and Gerald Segal, eds., *China Deconstructs* (London: Routledge, 1994); Jack A. Goldstone, 'The Coming Chinese Collapse,' *Foreign Policy* Vol. 99 (Summer 1995), 35–53.

[55] Yoshihara Kunio, *The Rise of Ersatz Capitalism in South-East Asia* (Singapore: Oxford University Press, 1988); Kit G. Machado, 'Proton and Malaysia's Motor Vehicle Industry: National Industrial Policies and Japanese Regional Production,'

in Jomo K. S., ed., *Japan and Malaysian Development in the Shadow of the Rising Sun* (London: Routledge, 1994), 291–325.

56 Edmund T. Gomez, *Political Business: Corporate Involvement of Malaysian Political Parties* (Townsville, Australia: James Cook University of North Queensland, 1994); Edmund T. Gomez and K. S. Jomo, *Malaysia's Political Economy. Politics, Patronage and Profits* (Cambridge: Cambridge University Press, 1997).

57 Mitchell Bernard and John Ravenhill, 'Beyond Product Cycles and Flying Geese: Regionalization, Hierarchy, and the Industrialization of East Asia,' *World Politics* Vol. 47 (1995), 171–209; Walter Hatch and Kozo Yamamura, *Asia in Japan's Embrace. Building a Regional Production Alliance* (Cambridge: Cambridge University Press, 1996).

58 James Cotton, 'The Limits to Liberalization in Industrializing Asia: Three Views of the State,' *Pacific Affairs* Vol. 64 (1991), no.3, 311–27.

Chapter 7

Korea's Importation of a Democratic Regime: Successes and Limitations

Korea was one of the earlier examples of a transition from authoritarianism and its replacement by democracy. But the question of how the post-authoritarian Korean political system is precisely to be categorized is widely debated. For some analysts it is a yet to be consolidated democracy, for others its present imperfectly democratic characteristics reflect perennial features of its political culture. Given the teleological approach of the 'consolidology' school in much Western political science, the more generally accepted view is that the form of politics practiced in the later 1990s will not be enduring, but will give way to a more mature, open, inclusive and accountable system of government.[1] For those who, by contrast, emphasis the 'imported' character of Korean democracy, its features are bound to be both more and less than its Western prototypes.[2] This chapter will review the transformation of Korea's regime type from the military authoritarianism of the Park era to the present, paying particular attention to analyzing the most noticeable features of the new civilian politics. However, bearing in mind that regime types are often transient but at the same time the most temporary political expedients sometimes prove surprisingly resistant to change—an attempt will be made to bracket the more overt teleological assumptions of the contemporary analysis of democratic consolidation.

THE KOREAN POLITICAL CONTEXT

Although the standard claim that Koreans often repeat that their country has a history of 5000 years is something of an exaggeration, there has been an identifiable Korean state for well over a millennium, making Korea one of the oldest continuous organized political communities in the world. This longevity did not however guarantee Korea's survival amidst the competing imperialisms of the 19th century, and the evident incapacity of the (by then) Confucian state contributed to a strong sense of uncertainty among the ordinary people many of whom converted to Christianity at the turn of the century (making Korea presently Asia's most Christian country after the Philippines).[3]

The Japanese colonial project (following direct annexation by Japan in 1910) sought to transform Koreans into Japanese, an impossible ambition but one the prosecution of which suppressed all open expressions of national political consciousness and aspiration. The mass public demonstrations of the *Samil* independence movement of 1919 are claimed by all political movements as their *fons et origo*, Rhee Syngman (later first president of the Republic of Korea) was a prominent member of the provisional government in exile formed as an outcome of the movement, and Kim Il-sung in the North claiming that his father was the leader of the *Samil* protestors in Pyongyang. What the heroic failure of 1919 did demonstrate was the reality that foreign support was essential for the attainment of independence, a strategy that was then adopted by various political movements of the left and right even despite the strong cultural rejection of foreign entanglements (as a result of Korea's long experience as a suzerain of the Chinese empire). Meanwhile with the expansion of the Japanese empire and Tokyo's preparations for the coming contest with the US, Koreans had their first taste of bureaucratic developmentalism, both in their homeland and also as a result of their forced service as industrial labourers in the Japanese home islands.

Korean independence was the result—almost the accidental if fortuitous by-product—of Japan's defeat in the Pacific War. But independence also brought division, since what had originated as a temporary occupation of the peninsula by the two major powers led to their fostering of inevitably competing client regimes when the Cold War supervened. The Korean War led to the creation of a numerous and well maintained military (thanks to the security reliance upon the United States) in the South, privileging and empowering this social force in a country then amongst the least developed in the world. The autocratic and ineffective government of Rhee Syngman did little to improve the prospects of democracy, even though Rhee endeavoured to govern with the trappings of

Western constitutionalism and in conjunction with various parties avowedly 'democratic' and 'liberal'. The reality behind these labels was that the Korean political class were principally scions of landed families, more often than not of Christian education and *yangban* (traditional gentry) lineage. Rhee, though a Princeton PhD, was himself a collateral member of the former royal family. Across the border, North Korea, rearmed and rebuilt with the support of the major communist powers, prepared openly for a renewal of armed struggle as a means of unification. In the alleged interests of national security, political debate and organization were constrained and controlled. Rhee was widely reviled, and his electoral manipulations eventually provoked a student led uprising which forced him into exile. But the parliamentary democracy that emerged to fill the political vacuum was the victim of bitter factional division and quite unequal to the many economic and security challenges facing the republic. Through this period the security guarantee—and concomitant economic relief—provided by the United States were crucial to the existence of the state. At this time, however, US specialists were convinced that Korea would be an aid dependent client for the foreseeable future and that the prospects for democratic development were singularly poor. It came as little surprise—even as something of a relief, given Korea's pivotal role in the network of US alliances in Asia—when elements of the military seized power in 1961.[4]

KOREAN AUTHORITARIANISM

Although the country was effectively ruled by former generals from 1961 to 1987, and then by an elected general until 1992, Korean authoritarianism may be considered as falling into three distinct phases. To this extent it is difficult to speak of a single 'authoritarian regime'. When Park Chung-hee came to power in the military revolution of May 1961 his clique of younger officers (most of whom were lieutenant-colonels) stepped into politics at a time of uncertainty and governmental paralysis, and his intervention engendered little active opposition. His program for economic reconstruction was then a spectacular success, and using his position as gatekeeper to his nation's entry into the booming Pacific economy he accumulated sufficient resources to support a powerful para-political apparatus and by carefully spreading largesse fostered a strong if selective public following. During this time, however, not only was there considerable media freedom but elections were contested, though opposition politics were so severely factionalized that Park did not face credible challengers.[5]

The circumstances of the early 1970s were very different. Park was no longer able to exploit Korea's participation in the Vietnam war, his program of industrialization had greatly swelled the numbers of the restive urban proletariat and the opposition had become temporarily united behind a new champion (Kim Dae-jung). In the uncertain international environment, consequent upon Henry Kissinger's visit to Beijing, Park's implacable anti-communism also began to appear dated. Public revulsion at the manipulated election result of 1971 forced Park to adopt a program of 'revitalising reforms' that, in effect, led to personal rule. Park resolved that Korea would be a heavy industrializing power; he also launched an ambitious scheme for remaking the national consciousness the core of which was the 'new community' movement. He relied increasingly upon a coterie of technocrats, his programs backed by military, bureaucratic and corporatized social forces, a position of power from which he was unseated by assassination, though only in a climate of labour unrest and civic protest. Through this period Korea's *chaebol*, with development funds guaranteed by the state, emerged to command the economic landscape though they never occupied a central position in the ruling group. Korea shared some, but by no means all, of the features of bureaucratic authoritarianisms of the Latin American type.[6]

The third period of authoritarianism was coincident with the rule of Chun Doo-hwan. Though he purged most of Park's personnel, Chun's method of rule was modeled on that of his predecessor. However Chun was in every sense a lesser man, corrupt where Park was austere and vacillating where Park was decisive. Moreover, his neo-liberal economic reforms undermined many of the state protected structures from which Park drew support. By this time Korea's continued economic growth had carried the nation to developed status, and the rule of a narrow military elite appeared more and more anomalous. Chun partially relaxed rules constraining political competition in 1985, but even the limited electoral competition thus permitted demonstrated his lack of legitimacy. He temporized with draconian measures, but in the event could not contain the wave of popular protest in which political dissidents, religious figures and underground unions provided the shock troops and the ordinary citizens of Seoul provided the foot soldiers.

IDENTIFYING KOREA'S REGIME CHANGE

It is at this stage that there is some room for difference on the precise endpoint of Korea's authoritarianism. In 1987 Roh Tae-woo was Chun's chosen successor, and in this role announced that the next elections for the presidency would be popularly contested in a liberal political atmosphere. There is no doubt that Roh's decision was taken in the context of a complex bargain that saw him gain a plurality of votes in November of that year and become (setting aside the very imperfect institutions of the First Republic) Korea's first popularly elected president and an example of Huntington's 'transplacement' mode of democratization.[7] Roh's triumph was facilitated by opposition divisions, but the full measure of the 1987 pact of the elites only became clear with the political realignment of 1990, which saw Roh, and Park Chung-hee's most important lieutenant and his political legatee Kim Jong-pil, join forces with oppositionist Kim Young-sam who in charge of their common political vehicle rode to power in the elections of 1992. Some analysts would regard 1987 as the break with authoritarianism, while some would contend that Roh's period in power was a prolongation of authoritarianism by other means—in retrospect, a judgement with some basis given the monetarisation of politics that occurred under Roh's tenure and his own accumulation of illicit political funds.

Kim Young-sam could claim to be the first genuine civilian to come to power for more than a generation, and his decision first to purge the military to extirpate all those general officers who had played a political role and then to allow prosecution of former presidents Chun and Roh for sedition and corruption seemed to mark a fundamental break with the past.[8] This interpretation of his presidency is supported by a consideration of the 'real name' financial reforms of 1993 that did much to prevent electoral (and taxation) malfeasance. However his subsequent disgrace in 1997 stemmed (aside from his ineptitude) partly from his use of similar methods to those of his predecessors but specifically from the fact that not only was he indebted to the political machines of the former authoritarians but he also used—as it came to be revealed—their funds to support his 1992 election campaign.

Therefore there are those who claim that only with the election of Kim Dae-jung was there a genuine turnover in political power to a proven democrat. In reality, Kim Dae-jung's credentials were also suspect, as his narrow plurality in the 1997 was facilitated by an unlikely alliance with Kim Jong-pil (along with other old regime retreads) who extracted the condition that not only would he serve as prime minister but would become effective executive head of the government when the constitution was changed to render the post of president largely honorific. Neither did his political practice vary greatly from that of his immediate predecessors, a point to be discussed subsequently. If Korea resembles, in Larry Diamond's judgement, a 'delegative democracy',[9] it is difficult to say precisely when it became thus. In this context it should be recalled that South

Koreans, when asked to rank their presidents, past and present, find Park to have been far and away their best leader since independence.

THE TRANSITION FROM AUTHORITARIANISM

Korean authoritarianism was undermined by many forces. The Republic of Korea had been conceived in 1948 as a republic of the Western style and though its constitution was transformed no fewer than six times between that date and 1987, this frequently revised document always proclaimed the principles of liberty, representative government and the rule of law. In this respect every usurpation of power could be represented as such, with Korea's rulers, unlike their state socialist counterparts, unable to hide behind the fig-leaf of historical materialism. Park's revitalizing reforms, though they did have a significant impact on the popular consciousness, never managed to supplant that republican discourse. Nevertheless Park's appeal to Koreans to rebuild their society and economy in order to achieve self-reliant independence struck deep chords in the national psyche. The idea of self-reliance or self-sufficiency has a long history on the peninsula, being one of the strategies proposed by Cho Man-sik and other nationalists in their attempts to resist by non-cooperation with Japanese rule. Humiliated by generations of external power interference, and still beholden to the United States for their security, South Koreans were undoubtedly attracted to the idea of building national strength in order to escape dependence. It is no accident that the chief slogan of North Korea's national ideology (*juche*) is a cognate term, and that charges of renewed and shameful national dependence were aired in Seoul when Kim Young-sam was compelled to seek assistance from the IMF during the financial crisis of 1997.

If Park's slogans held some attractions for his countrymen, their realization prompted consequences he could not manage.[10] The fundamental challenge to Park's rule was generated by the very social and economic transformation that was central to his program. This produced an educated and increasingly well-traveled middle class who chafed at the many restrictions of the authoritarian era. It also moved almost an entire generation from the countryside to the cities, Korea's cheap and controlled labour force being the main reason for the development of internationally competitive textile, clothing and footware industries which in the 1970s provided more than half of the nation's exports. As this industrial labour force grew it became restive at the rigid corporatists controls exerted by the state, and sought a greater share of the prosperity that the export economy began to produce. It was to these constituencies that Park's political opponents appealed. Draconian rules—at one point it became a serious crime to criticize the constitution or advocate its amendment, that document that Park changed at and for his convenience—produced reactions of increasing militancy. Although the full story of Park's murder has not been told, it is clear that in October 1979 there were deep differences among Park's supporters on the best way to deal with the strikes and demonstrations that were threatening both his program and his hold on power. The political arena was further complicated by the presence of radical dissidents with various degrees of sympathy with the communists in the North (who were then still credible competitors in a zero-sum contest for national legitimacy).

For a brief period it seemed that Korea might escape from its restrictive authoritarianism and come to enjoy a political status more in keeping with its newly industrialized economy. However major divisions between the most prominent of the former opposition politicians (Kim Young-sam and Kim Dae-jung) prevented concerted action, and an ambitious clique of military officers used the occasion to engineer a coup within their own ranks in order to prepare for an assault on political power. Their leader, Chun Doo-hwan, showed himself capable of using deadly force in the repression of a rebellion against his usurpation in Kwangju. Despite the presence of a combined military command on the peninsula the United States did nothing to obstruct his dispatch of special forces to that city, and Chun was later the first foreign leader to be welcomed to the Reagan White House.

In time Chun faced the same opponents as his more illustrious predecessor, and beyond sheer force he had neither the ideological nor the personal resources to counter those opponents. His rapacious extraction of political and personal funds from the *chaebol*—it later emerged that he amassed a political fund of 950 billion *won* ($1.24 billion at the then prevailing exchange rate)—alienated the industrialists who figured, especially once Chun had ruined the Kukje conglomerate after its owner failed to make a donation of the necessary size, that a more accountable regime would be less demanding and more predictable. In early 1987 Korean citizens took to the streets as never before, underlining the fact that authoritarianism had no real constituency. Meanwhile Korea's international situation had changed. Seoul's international image was on trial in the preparations for the 1988 Olympics which dissidents were determined to abort in a miasma of tear gas if Chun continued to resist democratization. With the advent of Gorbachev the Cold War was in its final throes and in East Asia the United States was less and less prepared to support manifestly unpopular regimes, as the demise of Ferdinand Marcos demonstrated.

The key to democratization was held by Roh Tae-woo, Chun's former class mate and coup conspirator and now his designated successor. Roh realized that the days of military rule were over. He may well have assumed that divisions between Korea's democratic champions would give him a chance in an electoral contest, especially if democratization came ostensibly on his own personal initiative. It later became clear that the two Kims were both subsidized at this time from regime sources, no doubt to encourage their contention. In the light of his 1990 alliance with Kim Young-sam it may also be conjectured that Roh had a particular future shape of Korean politics in mind when he announced his plan to stage elections for the presidency under a new constitution by the end of 1987. At any event, his victory in those elections, when he succeeded in securing 36.6% of the popular vote brought the old authoritarianism to an end.[11]

Roh's status as a transitional figure in Korea's political narrative is assured, though more precise descriptors for his regime are a matter of dispute. Roh relied not only on former military personnel but also on supporters from his home district ('TK'—Taegu, North Kyongsang) to staff his administration, thus helping to civilianise the political system. Controls on the media were eased, stimulating public debate. His 'Nordpolitik' successfully engineered openings to North Korea's communist patrons, thus setting in train the transformation of relations on the peninsula. But in retrospect a major characteristic of his rule was the monetisation of political life. He accumulated a vast political fund the use of which became scandalous. The source of this money lay in the *chaebol* whose owners vied for support in the form of state approved finance as well as a congenial role in the nation's industry policy. According to his critics, what Chun had achieved by force, Roh sought to gain by monetary leverage.

The political bargain of 1990 had the appearance of setting such practices as the norm. It should be noted that presents of 'rice cakes' and envelopes of money are standard practice in Korean society and to this extent Roh and his followers were building upon a pre-existing cultural predisposition. En route to the Blue House Kim Young-sam had to overcome the electoral challenge of Hyundai chief Chung Ju-yung who had at his disposal—as court action later established—considerable company derived funds. Despite posing as a champion of business against corrupt and self-serving civilian politicians, Chung was not able to rally the big conglomerates behind him, and his venture into politics ended in an ignominious defeat (with severe tax compliance problems for Hyundai to follow). Despite his alliance strategy, once in power Kim Young-sam evidently resolved to set politics on a new and less corrupt path. His methods however were unfortunately for his subsequent reputation too much of a mixture of the old and the new. His administration drew extensively on a coterie of supporters drawn from his home region ('PK'—Pusan, North Kyongsang) and despite his anti-corruption legislation he did not reform many of the restrictive rules inherited from the past. To take one example, despite many complaints, laws prohibiting unions from associating with, funding or supporting political parties or candidates for political office remained part of the legal code. He initially resisted an accounting with his predecessors but then pursued it despite doubtful legality, the outcome—prison sentences for both Chun and Roh for military rebellion and corruption—overshadowed by revelations that his own son had acted as an influence broker for the bankrupt Hanbo conglomerate the business failure of which heralded in Korea the onset of the 1997 financial crisis.[12]

It was in this sorry context that Kim Dae-jung triumphed in the contest for the presidency in December 1997. Kim was pledged to a new era of genuinely civilian and non-corrupt politics, but his narrow victory (from 39.7% of the vote, as against 38.2% from his nearest challenger) was as much the result of further political party machinations. Kim Dae-jung's unlikely alliance with Kim Jong-pil has already been noted. In addition his task was made easier by the split that emerged in Kim Young-sam's political machine with a former protégé in charge of a splinter party running against the party's mainstream candidate, Lee Hoi-chang, who had once served as Kim's prime minister. Kim Dae-jung subsequently left his stamp on Korean politics. The nature of his administration requires more detailed analysis if the present state of Korean democracy is to be determined.

CHARACTERISTICS OF KOREA'S DEMOCRACY

If Korea has evolved from authoritarianism to political arrangements where national leadership is determined by electoral contest, it would seem clear enough that Korea's politics are now democratic. This is true, but it is also a fact according to many analysts that Korean politics is a case of 'democracy with adjectives'.

Since 1987 the highest political office has been determined by elections. Though the presidency is a powerful office with independent political resources, as envisaged under the 1987 constitution power has been shared to a limited extent with the National Assembly, also elected though on a separate political cycle. Under Kim Young-sam local government has also been democratized, with regional governors and city mayors commanding their own budgets. Further, democracy is truly 'the only game in town' since there are no significant political forces committed to working outside or against this elected political context. The last gasp of anti-electoral politics was represented by the secretive military society, the *Hanahoe*, the extirpation of which was one of Kim Young-sam's first tasks as president. This of course is to exclude active supporters of North Korea from consideration. North Korean aligned student movements were still in evidence when Kim Young-sam came to power, but as a result of the manifest failure of the North Korean system and internal ideological bickering their numbers are now of no consequence. In addition there has been at least one turnover of power, which suggests that democracy has gained the necessary momentum.

However, from the perspective of students of comparative democratization, these changes, though significant, are not in themselves sufficient to indicate the consolidation of Korean democracy. Prima facie, there are some grounds for considering Korea another example of 'delegative democracy' or mere electoralism, with administration policy between elections having little references to popular demands, aspirations or expectations.

At this point it is necessary to determine what indicators would be taken as sure signs that a political system had evolved beyond electoralism. There is an extensive literature on this topic, with authorities focusing variously on the functioning of institutions, the prevalence of specific social norms and values, and/or the production of policy outcomes. Nevertheless there is some measure of agreement that a consolidated democracy possesses accountable political institutions animated by genuinely representative political parties and functioning in a predictable and routinized fashion.[13] On this view, the method and approach of democracy receives wide popular assent, participation in politics involves a range of social and interest groups, and actual government policies reflect citizen demands. What are the facts of the Korean case?

THE KOREAN CASE

The political record of the administration of Kim Dae-jung will now be examined to determine how far the main features of liberal democracy have become apparent. For the restricted purposes of this paper the analysis focuses on institutions and institutionalization, popular norms and attitudes, political behaviour and policy outcomes.

Institutions and Institutionalization

Since 1987 the Korean constitution, having endured many revisions for partial and partisan causes, has taken on a more settled character. This constancy would suggest that constitutionalism and thus predictable rules of the game are now the norm. However this predictability owes little to Kim Dae-jung's intentions.[14] He came into power with the avowed program of revising the constitution to introduce a parliament-based executive, and was only frustrated in this design by the opposition of the *Hannara* Party. When electoral reform to reduce the number of representatives was discussed, Kim's party floated the idea of introducing at the same time multi-member constituencies and a single transferable vote, a change that would maximize the representation of Kim's followers and allies, even though this form of electoral system was notorious as the source of corruption and factionalism in Japan (until it was altered there in 1992).

The 1987 constitution gives the National Assembly an independent role in Korea's government. On coming to power Kim had to deal with an Assembly where his supporters and allies did not command a majority, but it was clear from the first that Kim had little interest in making 'cohabitation' Korea-style work. The Assembly must approve the president's choice of prime minister. But there was no majority in favour of approving Kim Jong-pil for the post. The vote was delayed and then aborted, and for a period of almost six months Korea's executive was superintended by an 'acting' prime minister, an expedient undoubtedly against the spirit of the constitution. Meanwhile the government launched a series of anti-corruption and taxation probes, targeting members of the *Hannara* party. When he assumed office Kim's coalition commanded a maximum of 129 seats in the Assembly, with the opposition *Hannara* commanding 161 of a total membership at that time of 299. By September Kim's coalition had swelled, mostly be defection and cooptation, to 158, giving him a clear majority.[15] All this time the Assembly barely functioned and could hardly exercise the role assigned it by the constitution. Clearly Kim had no concept of a loyal opposition, or did not think it applicable to Korea's circumstances. Similarly, when following the Assembly elections in April 2000, the United Liberal Democrats (ULD—the party of Kim's ally Kim Jong-pil) performed so poorly that with 17 representatives they lacked the numbers to be officially recognized as a negotiating group in the legislature, Kim first sought to change the rules and when this tactic failed then prompted some defections from his own party so that the ULD would have the requisite minimum representation.

These maneuvers raise the issue of political parties in democratizing Korea. In Japan it used to be said that the dominance of the ruling Liberal Democratic Party endured for 'half a lifetime', and indeed despite the splintering of the party in the 1990s most parliamentary representatives are still drawn from the party or its remnants. By contrast in Korea parties change almost annually.[16] The most enduring feature of parties in Korea is that they represent dominant personal cliques. Typically they neither aggregate citizen demands nor mobilize voters for anything other than the most limited and electorally focused political involvement. At the present time, with the partial exception of attitude towards North Korea, there is no evident policy difference between the two major parties.

Since 1985 Kim Dae-jung has been the leader of four parties, starting a new party in 1995 when he decided to reverse his decision to retire and was not received back into active politics by the leaders he chose for his old party machine. In 2000 Kim renamed his party—it is now the Millennium Democratic Party—and sought to give it a new image by enrolling formerly non-aligned political figures. Throughout this time, however, Kim's successive political movements have been managed by the same personnel, typically individuals from Kim's native region (the Cholla provinces) who have been with him since the 1970s. In the behaviour of political parties it is not possible to discern the required features of liberal democracy, and Kim's presidency has done nothing to improve their record. In these circumstances it is perhaps unremarkable that only 57.2% of voters turned out for the 2000 National Assembly elections, the lowest figure in Korea's democratic history. Data from 1997 is revealing on the attitude of the public towards their elected representatives. While 72% of Koreans expressed trust in their military, the figure for the legislature was only 22% and for political parties 20%.[17] Political developments of the past decade have evidently had their impact on public opinion.

Outside formal political institutions and political parties, the media is probably the most important component of a democratic political system. There is no doubt that the influence of the media in Korea is very great, and since 1987 newspapers especially have played a key role in exposing (sometimes in unscrupulous ways) the misdeeds of politicians and the failures of political leaders. It would be fair to say that Kim Dae-jung's relationship with the press has not been harmonious. After sustained press criticism of Kim's new administration, the publishing firms controlling several major newspapers were subject to intensive taxation audits, and the owner of one of the nation's most prestigious newspapers, the *Chosun Ilbo*, was sentenced to a gaol term for tax evasion. The institutionalisation of a free press is a work still in progress in Korea.[18]

Norms and Attitudes

The evidence for a deepening of democracy from popular attitudes towards politics is mixed. The data from the Korea Democracy Barometer cited by Doh Chull Shin are revealing.[19] On the one hand, in 2001 support for 'the idea' of democracy was extremely high—91% of respondents were either supportive or very supportive of democracy. In addition, almost as many members of the sample (78%) were in favour of further democratization of their country. But when asked whether democracy was 'always preferable' to dictatorship, only 45% were sure that it was, and 37% considered that there might be circumstances where authoritarianism was preferable. As to whether democracy or dictatorship were better systems with which to manage economic problems, Koreans seemed to be equally divided. Aggregating these various measures, Shin claims that convinced supporters of democracy are in a minority and that Korea's comparative standing on commitment to democracy is low, by comparison with data from East Europe and Latin America.

The assessment by Koreans of how their own democracy is working in practice is especially sobering. Using the 2001 data Shin combines measures of the extent to which Koreans consider their democracy 'empowering' and 'responsive'. A clear majority—68%—are of the view that it is one or the other, but only 24% consider it to be both. Again this is a low figure in comparative terms. Significantly, Koreans more often than not rate their politicians as untrustworthy or corrupt, and view the system of government as generally unaccountable. Rose and Shin postulate that the problem may be traced to the fact that Korea achieved electoral democracy ahead of the rule of law and workable democratic institutions.[20] When trends in this data are considered over time it is very evident that support for democracy amongst Koreans has fallen significantly over time, the presidency of Kim Dae-jung contributing to rather than arresting that trend.

Political Behaviour

Turning from political attitudes to political behaviour, the most striking feature of Korean electoral performance is the dominance of regionalism. In a country where religious differences have rarely been manifest in the political arena, where there are no ethnic divisions and which is a single linguistic entity, it is remarkable that regional differences should have such important political consequences. This is a topic that has been the subject of extensive commentary.

Suffice it to say that regional origin (which is generally elicited by asking respondents in surveys to name the home province of their paternal grandfather—being Korea, grandmothers do not figure) is the best predictor of voting behaviour. Regionalism has been very much apparent in Korean electoral politics since 1987, and its logic has underlain the various party realignments from that time. In the 1997 presidential elections, Kim Dae-jung, though he won a bare plurality of the national vote, received an astonishing 90% of the votes in his home district, the Cholla region.[21]

What are the consequences of regionalism for Korean democracy? Clearly if regionalist sentiment is the most important standard by which politics is judged, then cross-cutting and overlapping affiliations of organizations and interests cannot arise. Rather, political outcomes must be seen as zero-sum. To return to Shin's 2001 data, it is most significant that (with Kim Dae-jung the incumbent president) residents of the Cholla provinces are almost twice as likely as those from Kyongsang to view the performance of the current system as satisfactory.[22] And it should be noted that successive administrations have done nothing to mitigate this regionalist view.[23] The Cholla region accounts for a little less than a quarter of the Korean electorate. Yet of the 17 cabinet level members initially appointed in Kim Dae-jung's administration, 11 were from Cholla.

In additional to regionalism, Korean politics is also marked by a deep patriarchal bias.[24] In the 2000 National Assembly the representation of women was modestly augmented, from 3.0% to 5.9%, but women in local governing bodies and in the political parties are almost non-existent. While activity in politics correlates with education, it is striking that Korean males with poor education are still more active in politics than college educated women. During Kim Dae-jung's tenure of office, women's groups campaigned for a change in the law relating to households which requires all women to be registered as members of a family group with a male 'family master' (*hoju*) as the legally recognized head. This law more than any other measure is emblematic of the subordinate status of women. However Kim's administration has been more receptive to Confucianist pressure groups who have represented such a reform as threatening to the national culture. The constitutionality of this law was the subject of a court action in 2001.

A vibrant civil society is considered a prerequisite for a healthy democracy. There is no doubt that civil society played a major role in the demise of authoritarianism. In the Kim Dae-jung era groups such as People's Solidarity for Participatory Democracy have campaigned for higher standards in political and public life. However, civil society has still to make the transition from 'protest to policy advocacy'.[25] Civil society groups have proliferated, but citizen commitment is frequently nominal and effective leaders are often co-opted by established political parties.

Policy Outcomes

A democracy should produce democratic policy outcomes, that is, outcomes that address public demands, are the result of a transparent process and do not favour special interests. The personnel in charge of policy making should be competent and corruption free. How did the Kim Dae-jung administration rate according to these criteria? Kim Dae-jung's most urgent challenge was undoubtedly dealing with the financial crisis.[26] Kim quickly established a Financial Supervisory Commission to reorganize the many indebted and insolvent insurance companies and banks that littered the economic landscape. Using its extensive powers numerous financial institutions were merged or their assets sold, though not without the state in effect taking on the control of a number of major banks. A program for the reorganization of the *chaebol* was also pursued, again with mixed results. Company holding structures were drastically simplified and the number of domestic producers in key export markets (including motor vehicles and computer chips) were reduced, but the net effect was actually to increase (if only relatively marginally) the *chaebol* domination of the economy. Moreover reforming Korea's financial institutions involved an exercise of bureaucratic power of which Kim's predecessors would have been proud, with the FSC answerable only to the Blue House and quite independent of the Finance and Economy Ministry. Similarly the complex negotiations to rationalize the conglomerates were conducted by presidential staff behind closed doors, something of an irony given the fact that Kim's most famous authored work is a book advocating a 'participatory economy'.[27]

Kim's greatest policy innovation was undoubtedly manifest in his approach to North Korea. Kim's meeting with North Korean leader Kim Jong Il in June 2000 was largely a consequence of his conciliatory 'sunshine policy' which had the potential to reshape the international politics of Northeast Asia.[28] The announcement that he would travel to Pyongyang, however, was made a matter of days before the April 2000 elections, which led to the suspicion that the timing was chosen for partisan advantage. It was also by no means clear what inducements North Korea had been promised in order to facilitate the visit. In no sense was this strategy the result of a bi-partisan initiative, and one of the consequences was a fierce attack in the North Korean official press on the leaders of the *Hannara* as unpatriotic and hirelings of external forces. Kim won the Nobel

Prize for his efforts (an ambition he had long harboured), but the subsequent course of North-South exchanges produced little tangible results, an outcome reflected in growing public disenchantment. The revelation in 2001 that the failing Hyundai tourist venture to North Korea would be subsidized by tax payers' funds was greeted with dismay, since the revenues (already around $800 million) paid to the North went straight to Kim Jong Il. Kim's handling of this sensitive and vital issue was criticized by many Koreans for its secretive and partisan character.

In light of the extensive corruption in the Roh Tae-woo and Kim Young-sam administrations, Kim was adamant that he would expect the highest standards of probity from his cabinet and top officials. Since 1998, however, there have been a series of scandals that seem to indicate that little is changed. It is unnecessary to recount them in any detail. In late 2001 the principals of two failed financial firms were placed under arrest for malfeasance. With the investigations still underway, so far the Vice Minister of Justice, a senior member of the MDP and the younger brother of the Prosecutor General have been arrested, and the Prosecutor General and the Deputy Director of the National Intelligence Service have resigned, both cases involving bribery of officials and politicians in order to conceal stockmarket manipulations or avoid taxation probes.[29]

The extensive public distrust of figures in political life is undoubtedly a consequence of cases such as these and has prompted civil society activists to campaign for a new political era in which individuals tainted by such conduct should be ineligible for elected office. In pursuit of this objective the People's Solidarity for Participatory Democracy and other NGOs organized the 'Civil Action for the 2000 General Election' movement which sought to inform voters of candidates for election to the Assembly who had corrupt records, had violated the Election Law, had been involved in past military coups or cases of human rights abuse, or who were not diligent parliamentarians. Despite substantial public approval, this campaign was not well received by the government and in 2001 its organizers were prosecuted and fined for damaging the electoral process.

EXPLAINING THE KOREAN TRANSITION AND ITS PROSPECTS

The teleological aspect of much current scholarship on transitions to democracy has already been noted. Given the historical context of the 'third wave', this is unremarkable. Most of the political systems democratized during this era were clearly temporary political way stations, being military dominated, or communist autocracies, or personal dictatorships. In many instances (though not always) they were associated with ineptitude and economic stagnation. In respect of the communist systems in Eastern Europe they were ultimately maintained only by external pressure. Democratisation was therefore to be conceptualized simultaneously as change of regime and also as progress to a sustainable regime type.

South Korea's authoritarianism is to be contrasted with many of these defunct regimes.[30] Its demise was a product more of its success than its failure, which is one reason why authoritarian rule—and Park's rule in particular—has not been utterly repudiated as a possible expedient by all Koreans. In this context it should be recalled that Park's rule was excused at the time as the necessary response to the very palpable security threat posed by North Korea. However, the developmental project espoused by Park Chung-hee produced the very social strata and civil society whose protests made the sustaining of authoritarianism impossible, while embedding the principles of private property that helped facilitate democratic practices. This is not to deny altogether the role of the US security connection in helping maintain Park in power during the height of the Cold War, especially since counsels from Washington in 1987 helped persuade Chun Doo-hwan and Roh Tae-woo that the time had come for political transition.

The subsequent history of Korean democracy has seen the emergence of a stubbornly imperfect democratic electoralism. Neither politicians nor parties seem in any hurry to make their activities more transparent, responsive or accountable, and ordinary citizens have responded both with skepticism about the actual practice of their democracy and also with a degree of nostalgia for authoritarianism. The most common explanation for this political trajectory has been the claim that the practice of indefinite and largely unchecked power by remote figures is an adaptation of pre-existing political culture.[31] This must be placed in the context already noted, that Korea's authoritarianism was by many measures (and especially in nostalgic afterglow) a positive contribution to nation building. The very particular zero-sum nature of Korean regionalism is undoubtedly also a factor in the poor performance of Korean democracy.

In short, the specifics of Korea's political experience and political culture discussed in this essay suggest that the path ahead will resemble neither that of East Europe nor of Latin America. Consideration of the (in general more democratic) political outlook of the younger generation, especially when set in the context of the further impact of globalisation, provides the grounds for a somewhat more hopeful prognosis. In time the Korean political consciousness may be transformed, with efficacious effects on the democratic character of the political system. However, the cosmopolitan consequences of globalisation cannot be assumed. The biggest obstacle to the post-1997 financial reforms has been the reluctance of foreign firms to buy insolvent Korean enterprises in the face of hostile protests by local unions. Against these somewhat optimistic trends, however, it may be argued that the very real prospect of unification may have quite a different impact. Presuming (though of course other courses may be adopted) that the North Korea system is at some point incorporated as a whole in that of the South, the effect would be to add some 12 million voters, highly conservative in their social outlook and xenophobic in their attitude towards the external world. Their forced reliance upon their bretheren in the South for aid, sustenance, employment and protection will do nothing for their susceptibility to cosmopolitan influences. The unification of Korea may set the nation's democratic clock back by a decade or more.

NOTES

1 Larry Diamond, *Developing Democracy. Toward Consolidation* (Baltimore: John Hopkins University Press, 1999).

2 Bertrand Badie, *The Imported State. The Westernization of the Political Order* (Stanford: Stanford University Press, 2000).

3 Ki-baik Lee, *A New History of Korea*, Trans Edward W Wagner (Seoul: Ilchokak, 1984).

4 Don Oberdorfer, *The Two Koreas: a contemporary history* (London: Warner, 1999).

5 Joungwan A Kim, *Divided Korea. The Politics of Development 1945–1972* (Cambridge: Harvard University Press, 1976).

6 James Cotton, 'Understanding the State in South Korea: Bureaucratic-Authoritarian or State Autonomy Theory?', *Comparative Political Studies* Vol. 24 (1991–92), no.4, 512–31.

7 Samuel P Huntington, *The Third Wave. Democratization in the Late Twentieth Century* (Norman: University of Oklahoma Press, 1991)

8 James Cotton ed., *Politics and Policy in the New Korean State. From Roh Tae-woo to Kim Young-sam* (New York: St Martin's Press, 1995).

9 Larry Diamond, *Developing Democracy. Toward Consolidation*, 86.

10 Sohn Hak-Kyu, *Authoritarianism and Opposition in South Korea* (London and New York: Routledge, 1989).

11 James Cotton, 'From Authoritarianism to Democracy in South Korea' in James Cotton ed, *Korea Under Roh Tae-woo: Democratisation, Northern Policy and Inter-Korean Relations* (Sydney: Allen & Unwin, 1993), 22–41.

12 Robert Garran, *Tigers Tamed. The End of the Asian Miracle* (St Leonards: Allen & Unwin, 1998), 119–136.

13 Hyug Baeg Im, 'South Korean Democratic Consolidation in Comparative Perspective', in Larry Diamond and Byung-Kook Kim eds, *Consolidating Democracy in South Korea* (Boulder & London: Rienner, 2000), 22–23.

14 Brian Bridges, *Korea after the Crash. The politics of economic recovery* (London & New York: Routledge, 2001), 32–45.

15 Byung-Kook Kim, 'Electoral Politics and Economic Crisis. 1997–1998', Larry Diamond and Byung-Kook Kim eds, *Consolidating Democracy in South Korea* (Boulder & London: Rienner, 2000), 173–202.

16 Byung-Kook Kim, 'Party Politics in South Korea's Democracy: The Crisis of Success', in Larry Diamond and Byung-Kook Kim eds, *Consolidating Democracy in South Korea* (Boulder & London: Rienner, 2000), 53–86.

17 Yun-han Chu, Larry Diamond and Doh Chull Shin, 'Halting Progress in Korea and Taiwan', *Journal of Democracy* Vol. 12 (2001), no 1, 130.

18 On institutionalisation more generally, see: Larry Diamond, and Doh Chull Shin eds., *Institutional Reform and Democratic Consolidation in Korea* (Stanford: Hoover Institution Press, 2000).

19 Doh Chull Shin, 'Mass Politics, Public Opinion, and Democracy in Korea', in Samuel S Kim ed, *Korea's Democratization* (New York: Cambridge University Press, 2002); c/f Doh Chull Shin, *Mass Politics and Culture in Democratizing Korea* (New York: Cambridge University Press, 1999); Rose, Richard, Doh C Shin and Neil Munro, 'The Tension between the Democratic Ideal and Reality: South Korea', in Pippa Norris ed, *Critical Citizens: Global Support for Democratic Governance* (New York: Oxford University Press, 1999), 146–168.

20 Richard Rose and Doh Chull Shin, 'Democratization Backwards: The Problem of Third-Wave Democracies', *British Journal of Political Science* Vol. 31 (2001), 331–354.

21 Hyeon-Woo Lee, 'Economic Voting in Korea: Analysis of the 15th Presidential Election', *Korea Observer*, Vol. 29 (1998), Winter, 635–662.

22 Doh Chull Shin, 'Mass Politics, Public Opinion, and Democracy in Korea', in Samuel S Kim ed, *Korea's Democratization* (New York: Cambridge University Press, 2002).

23 Sunhyuk Kim, 'Patronage Politics as an Obstacle to Democracy in South Korea: Regional Networks and Democratic Consolidation', in Howard Handelman and Mark Tessler eds, *Democracy and Its Limits. Lessons from Asia, Latin America and the Middle East* (Notre Dame: University of Notre Dame Press, 1999), 115–129.

24 Seungsook Moon, 'Redrafting Democratization through Women's Representation and Participation in the Republic of Korea', in Samuel S Kim ed, *Korea's Democratization* (New York: Cambridge University Press, 2002).

25 Sunhyuk Kim, *The Politics of Democratization in Korea. The Role of Civil Society* (Pittsburgh: University of Pittsburgh Press, 2000).

26 Brian Bridges, *Korea after the Crash*, 68–89.

[27] Kim Dae-jung, Mass-Participatory Economy. A Democratic Alternative for Korea (Lanham: University Press of America, 1985); Chung-in Moon and Sunghack Lim, 'The Politics of Economic Rise and Decline in South Korea', in Soong Hoom Kil and Chung-in Moon eds, *Understanding Korean Politics. An Introduction* (Albany: State University of New York Press, 2001); Yoon Young-Kwan, 'South Korea in 1999. Overcoming Cold War Legacies', *Asian Survey* Vol. 40 (2000), no 1, 164–171.

[28] Brian Bridges, *Korea after the Crash*, 90–110.

[29] *Korea Herald* (Seoul), 7 January 2002, 17 January 2002.

[30] Richard Rose, William Mishler and Christian Haerpfer, *Democracy and Its Alternatives: understanding post-communist societies* (Cambridge: Polity Press, 1998).

[31] Geir Helgesen, *Democracy and Authority in Korea. The Cultural Dimension in Korean Politics* (London: Curzon, 1998), 221–244.

Chapter 8

CHINA'S COASTAL DEVELOPMENT STRATEGY: JILIN PROVINCE AND NORTHEAST ASIA[1]

> Further opening of the economy to the world will be the strategic choice of our province in the Eighth Five Year Plan and through the whole of the 1990s... The development, opening and construction of the Tumen River region is an important matter that has profound significance... We should exert every effort to strive for the opening to free navigation of Hunchun port for the passage of goods and personnel, so that we can make Hunchun our window on the world. We should actively take part in international efforts to develop the Tumen River region as the economic and trade centre of Northeast Asia.[2]

At its closest point, China's Jilin province is a mere 15 kilometres from the Sea of Japan.[3] Indeed, Hunchun (close to the point where the Russian, Chinese and Korean borders meet) enjoyed brief prominence as a 'Treaty Port', with the Qing authorities opening a customs post there in 1910. On the banks of the Tumen River at Fangchuan and within sight of the sea, there are now inscribed in stone texts by (then) Premier Li Peng and President Jiang Zemin, expressing regret that China's way to the sea should be barred by such an arbitrary border, and one created by the annexation of territory which was once part of 'Jilin'. Jiang, Li and other central leaders visited the region in 1991 at the time when the centre was deciding whether and to what extent to extend 'open' status to this locality. From the perspective of the centre, the denial to China of strategic coastal territory in this region is undoubtedly the principal reason for the sentiments they expressed. From the perspective of the province, at least since the reform era began in the early 1980s, Jilin's lack of coastal status has been the most important reason for the province's slow growth and incomplete adaptation to the demands and opportunities of the market.

After experimentation beginning in 1979 with the introduction of Special Economic Zones, and continuing through the announcement in 1984 that 14 locations would become Open Coastal Cities, in February 1988 the 'Coastal Development Strategy' became Chinese Communist Party (CCP) policy.[4] As a consequence, the State Council instructed coastal localities generally to take advantage of their abundant labour resources and geographical locations to assume the leading role in development. Raw and semi-finished materials should be imported, to be exported after processing and finishing, joint ventures should be facilitated, and large and medium sized state enterprises should be encouraged to produce for export.[5] This policy, in giving unambiguously to the coastal regions the vanguard role in the development of China, further underlined the central government's then acceptance of the growing differential that was bound to emerge between the level of development of coastal China and the inland provinces. According to this policy, as a land-locked province, Jilin would have to rely upon linkages to coastal provinces (especially Liaoning) and would have to wait for a transfer of technology and capital from those provinces until development there had reached a point where they could be exported. This policy was most closely associated with former Premier Zhao Ziyang, who promoted it on high profile visits to the coastal regions. After the Tiananmen incident there were some indirect criticisms made of the privileged position enjoyed by the coast, but the policy document on the future directions of China's reforms stated that, 'the opening of special economic zones, coastal open cities and areas, [and] cities along the Yangtze River' were specified as major objectives.[6]

In the earliest days, Jilin's economy rested upon the production of soy-bean oil, grain, and timber. The industrial development of Jilin was largely due to the efforts, first of the South Manchuria Railway Company and then (in the Manzhouguo era under Japanese control) of the Manshu Heavy Industries Development Company.[7] Iron and coal mines in the province were developed as sources of supply for industry in the centres of Liaoning, and various light industries were established in Changchun, which grew in importance after it became the 'capital' of Manzhouguo, from a transportation centre (with a population of 133,000 in 1931) to a major administrative city (with a population of 862,000 in 1945). The construction of a major hydro-electric generation facility at Fengman led, given the proximity of a cheap source of power, to the development of chemical industry in nearby Jilin city. However, the principal orientation of the province was as a subordinate part of the Manchurian industrial complex concentrated in neighbouring Liaoning.

Without fundamentally disturbing this orientation, Jilin's development was further deepened under the government of the People's Republic after 1949. By 1960, the province accounted for around 1.6% of China's industrial capacity (as compared to 8.75% for Liaoning).[8] Transport infrastructure was improved, further mineral extraction occurred, and Jilin city became a major producer of chemicals and paper. Changchun, which was restored as the provincial capital in 1954, was favoured with the establishment of automotive and railway equipment plants. Prior to the reform era, Changchun was the locality where the largest number of motor vehicles in China was produced.[9]

JILIN UNDER REFORM

Jilin in the 1990s was a province of the middle rank. Comparative data (Table 1) reveals that it was a relatively industrialised province with a relatively well educated population, though there had been some erosion in its standing as compared to the 1980s.

Table 1: The Rank of Jilin in China's 30 Provinces

		1985		1990		1991	
		Number	*Rank*	*Number*	*Rank*	*Number*	*Rank*
Population	10000person	2298	20	2440	20	2460	20
GOIA[1]	100mil.*yuan*	327	15	680	15	741	16
GOIA per capita	*yuan*	1427	8	2816	8	3026	8
AO[2]	100mil.*yuan*	86	17	189	17	188	17
Cultivated land area	10000*mu*[3]	5999	9	5908	9	5907	9
Grain output	10000 *ton*	1225	13	2047	10	1898	9
IO[4]	100mil. *yuan*	241	16	492	16	553	16
Total workers and staff members[5]	10000person	449.5	12	517.3	11	533.4	11
Average annual wages:	*yuan*	1081	21	1888	25	2045	26
State-owned	*yuan*	1175	14	2068	23	2233	23
Collective-owned	*yuan*	880	21	1456	23	1596	23
SU/P[6]	person/10000 persons	5.95	13	7.28	14	7.25	14

Notes: 1. GOIA=gross output value of industry and agriculture.
2. AO=agricultural output value.
3. 15mu=1 hectare.
4. IO=industrial output value.
5. At the end of the year.
6. SU/P=number of students in university to the total population.

Source: Jilin Provincial Statistical Bureau (Changchun): *Jilin Statistical Yearbook 1992*, 637–9.

Jilin's population (Table 2) was concentrated in a few major centres, with the capital, Changchun, and Jilin city accounting for over 40% of the total. This population included significant numbers of the Mongol and *Manzu* 'nationalities'; it also includes a sizeable number of ethnic Koreans. The Koreans were concentrated in the Yanbian Korean Nationality Autonomous Prefecture; they also made up the bulk of the population in several autonomous Korean counties and townships elsewhere in the province. Of the almost 2 million inhabitants of Yanbian, slightly more than half were Korean. Prior to the reform era their political and economic role was not prominent, but once opening became national policy their presence gave the province the potential for closer cooperation with one of the region's dragon economies. Consequently, the provincial and local governments took steps to encourage Korean investment, with some success. This part of the province had also been able to take advantage of Korean tourism, with Changbaishan (Paekdusan) being a site of major historical and cultural significance for the Korean people.

Table 2: Population

Region	1986		1993	
	1000 persons	% of total	1000 persons	% of total
Total	23153	100.00	24961	100.00
Changchun	5951	25.70	6510	26.08
Jilin city	3965	17.13	4193	16.80
Siping	2824	12.20	3045	12.20
Liaoyuan	1152	4.98	1208	4.84
Tonghua	2094	9.04	2196	8.80
Hunjiang	1182	5.11	1263	5.06
(Songyuan)	(withBaicheng)	—	2490	9.98
Baicheng	4032	17.41	1918	7.68
Yanbian	1953	8.44	2138	8.57
In Yanbian:	2091 (1991)	8.50 (1991)	(% of Yanbian)	(% of Yanbian)
Yanji	294	14.06	330	15.43
Tumen	139	6.65	140	6.55
Hunchun	175	8.37	199	9.31

Source: Jilin Provincial Statistical Bureau (Changchun): *Jilin Social and Economic Statistical Yearbook 1987*, 314; *Jilin Statistical Yearbook 1992,* 113; *Jilin Statistical Yearbook 1994*, 86–88.

The contribution of the various localities to the provincial economy is revealed in the following data. It is clear (from Table 3) that the heavy industry concentrated in Jilin city declined in importance, and that the contribution of Yanbian increased:

Table 3: Gross Domestic Product (GDP, current prices)*

Region	1986		1991		1993	
	million yuan	*% of total*	*million yuan*	*% of total*	*million yuan*	*% of total*
*Total**	48211	100.00	43695	100.00	70398	100.00
Changchun	13164	27.30	11235	25.71	22090	31.38
Jilin city	10968	22.75	9553	21.86	13760	19.55
Siping	4924	10.21	4450	10.18	6824	9.69
Liaoyuan	2427	5.03	2154	4.93	2924	4.15
Tonghua	4041	8.38	3724	8.52	5803	8.24
Hunjiang	2289	4.75	2199	5.03	3471	4.93
Songyuan*					4929	7.00
Baicheng	6397	13.27	5811	13.30	3464	4.92
Yanbian	4001	8.30	4569	10.46	7133	10.13
In Yanbian:						
Yanji			969	21.21	1798	25.21
Tumen			335	7.33	494	6.93
Hunchun			286	6.26	916	12.84

Sources: Jilin Provincial Statistical Bureau (Changchun): Jilin Social and Economic Statistical Yearbook 1987, 315; Jilin Statistical Yearbook 1992, 88–89; Jilin Statistical Yearbook 1994, 65–66.

* There are some small inconsistencies in regional and provincial data as reported in these sources. 1986 data is calculated according to the value of Total Social Output. For statistical purposes, Songyuan was separated from Baicheng from 1991.

At the beginning of the reform era, Jilin accounted for around 2.6% of the Chinese economy (calculated on the basis of the Gross Output Value of Industry and Agriculture). This declined to 2.3% in 1990 and 2.0% in 1993. During this period the Jilin economy grew rapidly, but not as rapidly as the country considered as a whole. The province's difficulties in keeping up with reform were many. Much of China's growth at this time was the consequence (directly or indirectly) of foreign investment, or of the reorientation of Chinese industry towards export activity, or of the reanimation of the private and collective sectors.

There were obstacles to the province in all three of these areas. Foreign investment was principally aimed at the coastal provinces, either because of incentives created by the government or because of proximity to markets. Not only was Jilin an inland province, but access to ports in neighbouring provinces became more difficult and expensive as China's export orientation strained transport and shipping infrastructure. Any goods travelling to or from the province within China were required to transit Dalian, Yingkou, Qinhuangdao, or Tianjin (or more distant ports). The use of alternative foreign ports—in North Korea or the Russian Far East—was obstructed by political factors. This predicament also did not favour indigenous export activity. With the opening of the Russian Far East to border trade, the province was able to take some advantage of its geography, though only to the extent that the small common border (some 130 kms), poor transport infrastructure, and limited demand capacity would permit. In addition, Jilin suffered to a degree from the political and social legacy of the pre-reform years. The industrial Northeast was favoured during the Mao period as one of the bastions of modern industry, with many important industries being run from Beijing and devoted to heavy and chemical production. It has only to be recalled that the Anshan Iron and Steel Corporation in Liaoning—the largest enterprise in China before 1980—was considered an industrial model for the whole country. Other forms of economic activity were neglected or discouraged, and it was therefore difficult to find sufficient leadership or resources when the focus of China's modernisation effort shifted.

Jilin's position in the reform era of the first half of the 1990s is represented in the following comparative data (Table 4).

Table 4: Industrial Enterprises and their Output by Ownership

		Quantity			Shares %		
		State	*Collective*	*Priv./others*	*State*	*Collective*	*Priv./others*
		Number (1000 Enterprises)					
1980	Jilin	2.31	8.68	0.004	21.0	79.0	—
	China	83.4	293.5	0.4	22.1	77.8	0.1
1990	Jilin	2.88	20.94	154.8	1.6	11.7	86.7
	China	104.4	1669	6185	1.3	21.0	77.7
1993	Jilin	2.84	22.82	168.5	1.5	11.7	86.8
	China	104.7	1804	8003	1.1	18.2	80.7
		Gross Output (Billion *Yuan*)					
1980	Jilin	10.59	2.86	0.01	78.7	21.2	-
	China	393	103	3	78.7	20.7	0.6
1990	Jilin	38.87	12.44	3.92	70.4	22.5	7.1
	China	1306	852	234	54.6	35.6	9.8
1993	Jilin	67.58	20.73	15.01	65.4	20.1	14.5
	China	2272	2021	975	43.1	38.4	18.5

Sources: Number of enterprises and Gross Output are from: Jilin Provincial Statistical Bureau, *Statistical Yearbook of Jilin* (*Jilin Tongji Nianjian*) (Changchun, 1987 and 1994), 147 and 306–9; and State Statistical Bureau, *Statistical Yearbook of China* (*Zhongguo Tongji Nianjian*) (Changchun 1986 and 1994), 189, 224 and 373. Shares are calculated from the above data.

In 1980, the division of the province's gross output between the state, collective, and private sectors was very close to the national average. But by 1993, the province's reliance upon the state sector was some 50% higher than the national norm (65.4% as compared with 43.1%). Correspondingly, the collective sector was little more than half the size of the national norm for the collective sector. While the comparative data shows that the province had kept up in the formation of collective and private enterprises, and also in the proportion of the work force employed in those enterprises, these had failed to generate the goods and services seen in other parts of the country where reform had greater success. When it is recalled that the agricultural sector in the province pre-reform was proportionately smaller than the national average, this failure on the part of a relatively urbanised and industrialised region to take advantage of the opportunities for industrial innovation is striking.

The comparative data also show that even with Jilin's development strategy in its early phase, Yanbian was already relatively advanced in relation even to the provincial capital. The per capita contribution to the provincial economy (measured in terms of both GDP and National Income—Table 5) indicates that the centres of Yanji and Hunchun made a particular contribution, and that the growth in Hunchun's contribution was especially marked.

Table 5: GDP Per Capita and NI Per Capita (*yuan*/person)

Region	GDP per capita			NI per capita		
	1986	*1991*	*1993*	*1986*	*1991*	*1993*
Total	2082.279	1776.436	2820.32	845.5492	1493.068	2296.743
Changchun	2212.065		3393.241	843.7237		2706.452
Jilin city	2766.204		3281.66	1052.207		2618.65
Siping	1743.626		2241.051	720.6091		1786.207
Liaoyuan	2106.771		2420.53	819.4444		1748.344
Tonghua	1929.799		2642.532	785.5778		2476.321
Hunjiang	1936.548		2748.219	893.401		1956.453
Songyuan			1979.518			1763.855
Baicheng	1586.558		1806.048	749.752		1657.456
Yanbian	2048.643	2185.079	3336.296	860.7271	1756.576	2665.575
In Yanbian:						
Yanji		3296	5448		2646	4527
Tumen		2410	3529		1942	2857
Hunchun		1634	4603		1280	3668

Source: Calculated from previous table.

Overall, the province attracted some foreign investment (detailed in Table 6), the bulk of which derived from Hong Kong (though this was likely to conceal investments actually originating in China). It is significant that investment from Korea was the second largest contribution to the provincial total.

Table 6: 1990–1993 Foreign Direct Investment (Agreement Amount)

Country or region	Newly signed FDI agreement	FDI (agreed amount) US$ 100 million	% of total agreement amount	FDI (actual amount) US$ 100 million	Number of countries & regions
1990					
Total	52	0.216	100	0.169	6
1991					
Total	121	0.393	100	0.180	12
Hong Kong		0.149	38		
US		0.067	17		
Korea		0.054	14		
Taiwan		0.053	13		
Japan		0.032	8		
sum of 5		0.335	90		
1993					
Total	1434	7.7	100	6.5	40
Hong Kong	610	4	51.7		
Korea	237	0.9	11.3		
US	143	0.7	9.6		
Japan	119	0.4	4.8		
Taiwan	114	0.4	5.5		
sum of 5	1223	6.4	82.9		

Source: Jilin Provincial Statistical Bureau, *1991 Jilin Economic and Social Development Statistical Bulletin* (Changchun: 1991), 56; *1993 Jilin Economic and Social Development Statistical Bulletin* (Changchun: 1993), 5; 'Social and Economic Review', in *Jilin Statistical Yearbook 1992* (Changchun: 1992), 37.

It is even more noteworthy that investment patterns in Yanbian were somewhat different from the aggregate represented above. The biggest source of investment in the prefecture was the Republic of Korea, with investments concentrated in light industrial ventures.[10] At this point in its development, it can be seen that in addition to the geographical factor, the province and locality had also sought to use the potential of the Korean connection. Though some investment preceded the normalisation of relations between Beijing and Seoul, when these were established in August 1992 South Korean capital arrived in the region in an ever increasing volume. For these reasons, Yanbian/Tumen were the focus of much endeavour from the late 1980s in Changchun, Yanji, and elsewhere to create an investment and infrastructure niche for the province. The Yanbian region generally, and Hunchun in particular were the chief beneficiaries.

JILIN'S ROLE IN THE ORIGINS OF THE TUMEN COOPERATION SCHEME

Personalities and institutions in Jilin were at the forefront of advancing the notion of Tumen region cooperation. As early as 1988, the provincial government had argued for the introduction of a special economic zone in the area around Hunchun, and as a result of research carried out in the province, China sought to re-negotiate with the (then) Soviet Union the navigation rights which she had enjoyed until Soviet-Japanese hostility had closed the river to maritime shipping in 1938. These rights were restored in 1991. The first conference on Northeast Asian economic cooperation was convened in the provincial capital, Changchun, in July 1990, on which occasion academics and specialists (including members of the Jilin Academy of Social Sciences and the provincial government) reviewed new possibilities for regional and cross-border development. This was a stimulus to the United Nations Development Program (UNDP) sponsored July 1991 Ulan Bator meeting, where delegates from China, Mongolia, North Korea and South Korea affirmed the need for a Tumen River Area Development Program (TRADP). This was discussed at the second Changchun conference held in August 1991. The UNDP then convened a further meeting in Pyongyang, in October 1991—by this time also eliciting participation from Russia and Japan—where there was an agreement to draft a detailed regional development plan, to be managed by a Program Management Committee. This Committee met in Seoul in Feb 1992 and again in October of that year in Beijing, by which time two 'cooperation triangles' had been proposed, the smaller including Hunchun, and the larger including also Yanji.[11]

It is no accident that the first of the regional conferences was convened in Changchun. Amongst the originators of the intellectual concept of Tumen River cooperation were Mr Song Jian, (then) Minister in charge of the State Science and Technology Commission of China, and Dr Cho Lee-jay of the East-West Centre, Hawaii. Minister Song instructed Professor Ding Shicheng, then a member of the Jilin Province Science and Technology Committee (and subsequently Deputy Secretary-General of the provincial government and a National People's Congress deputy), to study the issue of economic cooperation and draft a proposal for the region.[12] Under instructions from the (then) provincial governor (Wang Zhongyu), at the second of the two Changchun meetings, Professor Ding, after reviewing the complementarities of the Northeast Asian economies and the experience of economic cooperation elsewhere, advanced the claim that the lower reaches of the Tumen River would be the 'golden delta' (*jin sanjiao*) of the region in the future. Professor Ding's proposal also outlined the concept of the two regional 'triangles', though at this time the smaller did not incorporate Hunchun, but only that territory which lay at the very mouth of the Tumen River. This was because he was then a proponent of the view that China should construct a seaport at Fangchuan which, with dredging work on the river (and the re-engineering of the North Korean-Russian railway bridge), could accommodate 2000 tonne ships. His proposal recognised that several forms of cooperation—bilateral or multilateral—would be feasible, but all would require extensive investment especially in transport and communications infrastructure.

The impact of these proposals upon the eventual plan which emerged for Tumen River cooperation—involving North Korea, China, Russia, South Korea, and Mongolia—was considerable.[13] The second of the Program Management Committee (PMC) meetings, held in Beijing in October 1992, agreed to prepare an extensive pre-investment feasibility survey of the proposal, funded by $3.8 million from the UNDP. The studies which emerged embraced many of the specifics of the Chinese proposals of 1991, including transport infrastructure upgrading, though finding that a port at Fangchuan would be an extensive project which would not reap as much return as the augmentation of port facilities in North Korea (at Rajin-Sonbong) and the building of further links between these facilities and China. China was compensated, however, with a proposal for the construction of an inland railway and warehouse hub located in Hunchun.

The subsequent progress of the UN sponsored Tumen scheme was erratic, failing to achieve the major objectives of the provincial planners. It is fair to say that some of the scheme's proponents, including Professor Ding, sometimes advanced unrealistic proposals for the region that tended to undermine the confidence of potential investors. In May 1993 the third PMC agreed to establish a multi-lateral corporation (the Tumen River Area Development Company) which would lease land upon which port and infrastructure facilities would be constructed.[14] This plan ran into difficulties for a variety of reasons, including the lack of any Russian legislation that would permit such an arrangement. The fourth PMC (held in Moscow in July 1994) was disrupted due to the death of Kim Il-sung and the withdrawal of the North Korean delegation.[15] Subsequently, on May 30 1995, the five participating countries agreed to establish a new coordinating committee to reanimate the project. Meanwhile, the early and very ambitious proposals of the UNDP to reconstruct the entire infrastructure of the area at a cost of US$30 billion was shelved in favour of a more modest program aimed at the harmonisation of existing projects and initiatives. It is clear that it was only when the larger regional cooperation scheme encountered serious problems that Jilin province pushed ahead with its own development proposals.

In an attempt to revive the fortunes of the Tumen scheme, the nations concerned agreed, in December 1995, to form a new five nation consultative committee, especially to address outstanding problems including the provision of a legal basis for trans-border commercial activities by foreign businesses. In addition, and mindful of fears expressed by UNDP specialists and others regarding the possible impact of development on the region's relatively fragile ecology, at the same time the Tumen participants signed a Memorandum of Understanding on Environmental Principles which would govern all future projects. And China, Russia, and North Korea also established a committee to oversee common security problems in the Tumen region including border transit.

INSTITUTIONS AND INTERESTS IN TUMEN COOPERATION

Centre, province, and locality all developed institutions to manage Tumen development and cooperation.[16] The 'Tumen River Area Leading Group' under the State Council and the State Science and Technology Committee, which also included members from other Beijing ministries as well as representation from the provincial government, generally met once or twice a year to coordinate overall Tumen policy. In addition, in April 1994, the provincial government inaugurated a new office, the 'Tumen River Area Development Administration' under the direction of Professor Ding Shicheng to coordinate Tumen policy from Changchun. There was some overlap in membership between the central and provincial bodies; the means by which the Chinese authorities chose delegates to the Tumen PMC involved something of a contest between centre and province. With the decision to shift the development focus to Hunchun, the 'Hunchun Border Economic Cooperation Zone Administration Committee' was inaugurated on May 28, 1993. The Zone was also serviced by a centre in charge of foreign business, which was conceived as a 'one stop' organisation to manage all negotiations and approvals involving foreign business entities.

It is clear that a number of interests intersected in the development of the Tumen region. Centre and province both had a stake: the centre in so far as the broader objectives of coastal and border development served the government's economic objectives, the province in that this scheme permited Jilin to overcome its landlocked status. Beyond these interests, other actors were crucially involved, though the goals they pursued did not necessarily coincide. As studies of the political economy of local governments and enterprises elsewhere have shown, local officials in particular may derive many advantages from the access and connections that the opening of their locality may offer.[17] Evidence is lacking, but in the case of Hunchun, the predominance of investment from Hong Kong in joint ventures suggested that many of the 'foreign' partners in the joint ventures may ultimately have been from China itself.

Until 1993, in the Tumen region itself, development was managed in Yanji, the seat of the Yanbian Korean Nationality Autonomous Prefecture. But with the status of Hunchun upgraded to that of 'open border city', and the formation of the Hunchun Border Economic Cooperation Zone (HBECZ) Administration Committee to manage the activities of Hunchun municipality within the HBECZ, Hunchun effectively bypassed Yanji to deal directly with the provincial level government. To a significant extent Hunchun was thereafter in competition with other localities in Yanbian. An article in the *Jilin Ribao* reminded readers that if the area did have an established port, then that was Tumen city (on the river of the same name itself, though upstream from the Hunchun district), from which goods regularly transitted North Korea by way of the port of Ch'ongjin.[18] This author's experience in dealing with the various authorities suggested that those in Yanji would like to restrict access to Hunchun and its district, perhaps to underline the primacy of the regional capital.

THE IMPACT OF TUMEN DEVELOPMENT IN JILIN

By 1995, in the Yanji area (including Tumen and Longjing as well as Yanji city) there were 586 foreign investments of various types, including 80 wholly owned companies and 447 joint ventures. South Korea (293) and Hong Kong (111) accounted for the bulk of these investments, most of which (74.2%) were in industry. Out of a total projected foreign investment of \$339.42 million, \$79.89 million (23%) had so far been committed.[19]

Whereas the initial development focus within Yanbian was on Yanji, by 1992 that focus had moved to Hunchun. Hunchun city was raised by the State Council to the status of an 'open city' in November 1991 (prior to that time it was off-limits to foreigners), and to that of 'open border city' on 9 March 1992. Under the terms of the latter decree, the city was empowered to establish a border economic cooperation zone, in which entrepot and export oriented commerce and industry was to be concentrated, and to which foreign investment was to be attracted.[20] The new status of the city was important in as much as it was from that time able to exercise much more initiative than formerly—for example, to nominate individuals to go abroad on city business—whereas previously such decisions were made in Yanji.

In October 1992 construction of facilities within the newly declared Hunchun Border Economic Cooperation Zone (HBECZ) was initiated. Activity in the Zone (with a total area of 88 squ.kms.) was financed both by local revenues and by a special loan from the centre of 10 million *yuan* annually for each year of the five-year national plan. It was administered by an Administration Committee under the authority of the Hunchun municipal government. Within the HBECZ, a 5 squ.km. area was designated for immediate development. By 1994, this area contained office development and a market built and administered by the Hunchun International Trade and Tourism City Development Company. Transport and other infrastructure was also under development. Attracted by the conditions available—including land available for 70-year industrial lease at 45 *yuan* per squ. m., and 45-year commercial lease at 80 *yuan* per squ. m.—some 99 foreign and joint venture companies (mostly the latter) had registered for business in the zone by 1995. The foreign participants included 29 companies domiciled in Hong Kong, 25 from South Korea, 9 from Japan, 8 from Russia, and 7 from Taiwan. Projected investment by foreign and joint venture companies in the zone was US$160 million, of which US$40 million had been invested by 1995.

An example of a successful joint venture in the Hunchun BECZ was Dongyi/Tongil Textile. The foreign partner was a Korean garment manufacturer; the local partner was Hunchun city. Dongyi was established to manufacture underwear in a plant constructed in 1992. Total registered capital investment in the plant was 33 million *yuan*, the workforce numbered 360 by 1995, and the projected output of the factory was 1.5 million pieces of underwear per year. Its specialty was underwear produced to cope with especially cold climates. It was originally intended that 70% of the production would be for export, but as the product (incorporating a triple thickness synthetic-natural fibre mix) was not otherwise available in China, after some negotiation its sale was permitted on the domestic market. The machines in the plant were all from South Korea as was the factory manager, otherwise the workforce was local, though many were ethnic Koreans (and all signs posted in the plant were both in Korean and in Chinese). A similar though smaller plant was reported in Richard Pomfret's study of the Tumen region. The Kangnam joint venture produced socks in the BCEZ. Employing a labour force of 82 and with a total registered capital of 10.28 million *yuan* (40% of this foreign), the venture produced from Chinese yarn items on machines imported from South Korea and under the supervision of a small Korean management team. Again, all the production found its way onto the domestic market, though the intention was ultimately to produce for export.[21]

Considerable effort was made to provide the Hunchun area with infrastructure. The Hunchun power plant came into operation in December 1988, and by November 1989 had an installed capacity of 200,000 KW. The road from Yanji to Hunchun was upgraded to national 'B class' standard, local telephone capacity was increased to 20,000 lines, and the construction of an international standard hotel was initiated. The consequence was that whereas before 1991 Hunchun was little more than a village with a GDP 18% below the provincial average, it became a substantial city that by 1994 possessed a GDP 60% over the provincial average.

SUCCESSES AND PROBLEMS IN JILIN'S COASTAL STRATEGY

From the perspective of the central government, Jilin's coastal strategy fulfilled objectives beyond those relating to the development of the province. China-South Korea trade had grown exponentially since the two countries established formal diplomatic ties in August 1992. By 1994 (with total trade running at around $12 billion) China emerged as Korea's third largest trading partner. Between 1991 and 1994 Korea's exports to China increased six times, and Korean FDI grew at more than 100% per year. South Korea was seen in China as one of the best sources of reliable (but not the most advanced and therefore not the most expensive) technology; the South Korean model of development was also held to be one which had particular lessons for China.[22] By facilitating linkages with South Korea, and especially by employing its ethnic Korean population in the process, Jilin was also serving wider national ends. Border trade with the Russian Far East was also assisting in the Chinese penetration of that region, and the building of a port dedicated to Chinese trade on the East/Sea of Japan would restore the nation's presence on the littoral. And to the extent that development in the region also eased the transition to a market economy in North Korea, the stability of the North Korean system and thus of the whole Korean peninsula might be guaranteed.

The most accurate measure of the importance of these various objectives was to be found, however, in the extent to which these undertakings received central funds. For the most part, these funds were not forthcoming, though the central government was reported to have loaned Hunchun 10 million *yuan* annually. Hunchun's linkage with the national railway system was one of the most important elements in the province's program, yet not only was this constructed without a contribution from Beijing, but the central authorities then refused to pay for the signalling equipment, thus delaying for more than a year the operations of the railway. Similarly, the Yanji-Longjing-North Korea road was reconstructed entirely with local government funds. This relative lack of interest in the region was partly a reflection of the fact that many other localities were better placed to exploit their coastal situations; it was likely also to have derived from some of the limitations that emerged to the full realisation of the province's aspirations.

Jilin scored some successes in pursuing Tumen cooperation. The opening of trading relations with the Russian Far East were of some advantage. Although not so well placed as neighbouring Heilongjiang, the province was able to pursue barter and cross-border trade. The shipping of Russian automobiles and trucks via Hunchun for sale in other provinces—taking advantage of the former arrangements whereby national minority regions were permitted to import vehicles under reduced charges—was an example of this trade. Another example was the importation of Russian metal products for resale. But cooperation with Russia had its shortcomings. Capital was scarce and market capacity was low, and the congested conditions at existing Russian ports (Vladivostok, Nakhodkha and Vostochny) made access to them not greatly useful. In addition, there may have been political obstacles and uncertainties,[23] and historical legacies to overcome. Russian suspicion of Chinese traders and labourers was evident in the requirement that was introduced in the early 1990s whereby inhabitants of Jilin to visit Russia were directed to obtain a visa from the Russian consulate in Shenyang (for which they had to pay a fee in $US), thus requiring them to make a trip across an entire province. And a lack of both capital and political will were evident in the very slow progress of railway construction between Changlingzi (on the Chinese-Russian border) and Zarubino (a small port nearby on the Pacific coast of Russia), and in the failure to complete the reconstruction of port facilities in the latter location, as well as in the decision not to lay composite (multiple gauge) track on the Russian side of the border (thus requiring expensive trans-shipment facilities).

But the initial sanguine anticipation of the benefits of Tumen cooperation derived much more from the advantages that were expected to come from Jilin's access to North Korean ports. Here the problems were at least as great as those with Russia. On the one hand, differences between the participants in the UN regional scheme delayed the implementation of genuinely multi-lateral cooperation. The declaration of the Hunchun BCEZ may be understood partly to have been a consequence of this delay, as China was always the strongest supporter of the UN scheme. North Korea led the way in pursuing a separate and uncoordinated strategy with the establishment of the Rajin-Sonbong Free Economic and Trade Zone in December 1991. Even though North Korea chose to pursue its own priorities, the regulations for investment and trading in the zone, and the plans for the upgrading of the infrastructure introduced in 1992–93 seemed to indicate that Jilin could expect to derive advantage from North Korea's commitment to an opening policy.[24] However, while the reconstruction of Rajin port and the railways in the North Korean hinterland were principally designed to achieve closer economic integration with China, those in charge of North Korean policy were slow to adapt their approach to the new conditions.

On the one hand, North Korean port charges remained unacceptably high; on the other, according to a number of informants, experience with trans-shipment of goods through North Korea was not good, with items pilfered or damaged and even the railway trucks in which they were sent purloined by the North Korean railways for their own use. With the alternative railway route to Zarubino under construction the North Korean authorities became more interested in making their facilities available. Several experimental containerised cargoes having been shipped from South Korea and Japan by way of the North Korean port of Rajin to China, a company was established to provide such shipments regularly. A thriving cross border trade emerged, involving Koreans on both sides of the China-North Korea border who were provided with special permits to facilitate visa-free transit. It is significant, however, that despite repeated efforts on the part of China to renegotiate their status, North Korea consistently refused to accept China's right to navigate on the lower reaches of the Tumen River.

So far it may be concluded that Jilin's coastal strategy was a limited success, exploiting such rules and mechanisms as were available in the first half of the 1990s for the developments of border and coastal regions. Foreign investment was attracted, border trade was stimulated, and there was a measure of development in the Yanbian region generally and in Hunchun in particular as a result. However, the large scale reconstruction of the region under UN auspices did not materialise, and the pace and character of reform in China was not matched by commensurate changes in Russia and North Korea. Through the 1990s, Jilin's 15 kms. from the sea remained a crucial distance.

NOTES

1 I am indebted to the Institute of Asia-Pacific Studies of the Chinese Academy of Social Sciences and Professor Han Feng for organising a field trip to Jilin, and to Mr Wang Xiaolu for research assistance. In addition, Ian Davies (UNIDO, Beijing) was particularly helpful with materials and advice. An earlier version of

this paper was read at a conference on 'China's Provinces in Reform', organised by the University of Technology Sydney, and held in Suzhou in 1995. I am obliged to the participants and especially David S G Goodman for their comments. On approaches towards the new regionalism in China, see: David S G Goodman and Gerald Segal, eds., *China Deconstructs. Politics, Trade and Regionalism* (London: Routledge, 1994).

2 Wang Zhongyu, 'Report on the Eighth Five Year Plan, 5 March 1992', *Jilin Statistical Yearbook 1992* (Changchun: Jilin Statistical Bureau, 1992).

3 As a geographical entity, 'Jilin' has existed for over three hundred years. Until 1881, when restrictions upon Chinese immigration to the Northeast were lifted, the region was a frontier area, sparsely inhabited by *Manzu*, Koreans, and some Chinese. There were no towns of any size, though Jilin city was established as a small military fortress in 1673. The modern Chinese province dates from 1907, by which time ethnic Chinese were already the majority population. Jilin province has undergone many boundary changes in the twentieth century. The term is used here to refer to the territory and principal cities of the present province.

4 Tzeng Fuh-Wen, 'The Political Economy of China's Coastal Development Strategy. A Preliminary Analysis', *Asian Survey* Vol 31 (1991), 270–284; Dali L Yang, 'China Adjusts to the World Economy: The Political Economy of China's Coastal Development Strategy', *Pacific Affairs* Vol 64 (1991), 42–64; Jude Howell, *China opens its doors: the politics of economic transition* (Boulder: Westview, 1993).

5 Li Peng, 'Report on the Work of the Government (March 25, 1988)', in *Major Documents of the People's Republic of China* (Beijing: FLPH, 1991), 735–9.

6 'Decision of the CPC Central Committee on some issues concerning the establishment of a socialist market economic structure', *Beijing Review* Vol 36 (1993), November 22–28, 25.

7 Nakagane Katsuji, 'Manchukuo and Economic Development', in Peter Duus et al eds, *The Japanese Informal Empire in China, 1895–1937* (Princeton: Princeton University Press, 1989), 133–57; Kungtu C Sun, *The Economic Development of Manchuria in the First Half of the Twentieth Century* (Cambridge: Harvard University Press, East Asia Monograph #28, 1969).

8 Yuan-li Wu, *The Spatial Economy of Communist China* (New York: Praeger, 1967), 61.

9 T Shabad, *China's Changing Map*, revised edn (London: Methuen, 1972), 259–68.

10 United Nations Industrial Development Organization, *Promotion of Industry in the Tumen River Economic Development Area (TREDA): Industry Sector Profile, Development Opportunities and Constraints* (UNIDO: Report RAS/92/01D, 1994), 41; Kim Ick-Soo, 'Promotion of Cross-Border Trade and "Progressive Harmonization" of Investment Mechanisms', in Lew Seok-Jin ed, *Tumen River Area Development Project: The Political Economy of Cooperation in Northeast Asia* (Seoul: the Sejong Institute, 1995), 251.

11 On Tumen cooperation, see Michael Freeberne, 'The Northeast Asia Regional Development Area: Land of Metal, Wood, Water, Fire and Earth', *Geography* Vol 78 (1993), 420–31; Andrew Marton et al, 'Northeast Asian Economic Cooperation and the Tumen River Area Development Project', *Pacific Affairs* Vol 68 (1995), 9–33.

12 Interview with Prof Ding Shicheng, Changchun, 19 October 1994. See generally, Ding Shicheng, *Tumenjiang Dichu Kaifa* (Changchun: Jilin Renmin Chubanshe, 1993).

13 There is a considerable literature on the concept of 'growth triangles' in general, and Tumen/Northeast Asian cooperation in particular. See Chia Siow Yue and Lee Tsao Yuan, 'Subregional Economic Zones: A New Motive Force in Asia-Pacific Development', in C Fred Bergsten and Marcus Noland eds, *Pacific Dynamism and the International Economic System* (Washington: Institute for International Economics, 1993), 225–69; Myo Thant et al eds, *Growth Triangles in Asia. A New Approach to Regional Economic Cooperation* (Hong Kong: Oxord University Press/Asia Development Bank, 1994); Mark J Valencia, 'Economic Cooperation in Northeast Asia: The Proposed Tumen River Scheme', *The Pacific Review* Vol 4 (1991), 263–71; Gilbert Rozman, 'The Northeast Asian Triangle', *Orbis* Vol 39 (1995), 65–80.

14 United Nations Development Programme, *Interim Report. Conceptual Infrastructure Master Plan. Tumen River Economic Development Area (TREDA)* (Montreal: CPCS Ltd, May 1994).

15 J Lilley, 'Tumen Teeters', *Far Eastern Economic Review* November 10 1994, 46–49.

16 On approaches to the role of institutions and interests in centre-province relations, see, Jae Ho Chung, 'Studies of Central-Provincial Relations in the People's Republic of China: A Mid-Term Appraisal', *The China Quarterly* No 142 (June 1995), 487–508.

17 David Zweig, '"Developmental Communities" on China's Coast. The Impact of Trade, Investment, and Transnational Alliances', *Comparative Politics* Vol 27 (1995), 253–74.

18 *Jilin Ribao,* October 8 1995.

19 The information in this and following sections is derived from interviews in Changchun, Yanji and Hunchun held between October 19 and 23, 1994, with local officials, and also from the following sources: Administration Committee of Hunchun Boundary Economic Zone, *Boiling Hunchun* (Hunchun: 1994); Richard Pomfret, *Regional Economic Cooperation in Northeast Asia: The Tumen River Project* (Adelaide: University of Adelaide Centre for International Economic Studies, policy Discussion Paper 94/19, 1994).

20 On the privileges available to 'open cities', see the Ministry of Foreign Trade and Economic Cooperation, *Investment in China* (Beijing: Shangye Chubanshe, 1993),

193–210. It is perhaps significant that in this official bilingual handbook, Hunchun is not correctly located on the single map on which it appears.

21 Richard Pomfret, *Regional Economic Cooperation in Northeast Asia,* 22–23.

22 Jae Ho Chung, 'The Political Economy of South Korea-China Bilateralism: Origins, Progress, and Prospects', in Ilpyong J Kim and Hong Pyo Lee eds., *Korea and China in a New World. Beyond Normalization* (Seoul: The Sejong Institute, 1993), 257–309.

23 Peter Kirkow, 'Regional Warlordism in Russia: The Case of Primorskii *Krai*', *Europe-Asia Studies* Vol 47 (1995), 923–47.

24 James Cotton, 'Signs of Change in North Korea?', *The Pacific Review* Vol 7 (1994), 223–7.

Chapter 9

NORTH KOREA'S EXPERIMENTAL ENGAGEMENT WITH THE ASIA-PACIFIC ECONOMY

The pattern of North Korea's external linkages, from 1948 until the 1980s, contained several inter-related features. Soviet and Chinese patrons were cultivated to provide aid, trade, and armaments. North Korea sought to raise its profile in the Afro-Asian and Non-Aligned worlds principally to secure support in the United Nations General Assembly with the dual objectives of contesting the legitimacy of the Seoul government and of the UN role in the Korean armistice. And strategic alliances in West Asia were established to trade arms for energy supplies. Throughout, the North Korean stance was that none of these linkages contradicted the policy of self-sufficiency (*juche*) that has been (and remains) the watchword of the regime since 1955, though the record shows that Chinese and especially Soviet technical aid has been crucial for the building of industrial capacity. In particular, trade was never a major priority, and North Korea's reliance upon trade was comparatively low for a developing economy. The brief experiment in the early 1970s with internationally financed purchases of advanced technology from the world market ended in (still) unredeemed indebtedness.

The collapse of communism, and the conversion of China to the imperatives of the market, forced North Korean policy into uncharted waters. Neither patron could now be relied upon, and the seating of the two Koreas in the UN and the decline in the leverage of the third world in the General Assembly rendered obsolete much of the perennial North Korean strategy for the world body. Only North Korea's arms for energy trade remained, but heightened United States scrutiny and other developments relating to the countries involved tended to limit its scope. In this context, North Korea's trade and investment experiment for the Rajin-Sonbong area, initiated in the early 1990s, was evidently of crucial importance for the regime and its future prospects. On the one hand, it marked a radical departure from the pattern of decades. Stressing trade in general, and foreign investment to facilitate export-oriented development in particular, not only contradicted the notion of self-sufficiency but was a novel and previously untried expedient. In addition, and given the patent economic difficulties North Korea faced, the success of this experiment, together with the outcome of the 1994 nuclear deal with the United States, will determine whether the government in Pyongyang will be able to maintain an independent existence.

This chapter reviews the record and prospects of the Rajin-Sonbong experiment, and the relationship between this experiment and the other major priorities of the regime. It argues that a new willingness on the part of North Korea to cooperate with its neighbours, and also with the international market and with South Korea, was required if the experiment was to be a success. By its own idiosyncratic standards, however, North Korea seemed to indicate by this policy departure a new resolve to facilitate international economic cooperation.

The Rajin-Sonbong FETZ: Establishment and Progress

On 28 December, 1991, the Administration Council of North Korea declared (in decision No 74) that 621 squ. kms. of the country around Rajin City and Sonbong County would be constituted as a Free Economic and Trade Zone (FETZ). In addition to joint ventures, foreign owned enterprises would be permitted to operate within the FETZ. Rajin and Sonbong (and neighbouring Chongjin) were declared free ports, and various taxation benefits were offered to investors in the zone. The zone was enlarged to 746 squ kms in 1993, to give direct access to China via the Wonjong road bridge over the Tumen River. Management of the zone was entrusted to the Committee for the Promotion of External Economic Cooperation (CPEEC), a body previously in existence to regulate trade with countries with which North Korea does not have official diplomatic relations, under its (then) Chairman, Kim Jong U.

The basic regulations relating to the FETZ adopted in 1992–93 distinguished between equity and contractual joint ventures (i.e. ventures managed jointly or exclusively by the Korean partner respectively) and foreign enterprises. Foreign enterprises could only operate within the FETZ, whereas the other categories could operate in any approved venue on North Korean territory. While the regulations pertaining to the operation of equity and contractual ventures were somewhat general in nature, those regulating foreign enterprises contained a detailed account of the concessions available for such activities.

According to the law on foreign investment published in 1993, foreign enterprises were required to pay income tax, with the rate set at 14% within the FETZ, and 10% for certain preferred high-technology activities. Further, such enterprises (apart from those in the services sector) would be exempt from enterprise income tax for three years after the first profit-making year, provided that they had operated for a period of at least ten years. A taxation reduction of up to 50% (which might be discretionary) was also applicable. Other taxation incentives were offered regarding funds reinvested or used for the provision of infrastructure. The state undertook to provide labour (at a minimum wage of $76—160 *won* at the official exchange rate—per month, with employers liable for no welfare or other charges), with the provision that foreign enterprises might employ technical or similar personnel from outside the country (including South Korea).

From its inauguration through to 1998, North Korea adopted a series of laws and regulations to provide a coherent regulatory framework for the operation of the FETZ.[1] These included provisions relating to visa-free travel (November 1993), foreign resident business representatives (February 1994), civil proceedings (May 1994), the leasing of land (September 1994), external economic contracts (February 1995), insurance law (April 1995), and even advertising (April 1996) and the registration of vehicles (July 1996). This flurry of legislative activity also brought to light laws not previously publicised, most notably the law on the protection of the environment (adopted in April 1986, published in 1995).

Only usage will determine how these laws will operate. However, it is noteworthy that they permitted foreigners (including South Korean citizens) to enter the FETZ without visas, to reside in the FETZ, to buy and sell property, and to own and drive motor vehicles in and out of the FETZ. The refurbishment of the Wonjong bridge in 1996 led to a sharp increase in vehicular traffic in and out of the zone.

In order to foster foreign interest in the FETZ, and following a similar exposition in neighbouring Yanbian in 1995, the CPEEC, with the assistance of the UNDP funded Tumen Secretariat in Beijing and UNIDO (United Nations Industrial Development Organization), organised the Rajin-Sonbong Zone International Business and Investment Forum, which was held 13–15 September 1996. After arguments concerning invitations and funding, a large contingent of South Korean officials and businessmen stayed away. However, around 440 delegates from 26 countries attended, to hear addresses from Kim Jong U, Vice

Premier Kim Bok Shin, officials from China and Russia, and businessmen who were undertaking investment in the FETZ.

During the Forum the CPEEC took some trouble to facilitate business negotiations. These were successful to the extent that the event concluded with the announcement that new contracts and foreshadowed investments with foreign entrepreneurs relating to activities in the area would total US$840 million. Added to existing investments of $319 million (of which $43 million had been already realised), this carried the total foreign capital planned to flow to the Rajin FETZ to over $1 billion.

According to data released at that time, Pyongyang had invested 150 million *won* (US$71 million at the official exchange rate) of its own funds in upgrading facilities, sealing roads and completing hotel and conference facilities. Other investments were also in evidence, notably modernised telecommunications engineered and managed by NEAT&T, a subsidiary of the Loxley group of Thailand. A fibre optic cable had been laid from Hunchun in China to the FETZ to link North Korean communications with Jilin province. Direct dial international telephone calls could be made from the FETZ, using 'smart card' telephones. As a concession in order to undertake this communications modernisation, Loxley was given a thirty year monopoly on all telecommunications and media developments in the zone. One foreign bank, Peregrine, in collaboration with Pyongyang's Daesong Bank, established a presence in the FETZ in 1996, with the ING Bank to follow. In late 1995 trial shipments of containerised cargo from China were being sent abroad (including to South Korea) by way of the port of Rajin, using the Wonjong bridge to cross the North Korea-China border. The intention at that stage was to introduce a regular shipping service to South Korea and Japan. Fertiliser was being brought by rail from Russia transiting Rajin port using a purpose built terminal.

THE FETZ: EXPECTATIONS AND LIKELY OUTCOMES

The biggest obstacle in the 1990s to the realisation of North Korean plans for the Rajin-Sonbong FETZ was the poor state of South-North Korean relations. South Korean investment in the neighbouring part of China had played a major role in the rapid development of the Hunchun Border Economic Cooperation Zone, just across the Tumen River in Jilin province, and the same advantages and proximity might be expected to draw South Korean business to Rajin. These relations, however, were at a low ebb, and while they remained that way, South Korean investors would stay away or be excluded by their government, and international investors would remain very cautious. Setting aside such difficulties, however, North Korea's priorities for the Rajin experiment were potentially somewhat at odds with those of foreign investors.

North Korean plans envisaged three different types of development. First, Rajin was to become a major container port for the Northeast Asian region (with linkages to Mongolia and China, and ultimately to serve as the Asian terminus of the trans-Russian land-bridge to Europe). Other specialised ports were also to be developed in the zone: Sonbong as an oil terminal, and Unggi as a timber port. Second, the zone was to become a major tourist destination, with the construction of hotels and other facilities, and the exploitation of the natural beauty of the coastal environment. Third, the zone was to host export oriented industry that would ultimately employ a majority of the working population.

While North Korea would expect to earn appreciable amounts of foreign exchange through each of these developments, the biggest pay off for North Korea would come from the additional benefits of technology transfer and manpower skills upgrading which would follow from the establishment of export oriented industry. Overall, the technology and skills of North Korean industry are at least a generation out of date, and the industry in the FETZ was no exception.

North Korea was therefore seeking to attract foreign investment in new export oriented activities in the zone, or foreign participation in the upgrading of established light industries to render them capable of producing goods for export. But here North Korea faced particular problems. By the mid-1990s there were many potential export platforms offering low wages in Asia. North Korea was in competition with some locations where infrastructure was better established, and political conditions more predictable. Moreover, most local industry (perhaps with the exception of food processing for export) was so backward that it was unattractive to foreign investors. The North Korean authorities arranged inspection tours of the local petrochemical, foodstuffs, and consumer products plants, but no foreign partners or buyers could be found. Several major international concerns advised the North Koreans to scrap their facilities and start again, if they wished to achieve internationally competitive practice. This is not to say, however, that investments of this kind were out of the question. The experience of reform in China suggested that there might be some package deals involving both the upgrading of existing facilities and the construction of new enterprises, the former being undertaken in order to ensure the maximum cooperation from local authorities and suppliers.

Of the two other potential areas for development, port modernisation had made some progress. There was now container traffic between China and South Korea via Rajin, though as yet on a trial basis. This employed lighter vessels, though using a less than satisfactory road network rather than rail, pending a new agreement with China on cross-border rail traffic. Although Rajin enjoys undoubted geographical and regional advantages, a very large investment was needed if the envisaged container port (to be constructed on reclaimed land adjacent to a deepwater anchorage) would ever materialise. Further coordination with China and Russia—which could have been achieved if the Tumen River Area Development Coordination Committee, the first meeting of which was held in April 1996, eventually realised its program—would also be required.

It is significant that the largest single investment announced at the Rajin forum was in the tourist area. The Emperor Group of Hong Kong contracted to build a five-star hotel and casino on the coast, at a cost of $180 million (with an additional $30 million promised from the same source for a banking venture). The construction of this hotel was realised in 1999.

Speaking at the Rajin-Sonbong investment forum, (then) CPEEC Chairman Kim Jong U stated that all investments and activities in the Rajin FETZ were permitted, provided they did not harm national security, employ outmoded technology, or cause environmental pollution. When questioned specifically about the casino project and its possible impact upon North Korean morals, Kim Jong U said without hesitation that as it met these three standards it was completely legitimate and acceptable. [2]

In the absence of improved inter-Korean relations, tourism seemed likely to prove the biggest beneficiary of the investment climate in the Rajin FETZ. Though providing some benefits, this would undoubtedly entail costs. The bulk of such tourists were likely to be from China, and as any visitor to coastal China could verify, such tourism tends to bring in its train social ills such as drug abuse and prostitution. Already, Rajin boasted a Chinese managed and staffed 'International Club' which was in reality a massage parlour. In pursuit of foreign capital as well as technology and skills, North Korea might therefore reap fewer advantages than were initially envisaged. In the process, this shortfall might also discredit the strategy of those advocates within the North Korean administration who were committed to experimentation with an open door policy. It is no doubt underestimated in the outside world how difficult it must be, given North Korea's political dynamics, to create the conditions necessary for this policy, or how exposed, consequently, its advocates must have been.[3]

POLICY MAKING AND OFFICIAL RATIONALE FOR THE TRADE ZONE EXPERIMENT

North Korea's major policy goal has always been the construction of an independent and self-reliant national economy. What this has meant in practice, however, has undergone considerable change over time. In the early days of the DPRK, Kim Il Sung stated clearly that independence and self-sufficiency were not inconsistent with foreign trade, though the trade he had in mind was with the socialist bloc, and was of raw materials and heavy industrial goods that North Korea produced in large quantities. Later, Kim spoke in support of commodity trade with other nations, including those in the capitalist world, in order to meet a shortage of foreign currency and to supply the country with some items of advanced technology that were lacking.[4]

In 1984, the year of the original North Korean law permitting joint ventures with international enterprises, Kim went further to suggest that with a more modernized economy North Korea should diversify trade to include 'processing trade and reselling'. In order to derive the maximum advantage, the country required foreign trade officials with foreign language skills, and a good grasp of the trends of the international market and of international commerce. He states quite categorically, 'Building an independent national economy means laying down solid foundation for the expansion and development of foreign trade.' He also leaves his readers in no doubt as to his personal role in the momentous changes that the joint enterprise law portended:

> Only recently I emphasized the need to develop foreign trade at a meeting of the Political Bureau of the Party Central Committee and at several other meetings. A short time ago I saw to it that the Supreme People's Assembly adopted a decision on developing trade work still further.'[5]

Though the managers of the Rajin zone might have been engaging in a little hyperbole when they claim that the site was chosen and the scheme developed by Kim Il Sung personally, nevertheless his support for the 1984 innovations was a matter of record.

There are a number of factors which might have contributed to decision No 74 on Rajin, though as no evidence of any debate preceded it, which of these actually influenced the policy makers cannot be established. At this time, notions of regional cooperation were being promoted in other parts of Asia, and there were some prospects of international finance and of support from the UN (North Korea having already received some UNIDO funding for infrastructure upgrading). Further, 1991 was the year in which Pyongyang and Seoul were undertaking the negotiations that led to two inter-Korean agreements announced in December, which provided for comprehensive cooperation and nuclear disarmament and transparency. But a major cause must have been the crisis in Eastern European socialism and the reforms in China, both of which were severely affecting the established pattern of North Korean trade.

If policy making in North Korea remains a notoriously obscure process, one test of the significance and centrality of a policy is to review the personnel associated with its implementation.[6] The Rajin experiment, on this test, had support at the highest levels. Between 1988 and 1992 the local (North Hamkyong) Provincial Chief Secretary of the Korean Workers' Party was Kang Song San.[7] Kang had been Premier in the period 1984 to 1986, when he had overseen the original introduction of laws providing for joint ventures with foreign entrepreneurs. Kang had also conducted a number of high profile visits to special economic zones in China. When he was transferred to Chongjin to head the Provincial Party apparatus, Kang laid the foundations for the FETZ. He was commended by Kim Il Sung personally at a meeting of the North Hamkyong People's Committee (of which Kang was also Chairman) in September 1992, and was shortly thereafter returned to the position of Premier. It is significant that the official who followed Kang as Premier, Li Gun Mo, followed him also to what was evidently by that time a provincial position of some importance.

In North Korea, though technical specialists have their role, the inner circle is composed largely of Kim Il Sung's relatives. Although a technocrat (trained at the Prague Engineering College), Kang was much more than that, being a member of Kim Il Sung's family (on his mother's side) and thus of 'true bone' rank. By the same token, the Chairman at that time of the CPEEC, Kim Jong U, was another member of the Kim clan (apparently the son of Kim Il Sung's father's sister), and a classmate of Kim Jong Il from his days at Sungshil High School. Kim Jong U was also an individual with standing in other areas of policy, as is shown by the fact that at one point he was charged with superintending his country's negotiations with the United States in Berlin in the lead up to the October 1994 nuclear deal.

Some twelve months after the formation of the FETZ, and in the context of unprecedented challenges to the North Korean system, Kim Il Sung again indicated, this time just a few months before his death, his support for a new approach to the tasks ahead. The regime had already admitted, in December 1993, that the previous Seven-Year Plan had failed to meet its targets, though the 'frustration' of socialism elsewhere was blamed as the cause.[8] In his 1994 (and final) address for the new year, Kim indicated that there would be a shift in policy emphasis away from heavy industry to agriculture, light industry, and trade.[9] Having decreed that the 3 year period to the end of 1996 would be one of 'adjustment', Premier Kang Song San, in April 1994 in a speech to the Supreme People's Assembly, amplified Kim's remarks to state that the three-fold objectives of 'the agriculture-first policy, the light-industry-first policy, the trade-first policy' should have pre-eminence throughout the adjustment period, in order to improve the livelihood of the people. And for the trade objectives to be realised, he also indicated, this policy 'must be highly upheld in all sectors of the people's economy'.

This rather bald statement needs to be seen in context. Kang's comments on agriculture were devoid of any reference to socialist principles of organisation, but concentrated solely on meeting the needs of the people for food. Ever since Kim Il Sung's 'Rural Theses' of 1964, however, the socialist nature of North Korea's rural organisation had been lauded by regime spokesmen as its outstanding feature. Moreover, to displace heavy industry from the pre-eminence that it had enjoyed—as Kim Il Sung himself can be quoted, 'the industrial development of a country is judged by its steel output'[10]—was a reversal of form of monumental proportions. And for a system which prided itself in the cultivation of self-sufficiency, to accord first place to foreign trade was a remarkable innovation. Kang went further, in seeming to suggest that there was a role for market principles in this reorientation:

> In economic management, we should properly utilize economic leverages such as cost, price and profit; correctly implement the independent accounting system; and intensify control by *won*.[11]

In subsequent ideological pronouncements, however, the opening experiment did not receive an unambiguously positive assessment. Indeed, in his most considered reflections on the post-socialist (and post-Kim Il Sung) era, 'Socialism is a Science', Kim Jong Il castigated those who have focussed upon economic issues, to the exclusion of other matters:

> If the ideological remoulding of the popular masses is regarded as a matter of secondary importance and the work of strengthening the driving force of the revolution and enhancing its role is neglected in socialist society, while attaching decisive importance to the objective material and economic conditions and concentrating only upon economic construction, the building of socialism as a whole cannot be carried out properly and economic construction itself cannot avoid stagnation. These practices were very apparent in some countries that had been building socialism in the past.

> Taking advantage of this, the renegades of socialism carried out "reforms" and committed counterrevolutionary acts, destroying the socialist economic system itself.[12]

This statement reads as though it were a rearguard action against policies designed solely with economic improvement in mind. The younger Kim was accepting the need for the latter, but only if accompanied by ideological work. In fact, no positive endorsement of the Rajin experiment appeared from this quarter. Given the political climate in North Korea, this was not however unexpected. The sole reason for Kim Jong Il's succession to his father, on the official account, was his boundlessly filial loyalty. In addition, since the early 1970s, he sought to present himself as an authority on ideology in order to bolster his leadership claims. Accordingly, any ideological innovations which openly embraced the world market would not be forthcoming at the very time when he was maneuvering to solidify his hold on power, lest he offer up a hostage to fortune. While Kim Jong Il went on record as warning against the neglect of ideology in whatever the system's future course might be, the Premier of the Administration Council was asserting that the leading role should be given to foreign trade, and concessions be made to market mechanisms.

Specifically on the Rajin-Sonbong experiment, the North Korean exposition of the reasons for this initiative mentioned a number of factors, including the country 'making maximum use of its geopolitical advantages'.[13] Two reasons were adduced by the CPEEC for this innovation. In the past, the principal objective had been the 'building of a self-sufficient economy', further economic development now apparently required the expansion of external economic relations. In addition, the FETZ reflected unanticipated external developments:

> The sudden collapse of the socialist market, which had accounted for 70–80% of the total volume of the DPRK's foreign trade, necessitated us to take a new approach in adopting the form, method and subject of our external economic exchange. On the one hand, the end of the East-West cold war provided favorable conditions for developing economic exchanges on a wider scale with the countries in the region and the rest of the world. The establishment of the free economic and trade zone will also make a great contribution to maintaining peace and security in northeast Asia as it fosters an atmosphere of active economic exchange and cooperation ...[14]

Speaking at the Rajin Investment Forum, (then) Vice-Premier Kim Bok Shin, having acknowledged the economic dynamism of the region, endorsed the interdependence that the Tumen project would produce as contributing significantly 'to [the] peace, development and prosperity of the Northeast Asian region.' North Korea had always been in favour of such cooperation provided it furthered 'peace and friendship and [was pursued] on the principle of equality and mutual benefits.'[15] On the same occasion, Kim Jong U invoked the authority of Kim Jong Il to say that that the experience of other countries in developing economic and trade zones could be tried to see if it was suitable. If it was not, he added, 'we can spit it out'.[16] Having summed up this experience, and developed a Korean model for such undertakings, it could be extended to other parts of the country, though there were no plans to take the latter step at that stage.

A story circulating at the Rajin forum and in Beijing maintained that specialists were preparing a report on the social and political impact of the free trade zone experiment. If this impact was such that it could be contained, further zones were contemplated in Nampo (the port city adjacent to the capital) and Sinuiju (on the Yalu River border with China). But the North Korean authorities were wary that reform ideas should not spread too rapidly inside their borders, fencing the FETZ off from the rest of the country, ostensibly for customs purposes but no doubt in part to minimise the traffic in unwanted influences.

MODALITIES FOR REGIONAL COOPERATION

It has been demonstrated that the realisation of North Korea's Tumen objectives required multi-faceted regional and international cooperation, of a kind which was utterly foreign to the established pattern of North Korea's external policy. It was a measure of North Korea's commitment to new directions that Pyongyang had been an active participant from 1990 in the various institutional mechanisms and fora which focussed on this agenda. This commitment entailed unprecedented access for foreigners to North Korean territory, exposure of North Korean inhabitants to foreign commodities and artefacts, and the sending of specialists abroad to acquire international market oriented skills and knowledge. In a land in which the only hoardings and signboards extolled the Korean revolution and wished a long life to its supreme leader, the advertising signs which began to appear in the Rajin region were the most visible indication of this change. While they only carried the names of major communications firms and thus could not have any meaning for the local population, they were surely a portent of things to come.

It is somewhat ironic that the history of Tumen region cooperation goes back to Japanese plans to gain access to the Northeast Asian hinterland through the construction of Rajin port and its connection with the Manchurian railway network. The present Namsan Hotel in Rajin, latterly frequented by international businessmen and CPEEC officials, was used as a stopover by Japanese agents on their way to infiltrate China's Northeast, and Kim Il Sung's guerillas fought battles to obstruct the completion of the Chientao railway linking the region with Jilin.

In taking part from 1990 in the various deliberations regarding the Tumen scheme, North Korea was reacting to proposals for cooperation in the region originally developed by Chinese and American personalities.[17] As early as 1988, the Jilin provincial government had argued for the introduction of a special economic zone in the area around Hunchun, and as a result of research carried out in the province, China sought to renegotiate with the (then) Soviet Union the navigation rights which she had enjoyed until Soviet-Japanese hostility had closed the Tumen river to maritime traffic in 1938. These rights were restored in 1991. With assistance from the East-West Center, Hawaii, the first conference on Northeast Asian economic cooperation was convened in Jilin's capital, Changchun, in July 1990, on which occasion academics and specialists (including representation from North Korea) reviewed new possibilities for regional and cross-border development.

The Changchun conference was a stimulus to the United Nations Development Program (UNDP) sponsored July 1991 Ulan Bator meeting, where delegates from China, Mongolia, North Korea and South Korea affirmed the need for a Tumen River Area Development Program (TRADP). This was discussed at the second Changchun conference held in August 1991, where the Northeast Asia Economic Forum was also established. North Korea was sufficiently attracted by the prospects of regional cooperation as to host a follow up meeting under UNDP auspices in Pyongyang, in October 1991. By this time, with participation from Russia and Japan, there was an agreement to draft a detailed regional development plan, to be managed by a Program Management Committee. This Committee met in Seoul in Feb 1992 and again in October of that year in Beijing, by which time two 'cooperation triangles' had been proposed, both of which included North Korean territory.

The plan which eventually emerged for Tumen River cooperation was very much influenced by preparatory work undertaken in China (and especially in Jilin province) and also in the international policy community.[18] The second of the Program Management Committee (PMC) meetings, held in Beijing in October 1992, agreed to prepare an extensive pre-investment feasibility survey of the proposal, funded by $3.8 million from the UNDP. The studies that emerged embraced many of the specifics of the Chinese proposals of 1991, including transport infrastructure upgrading. They rejected on grounds of cost, however, the idea of a port at Fangchuan on Chinese territory in favour of the augmentation of port facilities in Rajin-Sonbong and upgraded links to an inland railway and warehouse hub located in Hunchun, thus meeting North Korean objections that its potential contribution was not being taken sufficiently seriously,[19] while also compensating China with new facilities.

Although UN sponsorship kept the Tumen scheme going, it did not make as much progress as originally envisaged. In May 1993 the third PMC agreed to establish a multi-lateral corporation (the Tumen River Area Development Company) that would lease land upon which port and infrastructure facilities would be constructed.[20] This plan ran into difficulties for a variety of reasons, including the lack of any Russian legislation that would permit such an arrangement, as well as North Korean reservations. The fourth PMC (held in Moscow in July 1994) was disrupted due to the death of Kim Il Sung and the withdrawal of the North Korean delegation.[21] On May 30 1995, the five participating countries agreed to establish new coordinating mechanisms to reanimate the project. Meanwhile, the early and very ambitious proposals of the UNDP to reconstruct the entire infrastructure of the area at a cost of US$30 billion had been dropped in favour of a more modest program aimed at the harmonisation of existing projects and initiatives.

With comprehensive regional cooperation proceeding slowly, each of the riparian countries established their own local zones. The Russian counterpart, the Nakhodka Free Economic Zone was established in August 1991; a Greater Vladivostok Free Economic Zone was mooted in the same year but later abandoned. In China, Tumen development was first concentrated in Yanji. In November 1991, however, Hunchun became an 'open city', being upgraded to an 'open border city' in March 1992, and became the centre for the 88 squ km Hunchun Border Economic Cooperation Zone later that year.[22] These zones were conceived as possible building blocks for cross-border cooperation, though each could also become a pole attracting foreign investment in its own right, and thus potential competitors. It is noteworthy that in developing their own plans for Rajin-Sonbong, North Korea adopted the Chinese term, 'Golden Triangle' (or more correctly, 'Golden Delta'), *Hwangkumui Samkakchu*, which appeared emblazoned on all their literature subsequently issued.

In an attempt to revive the fortunes of the overall Tumen scheme, the nations concerned agreed, in December 1995, to form a new five nation Consultative Commission, and a three nation Coordinating Committee (the latter with delegates from China, Russia and North Korea) especially to address outstanding problems including the provision of a legal basis for trans-border commercial activities by foreign businesses.[23] In addition, and mindful of fears expressed by UNDP specialists and others regarding the possible impact of development on the region's relatively fragile ecology, at the same time the Tumen participants signed a Memorandum of Understanding on Environmental Principles which would govern all future projects. In April 1996, the first meetings of these bodies were convened in Beijing. At the same time, a Tumen Trust Fund was established (with South Korea providing seed money of $1 million) to assist in financing inter-government cooperation.

Meanwhile, a new Tumen agenda emerged which would tax the commitment of most countries to regional cooperation, but posed particular difficulties for Pyongyang. In 1994 the Tumen River Area Development Programme commissioned a series of nine reports on various aspects of development in the region. Each of these reports, covering tourism, transport, water-supply, investment and other issues,[24] demonstrated the need for close coordination of all such activities in what was fast becoming (in Robert Scalapino's terminology) a 'Natural Economic Territory'. This coordination required North Korea to provide much statistical and other information not previously available, and also necessitated access on the part of foreigners to North Korean territory and facilities.

To take one example, the environmental report, prepared by the Chinese Research Academy of Environmental Sciences, pointed out that serious pollution of the Tumen River, caused chiefly by paper processing up-stream in China, and mining in North Korea, would have to be reversed if the local eco-system was to be revived.[25] In keeping with the objectives of the Memorandum of Understanding on Environmental Principles of 1995, North Korea would have to comply with such a local environmental regime (which was likely to entail joint planning, independent inspection of facilities, penalties for non-compliance, and the like). Similarly, any moves to harmonise customs or financial regulations, or power generation, or any other relevant activities would bring comparable international enmeshment. If North Korea had been resistant in avoiding the obligations of the international regime on the control of fissile material (though bound to observe them by virtue of its membership of the Nuclear Non-Proliferation Treaty), it is surely noteworthy that this prospect did not prevent Pyongyang's participation in the Tumen scheme.

But cooperation was an absolute precondition both for the realisation of the wider Tumen scheme as well as for the development of the FETZ. If the new Tumen management bodies were to be effective, North Korea would have to be prepared to have substantive issues involving matters of sovereignty decided by multi-lateral entities, one of which (the Tumen Consultative Commission) included a delegate from Seoul. This would be a real test of the capacity of the

North Korean system to accommodate change. The resolve of both Koreas to realise cooperative relations would also be challenged. The failure of Seoul and Pyongyang to agree on the size and composition of the South Korean delegation to the 1996 Rajin forum—an episode the details of which did not reflect well on either party—illustrated the difficulty of this test.

THE CONTEXT FOR CHANGE IN NORTH KOREA: TAKING INTERNATIONAL LINKAGES SERIOUSLY?

On some interpretations, economic reform is of only episodic importance for North Korea.[26] This view would see the North Korean system consisting of a number of parallel bureaucracies or structures—perhaps military, security, strategic industrial, external economic—with only weak horizontal linkages between them. Although these structures are coordinated, at least in principle, at the very summit of the political system, the imperfect information and understanding of the leadership, or possibly its failure to reconcile competing factions or opinions, makes it possible for one structure to operate without reference to or even on occasion in contradiction to the others. Those in charge of the CPEEC might therefore have to labour without the consistent and comprehensive support of the whole system and its leadership. Their achievements might be nullified or disowned, or they might have a major impact on the overall system, depending upon its complex operations.

A second view would see reform or policy innovation as, at best, a tactical measure. While the leadership or its technical experts have long recognised the system's crucial need for foreign technology and inputs of capital, the political costs of genuine reform have been reckoned as too great. Opening policies are bound therefore to be a sham, though their appearance might buy the system time. If the ruse was really successful, the United States might become persuaded, and drop its longstanding policy of trade sanctions, and perhaps even offer diplomatic recognition to the government in Pyongyang. Longer term, the security regime linking Seoul and Washington might even be weakened. CPEEC officials are, on this view, in charge of what is essentially a propaganda mission, though one which must have at least a little substance.

Thirdly, opening policies might be the first step in a learning exercise. The North Korean leadership might be thought, according to this interpretation, to be standing at a position equivalent to that occupied by the Chinese leadership in 1979–80, though with the additional knowledge of the Chinese and Eastern European experiences with reform in mind. They might wish to manage systemic transformation, and especially to insulate political from economic change, and have decided that the best means to reach these objectives was to begin cautiously, in a remote part of the country and with a small section of their population, before they moved closer to the capital.

All three interpretations of the North Korean system have their advocates. The first would be easier to sustain if there were more evidence of pluralism and of policy debate, and less of policy coordination, than presently exists in this most 'monochrome' of political systems. If Pyongyang is capable of the most careful management of the nuclear issue—which resulted after years of bargaining and brinksmanship in the winning of considerable concessions from the United States—then economic opening can also be managed. The most significant objection to the second is the fact that it presumes that most important elites in Pyongyang do not consider that their system has a fast impending 'use by' date, that it is confronting systemic crisis. Evidence for the acknowledgment of this crisis should be obvious, even if only from the appeals for assistance which were directed to the international community in response to the natural disasters and famine conditions of 1996. The third interpretation would appear to be supported by suggestions that additional free economic zones are being mooted for other localities, pending further progress and experience in Rajin-Sonbong. The decision taken by North Korea in 1997 to open its airspace to foreign aircraft was a strong indication that considerations of military security can now be outweighed by commercial advantage. If news of experiments in agricultural reform, entailing not only the revival of 'farmers' markets' but the drastic reduction in size (in selected localities) of agricultural collectives, is correct, North Korea may be regarded as having entered a new phase in its external and domestic policy.

Against the last, the submarine infiltration incident of September 1996 has been cited, though it may be evidence for the first or second of the hypotheses set out above. Though this incident attracted a lot of attention, it cannot be decided whether this was a deliberate provocation, or a piece of espionage gone wrong. North Korea is certainly capable of overt provocations, as the maneuvers in the Panmunjom area during the South Korean National Assembly election campaign in 1996 demonstrated. A less costly provocation might well have achieved the same result, which suggests that it was not planned to be detected, though this leaves open the possibility that it was intended to gain intelligence for a large-scale incursion.

On balance, the changes made in external economic policy in North Korea seemed to amount to more than mere matters of style. North Korean documents and spokesmen were never more forthcoming than to say that the Rajin experiment accorded with the new and more cooperative conditions of the time, and made the most effective use of North Korea's comparative advantages. But the dovetailing of domestic innovations with a multilateral scheme directly involving South Korea went far beyond the various agreements made with Seoul since 1972, none of which ever moved much beyond paper. Tumen cooperation, irrespective of whether it was to be realised by government level committees or by piecemeal, practical, and market sensitive measures, was undoubtedly heading towards the creation of a regional regime. This regime, as with similar schemes in other parts of Asia, would involve access to North Korean territory, the provision of reliable data, the exposure of North Korean inhabitants to foreign technology, work practices and attitudes, and above all the modification of domestic policy. It should be recalled that in the socialist era Pyongyang resisted joining the Council for Mutual Economic Assistance (COMECON), despite its very great reliance upon Soviet trade and technology. Taking part in this type of regime was decidedly a new venture.

If North Korea was intent upon introducing at least some measure of reforms, then, just as the notion of 'our style of socialism' seemed to entail a very limited acknowledgment of the challenges that there have been to the whole notion of 'existing socialism' since the demise of the Soviet Union, so North Korea's engagement with the regional and international economy still appeared qualified and limited. But the paradox remained that for a system which has in the past claimed a flawless leadership and the coining of the only progressive ideology of the present age, and for which self-image is of supreme importance,[27] the admission of the need for even a small change to correct a shortcoming was in effect a large (and potentially embarrassing) act of self-disclosure.

The fate of the FETZ provides an indication of the real intentions of the North Korean regime. After 1996 Tumen cooperation encountered a series of obstacles and frustrations. In 1998 most of the TRADP development activities were devolved to the member states, a strategy which in part reflected the fact that by this time the local development activities of the three riparian states were more competitive than cooperative, and the expected international funding for the more ambitious Tumen projects had not materialised. In North Korea personnel and organisational changes were in evidence. Kim Jong U disappeared from the management of the CPEEC, according to one version of events because Kim Jong Il was dismayed that advertising hoardings in Rajin were more prominent than the signs proclaiming his father's ideological messages. Then the decision was taken to dispense with the 'Free' in the official title of the development region, and in 1999 new laws were published codifying the status of the re-named 'Rajin-Sonbong Economic and Trade Zone'.[28] The Rajin experiment did not become a model for a more general opening of the North Korean economy, and much of the capital investment anticipated by more enthusiastic proponents of the project was not committed. The region remains a transit and light manufacturing area fulfilling also a limited function as a tourist venue. This outcome suggests that the experiment remained an experiment and was either never intended as more than an extremely localised mechanism to secure foreign capital or was rejected as a more comprehensive plan because of its economic and/or social shortcomings.

NOTES

1 *Golden Triangle, Rajin-Sonbong: Collection of Laws and Regulations,* 7 vols (Pyongyang: CPEEC, 1994–96).

2 Kim Jong U, Press conference at the close of the Rajin-Sonbong Investment and Business Forum, Sonbong, 15 September 1996.

3 Stephen W Linton, 'North Korea under the Son', *The Washington Quarterly* Vol. 19 (1996), no.2, 12.

4 C/f Kim Il Sung, 'Some problems arising in bringing about a fresh upswing in socialist construction' [1958] *Works* vol.12 (Pyongyang: Foreign Languages Publishing House, 1983), 468; 'Concluding speech at the second enlarged plenary meeting of the fifth Central Committee of the Workers' Party of Korea' [1971] *Works* vol.26 (Pyongyang: Foreign Languages Publishing House, 1986), 130; 'On Improving the work of the Administration Council' [1976], *Works* vol.31 (Pyongyang: Foreign Languages Publishing House, 1987), 106–7.

5 Kim Il Sung, 'Let us thoroughly implement the party's policy on making foreign trade multilateral and diverse' [1984], *Works* vol.38 (Pyongyang: Foreign Languages Publishing House, 1993), 220.

6 Hyun-Joon Chon, 'Structure of the Power Elite of North Korea', *Information Service on the Unification Question of the Korean Peninsula* 1995–1 (National Unification Board, March 1995), 57–99; Moon Young Huh, Kyu Sup Chung, Hyun-Joon Chon, *The Advent of Kim Jong-il Regime in North Korea and Prospects for Its Policy Direction*, (Seoul: The Research Institute for National Unification, Policy Studies Report Series No 1, September 1994).

7 Chungang Ilbo, 'South Korean Paper Analyses North Premier's Position', *Summary of World Broadcasts* Far East/1773 A2/6–7, 21 August 1993.

8 'Communique of the 21st Plenary Session of the Sixth Korean Workers' Party Central Committee on the Status of the Fulfilment of the Third Seven-Year Plan', *Summary of World Broadcasts* FE/1868 S1/1–7, 10 Dec 1993.

9 Kim Il Sung, 'New Year Address', *Summary of World Broadcasts* FE/1885 D/3, 3 January 1994.

10 Kim Il Sung, 'All Efforts to Attain the Six Goals' [1961], *Works* vol.15 (Pyongyang: Foreign Languages Publishing House, 1983), 322.

[11] Kang Song San, 'On successfully fulfilling the tasks of socialist economic construction in the period of adjustment', *Summary of World Broadcasts* FE/1966 D3, D6, 8 Apr 1994.

[12] Kim Jong Il, 'Socialism is a Science', in Kim Jong Il, *On Carrying Forward the Juche Idea* (Pyongyang: Foreign Languages Publishing House, 1995), 387–8.

[13] Kim Mun Song, 'The Rajin-Sonbong FETZ, and the Policy of the Government of the DPR Korea', *Regional Economic Cooperation in Northeast Asia. Proceedings of the Sixth Meeting of the Northeast Asia Economic Forum, January 18–19, 1996, Honolulu, Hawaii* (Honolulu: Northeast Asia Economic Forum/Hawaii Asia-Pacific Institute, 1996), 71.

[14] *Questions and answers for investment in the Rajin-Sonbong Free Economic and Trade Zone* (Pyongyang: The Committee for the Promotion of External Economic Cooperation of the DPR of Korea, June 1996), 10.

[15] 'Najin-Sonbong Zone International Investment and Business Forum Opens,' FBIS, *Daily Report*, EAS–96–179, 16 Sep 1996, Pyongyang KCNA in English, 1006 GMT 13 Sep 96. Vice-Premier Kim was correct in saying that North Korea had always sought international cooperation on the basis of 'equality and mutual benefit': in the past, however, the third leg of this stool was not peace and friendship, but 'proletarian internationalism'. C/f Kim Il Sung, 'Let us embody the revolutionary spirit of independence, self-sustenance and self-defence more thoroughly in all branches of state activity' [1967], *Works* vol 21 (Pyongyang: Foreign Languages Publishing House, 1985), 456.

[16] Kim Jong U, Press conference at the close of the Rajin-Sonbong Investment and Business Forum, Sonbong, 15 September 1996.

[17] On Tumen cooperation, see Michael Freeberne, 'The Northeast Asia Regional Development Area: Land of Metal, Wood, Water, Fire and Earth', *Geography* Vol 78(1993), 420–31; Andrew Marton et al, 'Northeast Asian Economic Cooperation and the Tumen River Area Development Project', *Pacific Affairs* Vol 68(1995), 9–33; Mark J Valencia, 'Economic Cooperation in Northeast Asia: The Proposed Tumen River Scheme', *The Pacific Review* Vol 4(1991), 263–71; Gilbert Rozman, 'The Northeast Asian Triangle', *Orbis* Vol 39(1995), 65–80.

[18] On the concept of 'growth triangles': see Chia Siow Yue and Lee Tsao Yuan, 'Subregional Economic Zones: A New Motive Force in Asia-Pacific Development', in C Fred Bergsten and Marcus Noland eds, *Pacific Dynamism and the International Economic System* (Washington: Institute for International Economics, 1993), 225–69; Myo Thant et al eds, *Growth Triangles in Asia. A New Approach to Regional Economic Cooperation* (Hong Kong: Oxford University Press/Asia Development Bank, 1994).

[19] Burnham O Campbell, 'Introduction', in Won Bae Kim and Burnham O Campbell eds, *Proceedings of the Conference on Economic Development in the Coastal Area of Northeast Asia, 1991 Changchun*, (Honolulu: East-West Centre & Sasakawa Peace Foundation, 1992), 6.

[20] CPCS Ltd, *Northeast Asia's Tumen River Economic Development Area 1994: Collected Papers: Report G— Conceptual Infrastructure Master Plan.* (New York: UNDP, 1994).

[21] J Lilley, 'Tumen Teeters', *Far Eastern Economic Review* November 10 1994, 46–49.

[22] Gaye Christoffersen, 'The Greater Vladivostok Project: Transnational Linkages in Regional Economic Planning', *Pacific* Affairs Vol.67 (1994–95), 513–31; James Cotton, 'Jilin's Coastal Development Strategy: China and Tumen River cooperation', *Asian Survey* Vol.36 (1996), 1086–1101.

[23] Ian Davies, *Regional Cooperation in Northeast Asia. The Tumen River Area Development Program, 1990–2000: In Search of a Model for Regional Economic Co-operation in Northeast Asia* (Vancouver: Program on Canada-Asia Policy Studies, University of British Columbia, 2000).

[24] *Northeast Asia's Tumen River Economic Development Area 1994: Collected Papers* (New York: UNDP, 1994).

[25] Chinese Research Academy of Environmental Sciences, *Northeast Asia's Tumen River Economic Development Area 1994: Collected Papers. Report G— Preliminary Environmental Study* (New York: UNDP, 1994).

[26] North Korean spokesmen resist the use of the term 'reform', but it is still appropriate. For discussions of recent analyses of reform, see: John Merrill, 'North Korea's Halting Efforts at Economic Reform', in Chong-Sik Lee and Se-Hee Yoo eds, *North Korea in Transition* (Berkeley: Institute of East Asian Studies, University of California, 1991), 139–53; Byung-chul Koh, 'Prospects for Change in North Korea', *The Korean Journal of National Unification* Vol.3 (1994), 237–55.

[27] Samuel S Kim, 'North Korea and the Non-Communist World: The Quest for National Identity', in Chong-Sik Lee and Se-Hee Yoo eds, *North Korea in Transition* (Berkeley: Institute of East Asian Studies, University of California, 1991), 17–42.

[28] *Collection of Laws and the Regulations (Foreign Investment)*, (Pyongyang: CPEEC, 1999).

Chapter 10

AUSTRALIA'S REGIONAL POLICY: FROM 'ENGAGEMENT' TO 'NATIONAL INTEREST'

HISTORICAL BACKGROUND

Discussing the evolution of Australia's regional policy involves making some assessment of conflicting partisan claims as to its invention and promotion. Former Labor Prime Ministers Paul Keating (1991-96) and Gough Whitlam (1972-75) both claim to have invented the idea of pursuing engagement or community in the Asia Pacific region and both wrote books advancing their respective claims.[1] On the conservative side of politics, Percy Spender (Foreign Minister 1949-51) and R G Casey (Foreign Minister 1951-60, later head of state) paid great attention to diplomacy in the Asian region and also wrote books on this theme[2]. Nor is this a matter only of historical interest. In the 1990s one feature of election rhetoric was the charge that one side of politics or the other could not be entrusted with government since they did not have regional credibility or, alternatively, could not advance Australia's regional interests without compromising important values.

Setting aside these partisan questions, Australia's regional policy rests on several key geo-political legacies. Australia is a largely European derived society on the fringes of the Asian land mass. It is sparsely inhabited yet its armed forces must defend an entire continent. Australia's security has traditionally been sought through alliances or cooperation with extra-regional powers, first with Great Britain and from 1942 with the United States. This strategy has generally served Australia well, and it is popularly believed that only the US commitment to defend Australia prevented a Japanese invasion during World War II. However there have been important occasions when there were doubts that these partners had Australia's security as their highest priority, an historical record that has also perpetuated a sense of strategic uncertainty. Perhaps the most famous episode was the attempt by British Prime Minister Churchill in February 1942 to divert Australian troops returning from the Middle East for the campaign in Burma when the Australian government was expecting their return for the defence of the homeland.[3] Similarly, Australian policymakers were disappointed to find, in 1961, that the United States was prepared to support the Indonesian acquisition of West Papua in the interests (as was the perception in Washington) of keeping Jakarta out of the communist bloc even though this was anathema to the Menzies government.[4] As a consequence, Australia then came to share an ill-defined border with Indonesia under the unpredictable and increasingly leftist leadership of Sukarno. Australia's commitment of troops to the Vietnam War (despite the domestic turmoil this generated) can be partly understood as an attempt to help secure long term US involvement in Australia's immediate region.[5] At that time, of course, it was not imagined that once committed the US would not prevail.

The other legacy that has had an enduring impact has been the radical reorientation of economic linkages. Even in the 1930s signs emerged of economic complementarity between Australia and Japan, though at that time Britain accounted for more than half of all Australia's trade and the majority of foreign investment. In the immediate post-war period Britain resumed its role as chief trading partner, but through to the 1970s this predominance of British linkages progressively declined. By 1970 Japan had become the single largest destination for Australian exports, a trend encouraged further by the loss of major markets when, to the dismay of many in Australia, Britain joined the (then) European Economic Community (EEC) in 1973. By this time trade with the US was very significant, and investment from the US and (later) from Japan grew to rival levels of British investment, an issue vital in a nation traditionally dependent upon the importation of capital.[6]

These security and economic developments need to be seen in a social context. For almost the first half of its life, the Australian federation was avowedly an Anglo-Celtic country. By degrees this position was abandoned, first regarding immigration from the European area, and then from Asia. By 1966 exclusions on immigration on the grounds of race were abandoned and in 1973 an explicitly non-discriminatory definition of Australian citizenship was enacted. By the early 1980s 'Asia' outpaced 'Europe' as the largest source of immigrants, and of the former group those from Hong Kong were the most numerous.[7] The era of Australian 'multiculturalism' had begun. This trend coalesced with what by now was the dominant cultural view that being 'Australian' entailed a distinctive and unique national consciousness.

If emerging economic complementarities and immigration trends were the most noticeable form of regional engagement, other developments were also important. Through the 1970s the foundations were laid for a defence relationship with Indonesia, involving joint training, technical assistance and a certain level of information exchange. Australia also maintained close security relations with Singapore and Malaysia under (from 1971) the Five Power Defence Arrangement, a legacy of the insurgency in the peninsula conducted by the Malayan Communist Party against the British colonial authorities.[8]

THE HAWKE-KEATING GOVERNMENTS

Under the Hawke Labor government (1983-91), the economic trends already discussed were enhanced by the movement towards the internationalization of the Australian economy. Not without political controversy and entailing significant dislocation to some industries, protection of domestic manufacturing was progressively abandoned. The Australian market was thereby opened to the rising industrial power of East Asia.

At this time Japan was already the world's second largest economy and, in part as a result of the export of Japanese capital, the Asian NIC economies were growing at an extremely rapid rate. Elsewhere in the Asia Pacific, some of the countries of Southeast Asia were experimenting with similar outward looking development models, and China's turn away from Maoist autarchy (from 1978) added enormous economic potential to an already large and increasingly integrated regional economy. The liberalization of the Australian economy drew in increasing imports from all of these economies while simultaneously Australia became a significant source for their exports of raw materials. By way of illustration, by 1990 a single company in Korea (POSCO) became the largest single importer of any Australian commodity (in this case, coal).

The Hawke government sought to manage these trends to maximize their advantage to Australia. In the late 1980s a number of official and commissioned reports set out the government's regional agenda. Regarding population, in 1988 the Fitzgerald Report recommended that Northeast Asia in particular be seen as a potential source of skilled immigrants.[9] In 1989 *Australia's Regional Security* anticipated the emergence of new and cooperative security modalities embracing the entire region.[10] The most important of these expressions of a distinctive approach to the Asia Pacific region was the 'Garnaut Report', *Australia and the Northeast Asian Ascendancy* – authored by a team chaired by Australia's former ambassador to Beijing, which appeared in 1989.

Garnaut's argument was that for Australia to take best advantage of the rapid growth in the Asia Pacific region, and especially in Northeast Asia, the domestic economy should be further liberalized.[11] Such liberalization should be accompanied by changes in training, travel, and education to make Australians more aware of the region and facilitate access to its cultures, cities and markets. Recognizing differences between Australia and its new partners in connection with political and social systems and values, Garnaut recommended taking a long term and pragmatic view. Rather than confront directly illiberal practices regarding human rights policy, or lack of free expression, he argued that as it was a general trend that the liberalization of social and political systems followed economic liberalization, therefore there would be a gradual convergence of these values. Meanwhile, Australia's most positive contribution in this area was to encourage a market orientation that, to an extent, required Australia to lead by example.

Though Garnaut's message received a good deal of bi-partisan support, it was also subjected to a variety of critiques.[12] Some commentators claimed that other lessons should be drawn from the success of the Asian economies, for example on the need for a targeted 'industry policy'; others suggested that the purported linkage between political and social liberalization did not always emerge in the unqualified way Garnaut suggested. But the breadth of support for many of his arguments indicated that Asia, and Northeast Asia in particular, were now major preoccupations for policy makers.

As to the modalities best suited to entrench and institutionalize the growing complementarities between Australia and the Asian region, the Hawke and Keating governments favoured multi-lateral means. Here it should be recalled that the global context for these policies was the end of the Cold War and the deepening of economic and security cooperation across Europe in such organizations as the CSCE/OSCE (Conference on Security and Co-operation in Europe) and the European Union. Accordingly, Australia was a founder member in 1989 of APEC (Asia Pacific Economic Cooperation) the conceptualization of which owed much to the Australian policy community. Similarly the (then) Foreign Minister, Gareth Evans, was one of the first advocates (in 1990) of a region wide security architecture that was eventually realized in the ASEAN Regional Forum (1994).[13]

Nevertheless, other strands old as well as new could be detected in the fabric of Australian foreign policy. The alliance with the United States remained fundamental in security calculations. In addition, Foreign Minister Gareth Evans became a prominent if not always dexterous practitioner of 'middle power activism' in connection with a wide range of issues, from global arms control

(Australia making an especially significant contribution to the negotiation of the Chemical Weapons Convention[14]), through the resolution of such perennial problems as the conflict in Cambodia to the building of international coalitions of agricultural producers to wrest fairer conditions of trade from the industrialized world.[15] And Australia remained committed to the defence of Malaysia and Singapore under the 'Five Power' security agreement, an inheritance from the end of the British empire.

From time to time there were signs that all these many objectives and modalities produced incoherences.[16] Strains emerged in the alliance with the US when the government sponsored an international inquiry—the Canberra Commission—that found the possession of nuclear weapons to have no moral basis, and correspondingly some of Australia's new security interlocutors remained skeptical of a country that espoused the notion of common security while relying upon links with a power perceived as a *de facto* regional hegemon. Neither were these policies without domestic controversy. Though there was much support in the wider political policy community and among élites for regional engagement, there was still some community skepticism and even unease that the 'Asianization of Australia' would follow.[17] Seen in the longer perspective, however, the considerable reorientation of Australia's external policy that occurred in these years was remarkably free of pain or controversy.

THE TRANSITION TO A LIBERAL-NATIONAL PARTY COALITION GOVERNMENT

Having run its course, the Labor administration was replaced by a Liberal-National Coalition government led by John Howard in March 1996. At the outset, the new administration adopted quite a different tone in its approach to external issues. It described its philosophical position as 'realist' and defined its principal objective in this area as a pursuit of 'the national interest' explicitly defined in terms of the physical security of Australia and its citizens and their economic prosperity. In the words of the 1997 government White Paper, *In the National Interest*,

> Preparing for the future is not a matter of grand constructs. It is about the hard-headed pursuit of the interests which lie at the core of foreign and trade policy: the security of the nation and the jobs and standard of living of the Australian people. In all that it does in the field of foreign and trade policy, the Government will apply this basic test of national interest.[18]

Whereas in the Keating era republicanism was on the political agenda and aspects of the British inheritance and historical record were derided, Howard rejected such re-evaluations as the 'black arm band' school of Australian history and, in a phrase that often occurred in public pronouncements declared: 'we do not have to chose between our history and our geography.' Accordingly, though the government did not reject the idea of 'engagement' with Asia, it was much more inclined to view this strategy as desirable only if it served 'the national interest' and if it did not require or encourage the abandonment of essential values and traditions—especially transparency and the rule of law. Nevertheless, Foreign Minister Alexander Downer (undoubtedly more internationalist in his outlook) tirelessly re-iterated the message that 'engagement with Asia' was still the country's most important diplomatic task.

In other circumstances, the pursuit of foreign and defence policy under the Coalition government might in practice have resulted in little substantive variation from that of its predecessor. The Australian foreign policy debate, after all, had been characterized for many years by a considerable element of bipartisanship. The Howard government, however, soon had to grapple with developments in the region that overturned many of the established assumptions of the foreign policy community. The regional financial crisis that began in mid-1997 negated the widely shared expectation, as expressed in *In the National Interest*, that an increasingly prosperous Asia would inexorably bring Australia into its economic orbit while compelling a more judicious and nuanced approach by Canberra to more self-confident and perhaps even more assertive and capable neighbouring powers.

Within the space of a few months, the relatively benign and predictable regional environment became turbulent and uncertain. The political repercussions of the crisis, especially the attempted democratisation of Indonesia, inevitably subjected past attempts to build bridges with regimes and leaderships in the region to new and critical scrutiny. But it was not just previous relations with individual regimes that came under question. The backlash of Asian governments against perceived Western indifference to their financial plight, and the stimulus this gave to the creation of an East Asian identity, threatened to undermine Canberra's attempts at fostering regional organizations across the Pacific Rim.

The financial crisis highlighted the ambivalence in the Coalition's approach to the region. On the one hand, the government responded quickly and generously to the international relief programs for Thailand, Indonesia and then Korea, contributing US$1 billion in each instance. On the other, the crisis provided an opportunity for the government to point to the distinctiveness of Australia's economic and even social systems as an explanation for why the nation was immune from the regional contagion.[19] As the Foreign Minister remarked of Australia's record, 'what other country in the region has managed, in the face of the toughest economic conditions for fifty years, to maintain both strong economic growth and successfully renew democratic institutions through the holding of a free and fair general election?'[20] From being a pupil of the Asian dragons in the previous decade, Australia now volunteered itself as an instructor in the ways of reform, though Australia's assumed role as tutor was not well received in many parts of the region. At the same time the government was successful in managing a significant reorientation in Australia's trade. In the first 12 months of the crisis, there was a 22% increase of exports to the EU and 40% increase in exports to the United States.

ASEAN and APEC proved ineffectual in dealing with the crisis, and Canberra's somewhat skeptical approach to regionalism manifest after 1998 was in part a response to this poor performance. However, the Australian government still sought to use the latter as a basis for encouraging those reforms that would prevent a further recurrence of financial crisis, and attempted to pursue closer trade relations with the former through a proposed link between the ASEAN Free Trade Area and the Closer Economic Relationship agreement between Australia and New Zealand (a linkage eventually rejected by ASEAN).

The ineffectiveness of APEC, the most important mechanism in the previous government's program of economic engagement with Asia, generated two responses from the region to which there was a slow and uncertain reaction. One was the formation of the ASEAN Plus Three grouping, which realized Malaysian Prime Minister Dr Mahathir's long-standing goal of creating a region-wide East Asian grouping specifically excluding Australia. The second development was a new interest, particularly on the part of Japan, Singapore, and Thailand, in the negotiation of bilateral discriminatory trade and investment agreements. The government first rejected the relevance for Australia of the ASEAN Plus Three grouping and then lobbied to join it. And after decades in which Canberra had opposed bilateral trade agreements in support of its preferred alternatives of multilateralism and 'open regionalism', the Howard government belatedly adopted this strategy by seeking to negotiate free trade agreements with the United States, Singapore, and Thailand. To this extent, regional engagement was to be much more selective than in the past.

The Howard government's preference for closer cooperation with traditional allies and a more discriminating attitude towards regional and global institutions was challenged by developments not just in the region but throughout the world system. The growing interdependence of states—reflected in the emergence of global issues and opinions, and in the strengthening of global institutions and regimes—threatened more restrictive conceptions of the national interest with obsolescence. Global warming, the entrenchment of human rights standards, the proliferation of weapons of mass destruction, all demanded comprehensive solutions beyond the capacity even of groups of states. The financial crisis itself demonstrated the vulnerability of important economies to a world financial regime constructed on the foundation of new technologies in the 1990s.

Domestic political developments also challenged the Howard government's policies towards the region and on important global issues. Even in the less turbulent times of Prime Ministers Hawke and Keating, Australian élites were in some danger of outpacing popular opinion on many of the aspects of Asian engagement, from security to immigration.[21] In a domestic development with significant and still continuing impact on Australia's external policies, the Howard government was forced to deal with a new political force seeking to mobilise voters in the name of what was alleged to be a growing gap between élite preferences and popular aspirations.

This force was manifest with the irruption of Pauline Hanson onto the political stage, first as an outspoken independent, then as the leader of a party that won some 23% of the vote in the 1998 Queensland state elections, and (more significantly) 8.4% of the vote in the federal election that returned the Coalition to office in that same year. Hanson was never clear on the policies to be used to achieve her goals, but she was outspoken on what she disliked. In her parliamentary maiden speech she complained of the actions of many malevolent agencies in Australia: 'financial markets, international organisations, world bankers, investment companies and big business people'. She also warned of the dangers of 'being swamped by Asians'. All of these phenomena could be traced to the impact of globalisation on Australia, and to the government's partial dismantling of policies of social protection.

Although her party, 'Pauline Hanson's One Nation', disintegrated and she lost he federal parliamentary seat, the revival of her movement at the end of 2000 and its undoubted influence on election results subsequently in state contests in Western Australia and Queensland illustrated that it might not be a transient phenomenon—and certainly that the fears that sustained such a populist movement were far from ephemeral. Moreover, it was a political force that posed the greatest threat to the Coalition, since those who voted for the party were largely individuals who had previously voted for the National or Liberal Parties.[22]

Hansonism presented the government with a powerful electoral motive to underscore its skepticism of regional engagement and its defence of a restricted conception of national interest. In what can be seen in retrospect as an extraordinarily active period in Australian foreign policy making, the government's performance and utterances from 1997 especially regarding the Asia Pacific region cannot be properly understood without a consideration of this domestic dimension. The most important policy innovation over these years was undoubtedly the decision to abandon support for Indonesian sovereignty in East Timor, a decision that led first to extensive and prominent support for the UNAMET (United Nations Mission East Timor) ballot in the territory and then to leadership of the September 1999 international military intervention in the territory.

The Implications of the East Timor Intervention

From a 'realist' perspective, Indonesia is the key to Australia's defence. It commands the nation's Northern approaches from which or through which any military attack on Australia would be launched. A stable and friendly Indonesia is therefore crucial for Australia's security. From a common security perspective, there are added (or perhaps alternative) reasons for fostering good relations with Jakarta. Indonesia is the key to any wider multi-lateralist strategies for creating regional order. Indonesia is the dominant power in ASEAN, and this group is both the core of the ASEAN Regional Forum and the pioneer of the modalities for cooperation adopted by APEC. From this perspective, the negotiation of the 1995 'Agreement on Maintaining Security' with Indonesia was widely regarded as reconciling two potentially different conceptions of regional security and thus finally resolving the most important issue in Australia's strategic neighbourhood.[23]

If there is one policy that has had broad bi-partisan support in Australian politics in the last 25 years it has been Indonesia's forcible annexation of East Timor.[24] In acquiring the territory Indonesia violated the international norm against aggressive and forcible action and also denied the right of the inhabitants to self-determination, these transgressions being reflected in the censure of Jakarta by the UN Security Council (in 1975 and 1976) and the refusal of the UN to recognize the acquisition as legitimate. Nevertheless, Australia under a Coalition government extended *de jure* recognition to the annexation in February 1979, a position reaffirmed by the Hawke Labor government. The reasons for this policy were an uncertain and variable mix of the perceptions of Indonesia noted above. The decision by the Howard government to overturn this bi-partisan legacy was the most significant development in Australian policy towards the Asia Pacific region since the Vietnam War.

Global changes constituted the background to (or preconditions for) this policy shift. These included the rise in the post Cold War era of the doctrine of intervention and also the fact that a democratizing Indonesia in economic crisis was more amenable than in past times to international pressure. But a novel understanding of Australia's regional role was undoubtedly a factor in the government's calculations. As the Prime Minister was reported to have said in a widely quoted magazine interview:

> [The East Timor operation] has done a lot to cement Australia's place in the region. We have been seen by countries, not only in the region but around the world, as being able to do something that probably no other country could do; because of the special characteristics we have; because we occupy that special place—we are a European, Western civilization with strong links to North America, but here we are in Asia.[25]

Australia's leadership of the INTERFET (International Force East Timor) intervention in the territory in October 1999 was a watershed event. The East Timor commitment had nothing less than a profound effect on many aspects of Australia's regional security and defence posture. Australian-Indonesian relations were placed on a new footing, past and future regional engagement became the subject of vigorous debate, and defence priorities were re-ordered.

Relations with Indonesia took a wholly new course with the intervention. Prior to 1999, there were expectations that the emergence of democracy in Indonesia, especially in the context of Australia's US$1billion contribution to the IMF relief package provided as a response to the regional financial crisis, would put relations with Jakarta on an entirely new basis. Australian support for the infrastructure necessary to stage the 1999 parliamentary elections was indicative of the awareness that the progress of democratic consolidation was vital for Australia's national interests. But this support counted for very little in the balance as against what was widely represented in the Indonesian media as Australia's 'arrogance' and 'betrayal' over East Timor. This perceived hostility stirred passions. A vehicle carrying the Australian Ambassador was shot at in Dili. After the Australian Defence Minister stated that all bi-lateral defence contacts with Indonesia were suspended, Indonesia announced on 16 September that the 1995 bi-lateral Agreement on Maintaining Security would be abrogated. The agreement was then dismissed by the government as of little consequence, but its demise marked the end of a defence relationship painstakingly constructed from the 1960s. As the INTERFET operation began, demonstrators gathered outside the Australian embassy and there were violent incidents. And President Wahid himself described Australian policy as 'infantile').[26]

Despite strenuous diplomatic efforts, including a visit to Jakarta by Foreign Minister Downer in February 2000, relations with Indonesia remained in an awkward phase. Ironically President Abdurrahman Wahid was personally very familiar with Australia and was also extremely fond of overseas travel, yet he could only be tempted to visit the country in the twilight of his presidency. It was therefore something of a surprise that Prime Minister Howard was invited to meet his successor, Megawati Sukarnoputri, immediately upon her taking office. The two leaders met again in 2002 when they agreed to measures of bilateral cooperation in the international campaign against terrorism. In the area of greatest concern to Australia, the transit through Indonesia of people smuggling networks, much work however remained to be done.

Finally, Australian intervention in East Timor was seen as a possible harbinger of future interference in Indonesia's internal affairs, especially in connection with West Papua, where a separatist insurgency had considerable indigenous support. Despite strenuous denials from the Australian government, this suspicion was encouraged by statements from Colin Powell, shortly after being nominated by President-elect Bush as the new US Secretary of State. In remarks he made during confirmation hearings, he signaled a new skepticism of humanitarian interventions, and indicated that more reliance would be placed on allies, specifically referring to Australia's decision to 'take the lead' regarding Indonesia.[27] These remarks found an attentive audience in Jakarta.

If there was uncertainty in Indonesia regarding Australia's intentions in the region, this was a consequence not only of the nation's role in UNAMET and INTERFET, but also a reaction to the very public debate that the latter engendered. While Australian forces were committed to Timor with the undoubted expectation that there would be loss of life, the success of the operation led to statements from political and military figures that seemed to imply a larger if indeterminate commitment to similar undertakings in the future. For a short period the 'Howard doctrine', by which this position came to be known, depicted Australia as playing a role as a 'deputy' to the US in keeping the regional peace.[28]

According to the government's account, the objectives of the East Timor intervention were threefold. First a perennial problem in Australia-Indonesia bilateral relations was being addressed. It was incontrovertible that the perception of Indonesia's human rights record in East Timor had been an obstacle to a more favourable public assessment of that country for a generation. Second, and in light of the fact that the UN still held Indonesian occupation to be illegitimate, a new status for East Timor would remove perhaps the single major obstacle to

Indonesia playing a positive role in the world, commensurate with its size and potential. Third, the intervention was a response to the very strong reaction from the Australian public that was prompted by the violence and suffering experienced by the East Timorese in the aftermath of the ballot.

It was the fate of the Timor issue, despite the very particular circumstances that led both to the Australian policy change and also to the INTERFET intervention, to tend to be generalised into a novel and path-breaking national approach to the region. In the parliamentary debate of 21 September 1999 on the issue the Prime Minister used the opportunity to outline some 'home truths' regarding Australia's position in the region. Though not so outspoken as the putative 'Howard doctrine', this statement represented the most distinctive and considered contribution by the Prime Minister to foreign policy discourse since he assumed office in 1996. The first of these truths was that foreign policy must be based on a clearer sense of 'national interest' and 'values'. The national interest requires Australia to pursue relationships on the basis of mutual interest and to recognise 'where they exist, differences in values and political systems.' Secondly, Australia occupies 'a unique intersection—a Western nation next to Asia with strong links to the United States and Europe' and therefore commands 'unique assets.'

> We have stopped worrying about whether we are Asian, in Asia, enmeshed in Asia or part of a mythical East-Asian hemisphere. We have got on with the job of being ourselves in the region. In turn, the region has recognised that we are an asset and have a constructive role to play in it.[29]

The assets listed include the ANZUS and Five Power security alliances, and also bilateral defence cooperation programs. However, the alliance with the US was then identified as a separate (third) truth, and was described as functioning 'very effectively', having helped deliver a significant US contribution in this instance. Adequate defence resources were the fourth truth, and as the prevailing security climate was 'uncertain', these resources were apparently insufficient, and additional expenditure was thus foreshadowed. The fifth and final truth was the need to take account of 'the values of the Australian community', and the inference to be drawn from this was that Australia should not seek 'a good relationship with Indonesia at all costs or at the expense of doing the right thing according to our own values.' In each one of these 'truths' may be detected a statement of the distinctiveness, by comparison with the region, of Australia's identity and interests.

Returning to the issue of Australia's regional assets, John Howard contrasted his approach with that of some commentators who maintained that under his tenure Australia would be excluded from regional frameworks and thus would never be accepted in Asia. This underestimated Australia's capacities and institutions, especially as demonstrated by the nation's positive performance during the Asian economic crisis:

> ... our economic, military and other credentials are respected and give us a capacity to help and constructively participate in the region. Just as we were in a position to assist our neighbours during the Asian economic crisis, so also on East Timor we have shown that we have the capacity under the United Nations to work with our regional partners in putting together a multinational peacekeeping force. It is an example of both our commitment to the region and our capacity to make a constructive and practical contribution to its affairs.[30]

On this understanding of Australian foreign policy, the Timor commitment was consistent with the national interest in two respects. Australian forces were being used in the service of international institutions and with Indonesian consent to assist the East Timorese to realise the choice they made in an internationally supervised ballot. And these forces by suppressing violence would restore regional order and end uncertainty. But the issue of whether Australia's putative 'assets' were entirely welcome in the region was not considered. Moreover, the enhanced military preparedness that would allow Australia to embark on a similar intervention in the future might conceivably be seen as a threat rather than a positive contribution to regional order, and was certainly represented as such by Australia's critics. Indeed, Malaysia's Prime Minister Dr Mahathir was forthright in his criticism of Australia's regional designs, though other criticism expressed in Southeast Asia was more muted.[31] However these developments could be interpreted, Australia's willingness to employ military force marked virtually the end of the policy of 'regional engagement' principally by way of participation in multi-lateral institutions and the practice of consensus diplomacy.

Finally, the East Timor experience had a powerful impact on security perceptions. Australian forces performed well during the crisis of 1999, especially given the immensely difficult logistics involved in inserting and supporting in a potential hostile theatre a multi-national force the components of which had no prior experience of working together. Yet the commitment revealed potential lack of capacity, and as a result the government's 2000 Defence White Paper stated a commitment to significant increases in expenditure (albeit over a ten year period).[32] Such expenditure increases were already expected, given the problem of block obsolescence in much defence equipment. What was unprecedented in the White Paper was the clear statement that after the defence of continental Australia, 'lower level operations' including peacekeeping are the next most important priority for the ADF (Australian Defence Force), and that other features of the East Timor experience may recur:

> This might require the ADF to contribute to regional peacekeeping and humanitarian relief operations and help evacuate Australians and others from regional troublespots. We should be prepared to be the largest force contributor to such operations. Our planning needs to acknowledge that we could be called upon to undertake several operations simultaneously, as we are at present in East Timor, Bougainville and the Solomon Islands.[33]

What scenarios are anticipated here? The White Paper underlines the strategic primacy of Indonesia, and states that Australia's security would be threatened by 'adverse developments' inside Indonesia, whether internally or externally generated.[34]

On East Timor, the White Paper signals nothing less than a continuing security commitment:

> Within a short time East Timor will pass from UN authority to full independence. Australia will seek to develop an effective defence relationship with East Timor ... East Timor faces formidable security challenges. Our aim will be to provide, with others, an appropriate level of help and support for East Timor as it builds the capabilities and national institutions that it will need to ensure its security and thereby contribute to the security of its neighbourhood.[35]

A week before the document was released to the public, the Defence Minister announced a $A26m aid program to help train and equip an East Timorese defence force, the core of which was drawn from FALINTIL, the guerilla resistance army that was for a generation the Indonesian military's most dogged opponents.[36] Nor will relations with independent East Timor necessarily be harmonious on this account or even in light of the A$150million of aid promised by the government in 2000 for a four year period.[37] In short, Australia is now committed to the protection and development of a country the birth of which constitutes Indonesia's greatest policy reversal in all of its history as a nation. In this context it should be acknowledged that the message of the intervention for the region was decidedly mixed. Some ASEAN states participated in the INTERFET operation, but there were also some expressions of dismay and distrust at what was presented as the humiliation of Indonesia and its armed forces by an external power.

In retrospect, this shift in policy is in part testimony to the weaknesses and limitations of those multi-lateral institutions that had been the preferred mechanisms for regional engagement prior to the 1997 regional crisis. Since 1967 ASEAN has been committed to principles of non-interference in the affairs of other states, the pacific resolution of disputes, and an avoidance of external power entanglements. Indonesia's invasion of East Timor violated all of these principles not least because the Indonesian military became dependent thereafter on US military materiel and assistance. Yet East Timor was never a matter raised within ASEAN; indeed, the ASEAN countries maintained a united international front on the issue.[38] The reasons for this solidarity are not far to seek, but this episode may be taken to illustrate that such principles are only as determining of state conduct as power relations permit. Even in September 1999 when faced with the most significant regional security crisis since Vietnam's invasion of Cambodia, the ASEAN role was marginal, the group's foreign ministers initially even resisting discussing East Timor at the APEC summit in Auckland. If this was a non-subject for ASEAN, then it was never likely to appear on the agenda of the ASEAN Regional Forum. Without pursuing this issue too far, it may even be argued that these institutions were part of the problem, since they legitimized the Indonesian regime as a credible actor and made its cooperation vital to regional order. The inability of the ASEAN Regional Forum even to discuss the Taiwan issue, despite the fact that (on some scenarios) it may lead to a major East Asian war is a further illustration of the limitations of such diplomatic mechanisms.[39] Now these arguments are not the kind that any government spokesperson is likely to articulate publicly, but their logic supports the realist turn that is evident in foreign policy pronouncements from 1996.

THE REGIONAL BURDENS OF ALLIANCE

The East Timor commitment constituted a significant test of Australia's alliance with the United States, while also appearing to underline the necessity for realist calculations in an environment where multilateral mechanisms are ineffective. Despite some anxious moments in Canberra, the United States agreed to join the INTERFET coalition and in announcing this policy President Clinton specifically cited the alliance with Australia as a major consideration in his decision.[40] It should be recalled that US arms supplies were indispensable in facilitating the pursuit by the Indonesian military of the East Timorese resistance army, and the US was associated from the very beginning with the annexation by virtue of (then) Secretary of State Henry Kissinger's encouragement of the policy.[41] And despite the relatively small number of US personnel involved, Washington's role in 1999 was crucial. US diplomatic leverage (not least within the Bretton Woods institutions) impelled the Indonesian government to sanction the INTERFET operation. In the uncertain and potentially hostile environment of East Timor, US intelligence assets and heavy lift capability were vital.[42]

Indeed, in 2000 and into the Bush administration, US spokespersons were willing to cite the Australian role in East Timor as an example of the more self-reliant alliance model they wished to see world-wide, with the local partner in the alliance relationship taking the initiative and providing many of the forces (and footing much of the bill) while Washington provided diplomatic, intelligence and logistics support. Comprehensive cooperation with Washington however requires 'interoperability' of platforms and systems, and in anticipation of further regional crises Australia now faces some difficult choices if it is to remain a full member of the alliance.

The Revolution in Military Affairs (RMA) promises to transform conflict into a contest in which superior technologies (and especially the command of information) deliver mastery.[43] Australia had traditionally relied upon the possession of advanced armaments and information technologies to offset the disadvantages of its small population and immense territory. As part of the 'UKUSA' network Australia has engaged in intelligence sharing with the United States since the early years of the Cold War.[44] To participate in the RMA, according to some specialists, not only must Australia source its most advanced systems exclusively from the United States but it must also be unambiguously part of a global partnership centred upon the United States the framework of which derives from the bilateral alliances forged during the Cold War. If realist calculations are presently influential in Canberra, then this outcome may have its attractions. However realism also may prescribe the maintenance of the current regional strategic balance that might, on some interpretations, be prejudiced by the development of such new systems as National Missile Defence. In addition, Australia's policy makers may be convinced that bans on such devices as chemical weapons, or biological weapons, or landmines may enhance global security, but may come under pressure to abandon their criticisms of them in the interests of alliance solidarity. These and other concerns were the context for the 2001 AusMin (ministerial) talks, conducted in Canberra in late July 2001.[45]

Setting aside questions involving specific security decisions made by the US, there is some room for the argument that close security cooperation with other US strategic partners in the Asia Pacific is not necessarily in the national interest.

Both Japan and the Republic of Korea are important economic partners of long-standing, and (at least on paper) Australia is still a guarantor of Korean security by virtue of its participation in the Korean War. Greater cooperation with these partners would be consistent with many national objectives. But if the United States is to revive its security relationship with the Philippines, then as part of a regional network of states Australia may find itself embroiled as part of a coalition in a conflict over conflicting territorial claims in the South China Sea. Similarly the informal alliance that binds the US to Taiwan may draw Australia into a dispute between the major regional powers. Again, Taiwan is an important trading partner and is now a prominent example of a regional democracy, but direct conflict with China cannot enhance Australia's national security.[46] Commentators in China were not slow to point this out, in response to the outcome of the July 2001 AusMin (joint ministerial) proceedings.[47]

CONCLUSIONS

Through the 1980s to the regional financial crisis of 1997, the idea that there was a natural complementarity between Asia and Australia—firstly understood in economic terms, but then with respect to immigration, security, and even diplomacy—became increasingly influential. Now this idea was never universally accepted, but it was often encountered and became something like the established view. This idea no longer represents majority opinion. In all of these areas there are far more uncertainties than was acknowledged at that time. As this paper has argued, the reasons for this shift are many, but include the failure of regional institutions to make a real impact on economic and security problems, the election of a government somewhat skeptical of the multi-lateralist predilections of its predecessors, and domestic political dynamics.

In assessing these changes some critical comments are in order. It may be that this change of emphasis reflects the demise of those conditions from the 1980s that provided the foundations for regionalism. In short, regionalism may be a moment whose time has passed. Globalisation—of finances, of information flows, of tastes and trends, of security—may have undermined the capacity of such organizations as ASEAN to have a real impact in the long run. Distance has always been Australia's biggest obstacle to progress. Australia more than any other nation needs to globalise. A specific regional attachment may no longer be appropriate or efficacious.

But the point remains that the regional financial crisis as much as the Hanson movement was a manifestation of globalisation. In a genuinely global era, the relevance of a narrow conception of national interest may no longer be applicable. However much a triumph of Australian arms or values, the East Timor intervention would never have been possible without the attention of transnational interest groups, the weakening of the Indonesian government as the result of the activities of the global financial system, and the continued concern about the issue maintained by the United Nations. In pursuit of a hard-headed national interest, Australian policy has inevitably been conditioned and constrained as well as facilitated by the growing interdependence of nations. Therefore a lack of attention to building institutions to deal with issues which, while they have a regional dimension are nevertheless truly global, including the environment crisis, refugee flows and human rights abuses, may no longer accord with national interest however this term is understood.

NOTES

1 E G Whitlam, *A Pacific Community* (Cambridge: Harvard University Press, 1981); Paul Keating, *Engagement. Australia Faces the Asia-Pacific* (Sydney: Pan Macmillan, 2000).

2 Percy Spender, *Exercises in Diplomacy* (Sydney: Sydney University Press, 1969); R G Casey, *Friends and Neighbors. Australia, the US and the World* (East Lansing: Michigan State College Press, 1955).

3 Jeffrey Grey, *A Military History of Australia*, revised edition (Cambridge: Cambridge University Press, 1999),168.

4 Greg Pemberton, *All the Way: Australia's Road to Vietnam* (North Sydney: Allen & Unwin, 1987), 70-106.

5 Peter Edwards with Greg Pemberton, *Crises and Commitments: The Politics and Diplomacy of Australia's Involvement in Southeast Asian Conflicts 1948-1965* (North Sydney: Allen & Unwin, 1992), 358-62.

6 David Meredith & Barrie Dyster, *Australia in the Global Economy* (Cambridge: Cambridge University Press, 1999), 192-221; Sandra Tweedie, *Trading Partners. Australia and Asia 1790-1993* (Sydney: University of NSW Press, 1994).

7 Jamie Mackie, 'The Politics of Asian Immigration', in James E Coughlan & Deborah J McNamara eds, *Asians in Australia. Patterns of Migration and Settlement* (South Melbourne: Macmillan, 1997), 18-24.

8 T B Millar, *Australia in Peace and War. External Relations since 1788*, 2nd edition (Canberra: Australian National University Press, 1991).

9 Stephen Fitzgerald, *Immigration: A Commitment to Australia* (Canberra: AGPS, 1988).

10 Department of Foreign Affairs and Trade, *Australia's Regional Security: ministerial statement* (Canberra: DFAT, 1989).

11 Ross Garnaut, *Australia and the Northeast Asian Ascendancy* (Canberra: AGPS, 1989).

12 James L Richardson ed, *Northeast Asian Challenge: debating the Garnaut Report* (Canberra; Department of International Relations, Australian National University, 1989: Canberra Studies in World Affairs no 27).

13 Des Ball & Pauline Kerr, *Presumptive Engagement: Australia's Asia-Pacific Security Policy in the 1990s* (North Sydney: Allen & Unwin, 1996).

14 Trevor Findlay, *Peace Through Chemistry: The New Chemical Weapons Convention* (Canberra: Australian National University, Peace Research Centre Monograph 14, 1993).

15 Andrew F Cooper, R A Higgott, K R Nossal, *Relocating Middle Powers. Australia and Canada in a Changing World Order* (Melbourne: Melbourne University Press, 1993), 50-82.

16 David Goldsworthy, 'An Overview', in James Cotton and Ravenhill eds, *The National Interest in a Global Era. Australia in World Affairs 1996-2000* (Melbourne: Oxford University Press, 2002), 10-30.

17 Ian McAllister and John Ravenhill, 'Australian attitudes towards closer engagement with Asia', *The Pacific Review* Vol 11 (1998), no 1, 119-141.

18 Department of Foreign Affairs and Trade, *In the National Interest. Australia's Foreign and Trade Policy* (Canberra: DFAT, 1997), iii.

19 Michael Wesley, 'Australia and the Asian Financial Crisis', in James Cotton and John Ravenhill eds, *The National Interest in a Global Era. Australia in World Affairs 1996-2000* (Melbourne: Oxford University Press, 2002), 301-24.

20 Alexander Downer, "Australia and Asia – A New Paradigm for the Relationship", Speech to the Foreign Correspondents' Association (Sydney: 16 April 1999) at <http://www.dfat.gov.au/media/speeches/foreign/1999/990416_aust_asia.html>.

21 James Cotton and John Ravenhill, 'Australia's "Engagement with Asia"', in James Cotton and John Ravenhill eds, *Seeking Asian Engagement. Australia in World Affairs 1991-95* (Melbourne: Oxford University Press, 1997), 12-13.

22 Simon Jackman, 'Pauline Hanson, the Mainstream, and Political Elites: The Place of Race in Australian Political Ideology', *Australian Journal of Political Science* Vol 33 (1998), no 2, 167-84.

23 Peter Hartcher, 'How the Enemy Became an Ally', *Australian Financial Review* (Sydney), 4-5 July 1996, 1, 18-19, 26-7.

24 James Cotton, 'East Timor and Australia - Twenty-five years of the policy debate', in James Cotton ed, *East Timor and Australia* (Canberra: ADSC/AIIA, 1999), 1-20.

25 Fred Brenchley, 'The Howard Defence Doctrine', *The Bulletin* (Sydney), 28 September 1999, 24.

26 *Antara* (Jakarta), 30 September 1999; Hal Hill and Chris Manning, 'Indonesia-Australia Ties – What Went Wrong', *The Jakarta Post* (Jakarta), 30 November

1999, 4; Ikrar Nusa Bhakti, 'Howard Sets Back RI-Indonesia Ties', *Jakarta Post*, 12 September 1999, 4.

27 *Sydney Morning Herald*, 19 January 2001.

28 John Lyons, 'The Howard Doctrine', *The Bulletin*, 28 September 1999, 22-24.

29 *Commonwealth Parliamentary Debates*, 21 September 1999, 10029.

30 *Commonwealth Parliamentary Debates*, 21 September 1999, 10031.

31 *South China Morning Post* (Hong Kong), 27 September 1999.

32 Department of Defence, *Defence 2000. Our Future Defence Force* (Canberra: Department of Defence, 2000).

33 Department of Defence, *Defence 2000. Our Future Defence Force*, 39.

34 Department of Defence, *Defence 2000. Our Future Defence Force*, 22.

35 Department of Defence, *Defence 2000. Our Future Defence Force*, 37.

36 *The Australian*, 24 November 2000.

37 AUSAID, *East Timor Update*, 17 January (Canberra: AUSAID, 2001).

38 Sonny Inbaraj, *East Timor. Blood and Tears in ASEAN* (Chiangmai: Silkworm Books, 1995).

39 Robyn Lim, 'The ASEAN Regional Forum: Building on Sand', *Contemporary Southeast Asia* Vol 20 (1998), no 2, 115-36.

40 James Cotton, 'Against the Grain: The East Timor Intervention', *Survival* Vol 43 (2001), no 1, 127-42.

41 The National Security Archive, 'East Timor Revisited', at <http://www.gwu.edu/~nsarchiv/NSAEBB/NSAEBB62/>.

42 Eric Schwartz, 'A reminder that friends in deed are friends indeed', *Sydney Morning Herald*, 24 July 2001, 12.

43 Eliot A Cohen, 'A Revolution in Warfare', *Foreign Affairs* Vol 75 (1996), no 2, 37–54.

44 Jeffrey T Richelson & Desmond Ball, *The Ties that Bind: Intelligence Cooperation Between the UKUSA Countries* (Boston: Allen & Unwin, 1985).

45 Brendan Pearson, 'Powell Floats Idea of Asia-Pacific Security Bloc', *Australian Financial Review* (Sydney), 31 July 2001, 1.

46 Robert D Blackwill and Paul Dibb eds, *America's Asian Alliances* (Cambridge: Massachusetts Institute of Technology Press, 2000); Hamish McDonald 2001, 'Don't mention the sleeping giant', *Sydney Morning Herald*, 31 July 2001.

47 Michael Dwyer, 'China Attacks "another NATO', *Australian Financial Review* (Sydney), 2 August 2001, p.10.

INDEX

A

B

F

G

H

I

J

K

L

M

Q

R

S

T

U

V

W

Y

Z